SQUEEZED AND SHAKEN

Thought-Provoking Meditations on Living Cross-Culturally

T.L. Murden

CONTENTS

ACKNOWLEDGMENTS

Thanks to the many people - more than I can name here - who are a part of my story and have influenced my life. To my family, friends and teammates who have challenged, encouraged, corrected and sharpened me throughout my journey – I hope you see yourselves in these stories.

Thanks to those of you who shared your stories, read, and edited my stories and encouraged me to write it all down in the first place – you know who you are!

A special thanks to Kayla Berninghaus who helped me make this self-published book a reality. Not only did Kayla design the book cover but she spent countless hours helping me edit the content for consistency, and she did all of the formatting. I'm grateful to her beyond words.

If you have any suggestions, changes, or comments you can write to me at squeezednshaken@gmail.com. I'd love to hear your feedback.

For security reasons names and places have been changed but all the stories are true.

WHY WRITE THIS BOOK?
Is there really anything new under the sun?

While it's been a life goal to write a book, I always wonder if I really have anything new to say. Walking into a Christian bookstore is one of the most overwhelming things I can do (way more overwhelming to me than living in another culture!). There are books on every topic imaginable.

At a conference a few years ago, the main speaker mentioned in passing Ecclesiastes 12:9-10. This nugget captured my attention because it gave me a biblical framework for the importance of passing on what we know and have experienced. You might be thinking, "*of course it's Biblical to pass on what we know.*" That's what discipleship is all about (2 Tim. 2:2). That's what Paul's letters in the New Testament are all about (1 Thess. 4:1-2). Passing on what we have seen and heard to others is God's chosen method to advance the Gospel (Luke 1:1-4). So what is so fascinating about this nugget in Ecclesiastes?

In *A Godward Life* John Piper writes, "*Books don't change people; paragraphs do. Sometimes even sentences.*"[1] Think about that. Have you ever read a book or an article and one sentence gets seared into your brain in such a way that it takes root and causes action? Or is there a book you've never read cover to cover but you have a favorite chapter that you read over and over because it just hits you where you live? Solomon's proverbs are one-liners based on practical experience; his experiences. Ecclesiastes 12:9-10 says,

> "*Not only was the Teacher wise, but also he imparted knowledge to the people. He pondered and searched out and set in order many proverbs. The teacher searched to find just the right words, and what he wrote was upright and true.*"

Solomon took his practical experiences and pondered them, thinking about their meaning beyond the specific circumstances. He searched for the just the right words to best communicate deep truth in a simple

---

1 *A Godward Life* by John Piper p. 13

manner. Then he set in order a collection of these proverbs. He wrote them down and shared them with the people. I resonate with Solomon's style - practical experiences summed up in one-liner truths that apply to a variety of people in a variety of circumstances. That's my goal for writing this book.

In 2001, God led me to Kochevnikstan.[2] The cross-cultural adjustment turned my world upside down and inside out. I was squeezed and shaken in ways I hadn't even thought about before. Old sins I thought I'd conquered resurfaced. I reverted to old habits and sinful styles of relating as a means of coping with the stress. Insecurities and weaknesses I thought I'd put behind me began to ooze out once again. What spilled out of me when I got shaken up was a result of what was deep inside of me. In addition to being squeezed and shaken emotionally and spiritually, I was also challenged in new ways mentally and philosophically. Everything I thought of as a "non-negotiable" in my life was challenged and I was forced back to the Scriptures to re-evaluate my convictions. As I was confronted with new experiences and moral dilemmas, I had to re-assess my perspectives and paradigms, and in some cases, shift them.

Throughout my time in Kochevnikstan I kept a journal – parts of those journal excerpts show up in this book. I also wrote down different cultural experiences as a way of expressing my own learning journey. When it was time to leave Kochevnikstan after 11 years, I started debriefing my experiences, frustrations, joys, and lessons learned by writing them down. This writing was my way of personally processing as well as being able to pass on what the Lord had done in my life. This book is the result of that process.

I don't claim to be as wise as Solomon was, but as I put in order this collection of personal stories and lessons learned from laboring crossculturally, I long to pass on practical life principles (principles, not just applications) learned from real life experiences (mine and others) in short, easy-to-remember nuggets and one-liners that are God-focused, relevant, and sometimes humorous.

---

2   Not the real name of the place I lived. It's been changed for security reasons. The full account of how God called me can be found in "My Unique Story."

Through the use of short stories, Scripture studies, practical resources, and applications, **I hope to encourage cross-cultural laborers in their initial transitions**. Although there is a logical progression that moves chronologically through specific challenges cross-cultural workers face during their first year, the book does not need to be read in order. Each mediation can stand alone. At the end of each meditation there is one of three application segments:

> **ON YOUR OWN** challenges you to reflect on the topic as it applies to your own life.
>
> **FOR FURTHER STUDY** gives additional verses from Scripture to go deeper into the topic.
>
> **LET'S GET PRACTICAL** suggests specific action steps you can take to implement this truth.

In these stories, my goal is to be a thought-provoker not a teacher who has the right answers. It is right and good that you should question and test whatever you read and measure it against the truth of God's Word as well as think through how it practically applies in your own life (Acts 17:11). Just yesterday I got a note from a good friend who had proofread one of the chapters in the book. She commented, *"if you never practice truths, you can hear them a thousand times and your life will never change or be transformed! May everyone who reads this, find the courage to be transformed in their thinking."* Information that leads to transformation is my prayer for you as you read through this book.

Just before I moved to Kochevnikstan in 2001, I was at a mission's conference and the guest speaker (a Jamaican I think – very passionate) said that if we are to live and labor cross-culturally we must have a great love for the people. I was a little shaken. I wouldn't have said my main motivation for moving to my new country was this overwhelming love for the people. I liked the place, the people and the culture, but at the end of the day my main motivation for deciding to go was simply because it was strategic and because God didn't say "No."

The Jamaican had his story. I have mine. They are different stories just as your story is different from both of ours – it's unique. I pray that as you read through various parts of this book that you will be able to learn from my experiences. But never forget that these are *my* experiences and don't necessarily have to be yours. It's not a matter of doing what I do or experiencing what I experience or even choosing as I have chosen. However, I do exhort you to be what I am - a child of God who longs to walk in radical obedience alongside her loving Father. God has written a story just for you; He even knows the end! Learn to listen to how He leads you and seek to understand how He is writing your own unique story.

MY UNIQUE STORY

How did I get to Kochevnikstan?[3] When people ask me this question I always hesitate. Everyone's story about how God works in his or her life is different. In all honesty, I don't really feel like I have a moment when I was "called." Early on, I made a few foundational choices that set a life path for me. The most important one was choosing to follow the Lord 100% no matter what He asked. When decisions like Kochevnikstan came along, it was as simple as "*If God is in this then I will do it.*" That's it. However, simple does not mean easy.

Everyone has a unique life story and I'm no exception. As I tell you my specific story, please keep in mind that there is no right way to obey God; no right way to hear His voice. However, it is always the right thing to obey Him in whatever He is asking of you.

I had been working in my college town for a few years after graduation in order to continue to get hands-on experience discipling women. After my senior summer in Thailand, I had set goals that in 3 years I wanted to go back overseas. As the 3-year mark approached I wasn't sure what to do. I had a few different options and, to be honest, going back overseas was not my first choice. My campus organization at the time didn't have overseas opportunities, so doing something internationally meant that I would have to go with an unknown organization, to an unknown place, with unknown people…and I was afraid. For me *unknown* is the most frightening word in the English language! But with counsel, I decided I needed to embrace the unknown and apply to a one-year international experience with a different organization. As the deadline for this one year stint got closer, I continued to wrestle with my fears. One evening as I was finishing up the application the Lord clearly said (not audibly, but clearly), "*Tammy, all of your fears can be answered with two words – trust me! A ship is safe in the harbor but that's not what ships were made for*" (the Lord brought that exact phrase about the ship to mind from an inspirational poster I'd had as a kid). So I signed the application, mailed it the next day and waited to see what would happen.

---

3   For security purposes people and places names have been changed

Now, the only place in the world my mother never wanted me to go was to Russia. She grew up during the Cold War and everything "over there" was Russia. It was all communist and dangerous (I think she would have been happier had I applied to go to the Middle East; her concept of danger was totally shaped by her own preconceived ideas). Of course, the only place I really wanted to go was to Russia. So on the application Russia was my first choice, and when I was accepted to the program, I was accepted to Russia. The group was comprised of about 50 people being sent in teams to multiple cities. I was expecting to be on a team going to St. Petersburg (still called Leningrad at that time). Through our entire preparation and funding time, I was in communication with a teammate going to St. Pete. I told people – lots of people – I was going to Russia. I read and studied up on Russian history specifically about St. Petersburg, Catherine the Great, and Peter the Great. I was prepared. I had a plan but God directed my steps – and He took me in a direction I could never have predicted! I didn't pursue Kochevnikstan. Kochevnikstan pursued me.

In August of 1991 there was a coup outside of Moscow and the Soviet Union's collapse became imminent. This world event affected me more than I could have ever dreamed. The team leaders of the year-long program called me less than a month before I was leaving for St. Petersburg.

"There's an opportunity that's opened up in Kochevnikstan and we would like you to consider going on that team."

My first response was, *"Where's Kochevnikstan?"*

This was a legitimate question since in 1991 Kochevnikstan didn't exist on any map. Kochevnikstan declared it's independence and became a separate country in 1991 – yes, I was there for this historic occasion. I could not have planned that if I had tried! I don't remember what I was thinking, but I trusted the leadership's recommendation and agreed to be part of the team to Orchard City, Kochevnikstan. That was the first time Kochevnikstan pursued me.

The second time was 10 years later. After my one year international experience, I returned to the U.S. and went on staff with a collegiate organization to pioneer a new campus ministry. When I left Kochevnikstan in 1992, I said "goodbye" fully convinced that I would never return. However, during my time on staff, my campus sent summer teams to Kochevnikstan. Several of the girls I discipled and campus leaders I knew well were part of those teams. This regular contact with Kochevnikstan kept it in front of me, but even after being part of the 1996 summer team, I never thought that I would go back long-term. It wasn't part of my plan!

Remember how I told you that I *always* plan ahead? Usually I've thought so far ahead that I have to put the brakes on and wait for my circumstances to catch up to my plan, but this wasn't the case with my decision to move to Kochevnikstan long-term. It only took 2 weeks from start to finish.

I knew it was time to move on from my campus staff position. I loved what I was doing - I was at the top of my game. But I knew that for my own personal development I needed some new challenges, some new risks that were too big for me so that I would be forced to step out in faith. Although my campus director, several of my good friends from our campus ministry, and close friends who were already living in Kochevnikstan were forming a team to pioneer a campus work there, the idea of my being part of that team never crossed my mind. Looking back on it, I cannot explain why it never occurred to me to consider joining this team – me who is always thinking ahead and considering every contingency. But through these circumstances, God made it very clear that Kochevnikstan was *His* idea, not mine. In later years when things got hard it was a great comfort to remember that God had clearly led me in this. There was no room to second guess myself.

As part of my systematic plan to investigate new possibilities, I went to visit the U.S. Center for World Missions (USCWM). I wasn't looking to go back overseas but was interested in being a missions mobilizer. The afternoon just before I flew out to California, my good friend asked me a simple question. *"Tammy, why haven't you thought about going to Kochevnikstan? You know everyone on that team."* I have no idea what I said to her but that simple question planted a seed. Three days later during my exploration week at the USCWM, one of my group mates – someone I had only met days before and who knew nothing about me – asked me out of the blue, *"Tammy, why wouldn't you think about going to Kochevnikstan with this team of people you know?"* I must have already mentioned to her that I knew people planning to go, but I don't remember it. You could have knocked me over with a feather. The same question came from two totally different people in totally different places in just 3 days! God was saying something, and I wanted to know what it was. That night, lying in bed in Pasadena, California I finally asked the question for myself, *"Lord, why wouldn't I go to Kochevnikstan – a place I love – with a team I love laboring with?"* And in that moment, I knew that was what I needed to do.

This thought had only been in my head for three days. Could this really be how God was leading me? In the same conversation with the Lord that night, I came up with three things that He would need to do to confirm this was truly His leading.

First, I would pray and fast for a week. The question was not whether or not God was calling me to Kochevnikstan, because I felt certain that He was. The week of praying and fasting was to ask the Lord if there was any reason I should *not* move forward in this direction. That week He was silent and I took that as a sign that God was in this move.

Second, my mom would have to agree to come visit me; remember, my mom thought Russia (it was all Russia in her mind) was the most dangerous place around. Although I was in my 30s by this point and didn't need my parent's permission, I very much wanted their blessing. My mom agreeing to come visit me was something only the Lord could do, and He worked in her heart. Not only did she agree to come visit (which both my parents did after my second year in the country), but she told me she always knew I would go back overseas. That was pretty insightful considering I didn't know I would ever go back overseas!

Finally, I needed an invitation to join the team. In my whirlwind of new thoughts about Kochevnikstan, it occurred to me that the team leader (my good friend and campus director of 10 years) had not invited me to be part of this team. So the week I got back from the USCWM, I set up a lunch appointment. When I asked about the possibility of my joining the team, he looked a little dumbfounded. Not only had the Lord been planting the idea in my mind but in his as well. He'd been wondering just that week why he had never talked to me about being on the team. We talked. He invited. I accepted.

So it was total of two weeks from the moment the idea first entered my mind to committing to be on this new team headed to Kochevnikstan. I can't say that anything like that had ever happened before or since. No other major life decision has ever caught me so off guard or come together so quickly. In fact, when I left Kochevnikstan after 11 years, it took me several months to even consider the possibility and another agonizing six months to make a final decision.

That's two different times that Kochevnikstan pursued me when I wasn't pursuing it. There's one last time (to date at least – who knows what the future holds!) that Kochevnikstan wooed me to itself. I won't go into detail here, but in 2006 my organizational team disbanded. I had a decision to make: move to another international location with the organization that I had been with for more that 15 years – an organization that was like family to me – or switch organizations and stay in Kochevnikstan? Left to myself, I would never have chosen to leave the organization I was with, but the pull to stay in Kochevnikstan was strong. Kochevnikstan pursued me once, and once again the choice came down to an issue of fearing the unknown. Staying within the boundaries of my current organization felt safer and more familiar to me. But in His gentle voice the Lord asked me – as he had many years before – to trust Him. And as I had trained myself to do over the years, I said "yes" to the Lord.

I stayed in Kochevnikstan another five years with my new organization. Then, as I mentioned earlier, I agonized over the decision to leave. Eleven years in Kochevnikstan had done much to develop my character, challenge my views of the world, humble me over my own self-importance, deepen my intimacy with the Lord, and in a small way, I hope, impacted the Kochevnikstani people I loved dearly (and still love). This book was born out of those 11 years living and laboring in Kochevnikstan. My last six months in country, I started to write down some of the life lessons I'd learned. It was my way of processing truths I didn't want to forget and truths I wanted to pass on as I started a new job preparing and mobilizing the next generation of lifelong laborers.

✏ ON YOUR OWN

Think about how God has led you in the past in making big and small decisions. What patterns do you see in how He leads you? Write down – in your journal or in a letter to a friend – a few of the ways you've experienced God's leading.

For example, with my charge-ahead personality God rarely needs to say "yes." If something is not good for me He usually says "no" clearly. No answer means move forward – as it did during my prayer and fast week. This is a pattern I see repeated in my life as I make big decisions.

Embracing the Adventure

0-3 months

EXPECTATIONS – WE ALL HAVE THEM
Even if we don't know we have them!

Expectations eat my lunch! Have you ever heard that expression? It's one of my personal favorites, because it's so true of my life. I have expectations – some I know about, some I don't – and when my expectations aren't met I feel disappointed, frustrated, and angry – like someone stole my lunch when I'm starving!

Moving overseas brings out expectations we didn't know we had. For example when I get up in the morning in America I expect to see someone I know (besides roommate or family) at some point during the day. I don't think about it, but still I expect it. I had a large network of relationships in the U.S., but when I moved to a new country I knew only a handful of people and it wasn't uncommon for me to go days without seeing someone I knew besides my teammates.

In a job in the U.S., I expect my boss to have some say about my life – when I can take vacation or what my salary will be. I do not, however, expect my boss to have a say on WHERE I go on vacation or HOW I budget my salary. But in a cross-cultural setting, issues of safety and security are much bigger (depending on your location), and it is much more likely that your boss WILL say where you can or cannot travel. And if you are on support and your budget affects your ability to be in the country and to actually do your job, then it's likely that your supervisor will be much more hands on with you about your personal finances. (I knew a couple who ended up leaving the field because no one was asking them about their personal finances which were in shambles. The husband had a key role on this pioneering team, and it didn't just affect his family when he left but all the families on that team and the team's long-term strategy for that country).

Relating to your teammates is another place expectations can catch you off guard. Words like "vulnerability" and "transparency" take on a whole new meaning when you live cross-culturally (it still amazes me how common "bathroom talk" is on a cross-cultural team!). In the U.S., in a "normal" job, you might expect your co-workers to show you care and concern. As long as you do your job, they won't do much prying into your personal struggles. But co-laboring on a cross-cultural team means that an individual's "personal struggles" affect more than just them. It affects the function of the whole team because the team is so small. You are more like a family than like co-workers. If roommates are fighting it becomes about more than just their disagreements – the whole team is affected because everyone is drawn into the tension felt between the two teammates. Teams overseas – because of smaller networks of relationships and fewer outlets to "escape" the relational conflicts – feel each other's struggles more than groups working together in the U.S. It means that everyone is much more "up in your business" than most people expect and are comfortable with.

My first time overseas for more than a few weeks, I was on a team of 6 people. I was young and not used to people being "up in my business" all the time. That year God started revealing to me how I was very self protective – meaning that if someone got too close, whether it was threatening or caring, I would pull away to protect myself from getting hurt. That was my coping mechanism for keeping people from seeing the "real me" behind the walls I had built up. The problem that year was that there was no place to pull away. I knew 6 people and I couldn't escape them for long. We lived in close proximity – physically and spiritually – and these 6 people kept bumping up against my walls until eventually, in His goodness toward me, God broke them down. The result was a greater level of intimacy, trust and fellowship than I had ever experienced, both in my relationship with people and with the Lord. But that was not my expectation going into that year. It was not only uncomfortable it was downright frustrating!

Once you've experienced the benefits of living in close community - vulnerability and transparency that really sharpens and encourages you - you get a taste for it. In some cases you move overseas expecting that kind of community, fellowship, and accountability and then don't get it. Especially for students coming out of a strong campus ministry where there is an emphasis on training, one can feel left out in the cold, like no one is thinking for you and you are supposed to just figure things out on your own. Maybe your expectation was for a lot of hands-on leadership, training, and shepherding and but that isn't how the international team you've joined functions. You are disappointed because your expectations aren't being met.

As you learn to live together – in community – you learn to talk about your expectations as they emerge and to develop new habits and new expectations on living together in your new community.

In these situations – whether your cross-cultural team is more "invasive" than you expected or less "directive" than you are used to – the point is the same. We all have expectations and when our expectations aren't met we feel disappointed at best, and at the worst, our expectations result in serious conflict with our roommate, teammate, or supervisor.

The key is to recognize that you do have expectations even though you might not be able to express what they are. Imagine that you just got married. In the wife's family the dad always took out the garbage. But in the husband's family it was the mom's job. Neither of you consciously thought about your expectations on who will take out the garbage when you're married. Yet both of you bring expectations to your marriage about who takes out the garbage. As you learn to live together – in community – you learn to talk about your expectations as they emerge and to develop new habits and new expectations on living together in your new community.

✏ ON YOUR OWN

What expectations did you know you had coming into your cross-cultural environment? What expectations have caught you by surprise?

Write down your definition/expectation of vulnerability, transparency, and accountability. Write down a few specific examples of how this definition might practically play out for you with your teammates. Do you think they have the same definition/expectation? As a team talk about what these three things (vulnerability, transparency, accountability) should look like on your team.

What expectations do you have for your leadership? Are you getting more or less leadership than you would like? In what ways specifically? Talk with your supervisor about what appropriate expectations are. Not only is it a leader's job to learn to lead you the way you want to be led, but it's your job as a follower to learn to follow your leader in the way he/she wants to be followed.

UPROOTED

Take a minute and think of all the people you know in America - your extended family, your neighbors, your teachers, coaches, friends and their families, people at church, classmates from school and college, your dentist and doctor, co-workers, all your supporters. If you were to make a rough estimate, how many people – by name or face – do you think you know in America? 500? 1,000? More?

Now think about your new country. How many people do you know – by name or face – in your new country? If you are like me the list is significantly lower! When I moved to Kochevnikstan, I knew 12 people - 7 adults and 5 kids – all of whom were my teammates. If you threw in a handful of new local relationships (like my language teacher, her husband, and a few students I met on a summer project) AND all the expats I knew in a city of 1.5 million, the number of people I knew might add up to roughly 25! And these were mostly NEW relationships – people with whom I had very little history or common experiences. In a matter of days I went from having easy access to a network of over a 1,000 people to a network of 25 people total – including the most casual of relationships.

My pre-field training warned me that my network of relationships would shrink significantly and need to be rebuilt over time. But even with this preparation I was caught off guard – I didn't realize just how many roots were deeply planted in all my relational networks in the U.S. The deeper the roots the harder it is to uproot! I went from a wide variety of people that I saw everyday at work, social activities, and church to seeing the SAME 7 adults. We lived together (myself and my teammate), worked together, studied language together, socialized together, studied the word together, and prayed together. I liked my team and I knew them better than most new teams know each other. We were like family. But after a few months - I have to be honest - I was sick of those 7 teammates! It wasn't until my networks were uprooted, that I realized how much joy and connectedness I found in something as simple as a casual conversation with someone after church, or walking into my doctor's office and the receptionist knowing my name (no one anywhere in my new city knew my name!).

I realize that in the 21st century the internet has completely revolutionized the possibilities to stay connected to people living all over the world. You probably have a 1,000 friends on Facebook alone. When I moved to Kochevnikstan the internet was not easily accessible. I had e-mail, but it was dial up (you probably don't remember those days), and international calling was complex and expensive. So communication with my network of friends in America, while possible, was limited. As I look back on those early days – frustrating as they were at times with my limited network of new relationships – I'm thankful that I was uprooted and forced to develop new relational networks in the place where God had placed me.

Jeremiah 1:10 says, "*See today I appoint you over nations and kingdoms to uproot and tear down to destroy and overthrow, to build and to plant.*" While the context of this passage is Jeremiah's ministry calling to uproot and rebuild nations, I look at this process and believe that God does the same thing in our lives as individuals; He uproots and tears down the places or people in whom we put false security; He destroys and overthrows idols in our lives; He builds and plants new patterns of trust and dependence on Him. The starting point for this process is uprooting.

God uproots and tears down the places or people in whom we put false security; He destroys and overthrows idols in our lives; He builds and plants new patterns of trust and dependence on Him.

DANGERS OF NOT UPROOTING

In this technological age of high speed internet, e-mail, Skype, Facebook, Twitter, and whatever the newest social media connection is, it's easy to never really feel "uprooted" from your old network of relationships. Depending on where you live (if you have internet access or not) you could spend half your time (or more) every day talking to old friends and staying in touch with everything they are doing. If your best friend is only a phone call away, then when you feel lonely and discouraged it's easier to call him or her rather than run to the Lord or to develop a deeper relationship with a new friend or teammate by honestly sharing your struggle. While talking to your friend in America for 5-10 minutes a day may not seem like a lot, it keeps your head (and your heart) engaged in another place. While that might "feel safe" in the beginning (and it IS safe), it can become a hindrance down the road. If you only partially uproot, it's difficult to be re-planted. You'll become like a tree that's been upturned in a storm: not planted where it was but not transplanted somewhere new, its roots are exposed and they have nowhere to grow, no way to get consistent nourishment, and eventually the tree dies.

Don't get so caught up in staying connected to your old life that you miss out on all the blessings God has for right where you are.

I'm not suggesting that you write off your old friends or that you don't stay in contact with your family. Modern technology is amazing. Use it, but use it wisely. Limit your time on Facebook and however often (or however long) you spend talking to the States in a week. Set goals that will help you intentionally interact and integrate into your new culture. The danger is using technology as a way to "escape" the difficulties of your initial adjustment. Especially for the first 3-6 months which, honestly, will be the hardest for you and the period of time you most want to talk to old friends who provide the security of the familiar. But, like the partially uprooted tree, if you don't fully uproot and re-plant, you'll only be prolonging the initial adjustment period.[1] Don't allow yourself to get so caught up in staying connected to your old life that you miss out on all the blessings God has for you right where you are.

In addition to setting goals for yourself, set right expectations for your family and stateside friends. Sometimes we want to let go of our "old

---

1   Internet wasn't my greatest temptation - English language TV/movies were my escape to the familiar. So I set a goal to not buy a TV my first 6 months and to only watch movies if it was in a big group.

life" but it won't let go of us. Since it's so easy to stay connected, often people have high expectations for you to do just that. I have a friend whose mom wanted her to call every day. That's not realistic. Even an expectation to talk every week can become burdensome when you are juggling a new culture, new language, and a 6-12 hour time change. Staying connected is good, but the reality is that we only have so much capacity – and overseas our capacity is already lower than usual. It can sometimes become overwhelming, even draining, to live up to the communication expectations people have for us. Just because we have the capability to stay connected does not mean we have the capacity to stay connected with everyone we know!

Being uprooted is hard. There's no way around it. You just walk through it trusting that as God uproots, He also replants; as He tears down, He also builds up.

✔ **LET'S GET PRACTICAL**

How do you feel about your shrunken network of relationships? How does this reality affect your relationships with your teammates?

Give yourself a visual reminder of your "uprooted" transition. Buy a house plant and put it in a glass jar with water so you can see the roots (no soil). Or draw a picture that expresses how you feel about being uprooted. Let these visual aids remind you that you are in process.

What goal(s) do you need to set for yourself in the area of internet communication? Other escapes?

What can you intentionally do to begin to put down roots in your new culture?

HOW DO I...?

I was headed to a local friend's house for dinner. I was proud of myself for knowing that culturally it was appropriate to take a gift and often that gift was flowers. So I wanted to buy flowers for my hostess. I went to a nearby flower lady and asked to buy six flowers – half a dozen is a good round number (actually I made gestures to indicate what I wanted since I didn't have enough language yet to actually ask). I wanted to communicate how much I appreciated this friend inviting me into her home. However, the flower lady would NOT sell me the flowers. At first, I thought she just didn't understand. But it was clear – I wanted six flowers and she wouldn't sell them to me. She finally turned away ignoring me completely and began to help another customer. In total defeat, I walked away with no flowers! Only later did I learn that in Kochevnikstan you only buy flowers in odd numbers – even numbers of flowers are for funerals! In her own way the flower lady was "helping" me to not embarrass myself by unintentionally saying to my hostess, "*I wish you death.*"

In another culture even the simplest of actions can quickly become overwhelming and defeating.

How do I...buy flowers? Who knew you couldn't buy an even number of flowers?

How do I...cook? Where are the boxed cake mixes? What do you mean I have to make it from scratch?[2]

How do I...clean? Why don't they have mops? How am I supposed to clean the floor without a mop?

How do I...hang pictures on the walls? The walls are solid concrete? Anyone have a drill?

How do I...use public transportation? What bus goes where? How do I get a taxi? How do I pay? How much should I pay?

---

2   The Wycliffe cookbook is a great resource for cooking from scratch. It even has recipes for making basics such as mayonnaise, ketchup, and syrup.

How do I...get money? Do they have ATMs? What if none of my cards work?

How do I...know how much money I need? What's the exchange rate again? How much is that in dollars?

How do I...rent an apartment? Are you sure I don't need a legal contract? Am I going to get cheated?

How do I...pay my bills? You mean they don't come in the mail? I have to pay at a bank?

How do I...set up internet? What documents and whose permission do I need?

How do I...know where things are? I'm lost somewhere in the city, but I don't know where I am!

How do I...know what kind of products are good? Where's the Tide and Lysol? What, no Charmin?

How do I...buy furniture or basic items? What stores are good? What is a good price? Help! Where's the local Wal-Mart?!

Living overseas is a constant learning cycle. Just when you think you've got something figured out (like how and where to pay your bills), there is some other new thing to learn (like getting your internet repaired). It's an ongoing process. But the initial "How do I...." feelings of frustration and defeat are perfectly normal and they WILL pass.

INTENTIONAL INVESTIGATION
This was one of the most helpful things that I did long-term. I can't encourage intentional investigation enough as a way of learning your new city.

My team's ministry focus was students, and we wanted to gather information about where universities were and what student culture was like in Orchard City. Since we couldn't find any accurate statistical information (or didn't know where to ask for it) we decided to do our own leg-work – literally!

We split the city into major east-west and north-south roads. We split our team into groups of two and assigned each group several roads. Then we literally WALKED EVERY ROAD IN THE CITY (a city of 1.5 million people) mapping out locations of universities and institutes of higher learning (there are over 100 in Orchard City). We also used this time as a means of praying for the city, claiming the promise God gave His people in Joshua 1 that *"every place where you set your foot I will give you as an inheritance."*

In addition to learning what we wanted to know about the number and locations of universities, this team exercise had personal benefits. As a result I knew, and still know, my city better than most of my local friends. When I started driving six years after I first arrived in country, that one exercise from years before was really helpful to me in feeling comfortable getting around on my own. I knew this city and when someone told me crossroads to a "new" place, I had a framework for thinking about how to get to where I was going.

While everyone, or every team, doesn't have to do such a drastic investigative exercise, it is really important and helpful to be purposeful in learning your city. Whether you do it as a team or simply on your own, intentional investigation can help you lower your stress level as you begin to feel more and more confident about your new city.

LOWER YOUR EXPECTATIONS

Journal entry from my three-month evaluation:

> *My capacity is low. I'm tired a lot. I seem, at times to have
> nothing to do, but then I never seem to have time to do all
> that comes up. EVERYTHING takes more time than I'm
> used to. Normal life activities (shopping, cooking, talking,
> thinking) takes more energy than usual. Although I know I
> am where I need to be I sometimes feel guilty for "not doing
> more" in any given day or week.*

A co-laborer in a Southeast Asian country told me once that it takes
25% of your energy just to live in another country, leaving you only
75% of your capacity available on a good day. 'Another worker in a
different Asian country told me, *"I've spent 30 years learning to increase my capacity [in the U.S.]. Now suddenly my capacity has shrunk
to about one third. I need to lower expectations; learn new capacities,
adjust goals; simplify my life and then begin increasing my capacity
again. Learn how the locals live and adjust to their lead."*

I am a task-oriented person. I like to get stuff done. I make lists for
fun, and my "to-do" list is my favorite list of all. So you can imagine
my frustration when I moved to this new culture and my ability to
accomplish ANYTHING on my "to-do" list shrunk to nothing.

In the U.S., I generally had 10 things on my to-do list for the day –
sometimes less but sometimes even more. And I could usually get
them all done. So when I got to Kochevnikstan, I would make my
"to-do" list for the day or the week. But unlike in the U.S. I rarely got
everything done – in fact I rarely got even close to everything done.
I felt SO unproductive. I felt like I rarely accomplished anything and
yet I didn't have time to do anything more. And everything made
me tired. I had to learn to lower my expectations on what I could or
couldn't do in a day.

I began to "re-define" what it meant for me to have a "successful" day.
I lowered my expectations for myself so that if I did ONE thing in the

morning, ONE thing in the afternoon, and ONE thing in the evening – that was a GOOD day! The ONE thing could be something as simple as having a quite time in the morning, talking to someone in the afternoon, and making dinner in the evening. As ridiculous as it might sound, those three things were exhausting (it might not sound ridiculous to you if you are also experiencing the "failure" of not getting done all you think you "should" be doing).

The quiet time in the morning would often be dealing with my own guilt over feeling unproductive: *Where does that come from? Why do I feel this way? Is there sin in my life? Can I trust God to do what HE has promised to and to not worry about the rest?* Wow, good stuff but it's emotionally tiring to fight sin and wrong perspectives! Talking with one person in the afternoon – if that happened outside my house - meant I had to GET there. That meant knowing what bus to take and getting off at the right place (which I often didn't) or psyching myself up to get a taxi by myself (which of course meant I had to use my limited language). Meeting ONE person might sound as simple as going to a place, having coffee, and meeting with them. But in a new culture there are all kinds of unexpected "detours" that make a "simple" task a monumental and exhausting endeavor.

Whatever your expectations...part of adjusting to your new culture is learning to lower those expectations.

Making dinner in the evening – that should be easy right? But do you know how many U.S. cookbooks call for a can of this or a package of that or a box of something else? I had to get rid of a few cookbooks because they were useless in helping me cook in Kochevnikstan where pre-packaged food was limited. Cooking requires not only thinking about what I am going to cook but also if I can get all the ingredients. If not, can I substitute items? Then I have to go to the grocery story or bazaar and find all those items in an unfamiliar place and speak (or try to understand) an unfamiliar language and finally check out using unfamiliar money. That's assuming that I could find all the right ingredients at one place (which more often than not wasn't the case). In a new culture something as simple as making dinner becomes an EXHAUSTING task. It's especially difficult for moms whose family expects to eat dinner every single night. As a single person, it was a little easier. It's amazing what you can make a meal out of if you are by yourself. There were plenty of days I ate boiled potatoes with bouillon just because it was simple!

Perhaps your new country is not quite so different as the one you come from. And perhaps it's not such a hard task for you to do several things in a day. Or perhaps you have an adventurous spirit (you have to have some sense of adventure to go overseas in the first place!), so all the unexpected things that force you to be flexible are really fun for you. But whatever your expectations – and trust me you DO have expectations even if you don't know what they are – part of adjusting to your new culture is learning to lower those expectations.

If I'm feeling overly lazy, lacking in discipline, or in an "escape mode" and I can't get out of it, I try to remember that these things usually pass with time (at least that's true for me). I'll give myself a "grace period" to just let my emotions ride themselves out. And I set an attainable goal and a deadline (often a Monday) to begin my new goal. Usually by the time my deadline rolls around I'm ready for it. I've given myself time to "rest" as well as set a right "expectation" for getting back in the game.

A verse I learned to pray for myself - even before I moved overseas - that specifically applies to lowering our expectations is from John 17:4. In speaking to his Father, Jesus says, "*I have glorified you on earth, I have finished the work you gave me to do.*" Jesus didn't do everything that could have been done – there were still sick who needed healing, lost who needed to hear the Gospel, and disciples who needed more training. But he was able to say – with a clear conscience before God – that he had finished everything that God had given him. My frequent prayer for myself is that every day I would "*do all that God has given me to do and nothing that He hasn't.*"

🖊 ON YOUR OWN

What kind of expectations do you have for yourself? Are they realistic? Ask your team leader, mentor, or teammates what realistic expectations to have during your period of cultural adjustment. It helps to hear other people's stories – not to compare but to "normalize" your experiences and remind you that you are not alone.

What is a realistic daily "to-do" list for you? Weekly to-do list?

What is a verse that you can begin to pray for yourself as you learn to lower your expectations in how much you can do in your new culture?

DIFFERENT MIGHT NOT BE WRONG...
But it sure is frustrating!

In all your pre-field training have you heard the crossing cultures mantra "*Different isn't wrong it's just different*"? Well, I want to propose that while different may not be wrong, it sure is frustrating! Frustration, according to one author, is nothing more than blocked goals. When you move into a new culture you have goals you don't even know you have and they get blocked in ways you could never have imagined!

For example, you might have a goal to buy an ice-cold Coke. You don't think of that as a goal because it is such a simple task. You walk to a nearby store expecting to accomplish your task, only they don't have Coke. You really want a Coke because it's been a bad culture day and you need a taste of America. You use your three words of your new language and a lot of gestures to ask where you can buy a Coke. The seller points to a nearby store. Thanking her and leaving with an adventurous attitude, you excitedly head toward the object of your goal – a cold American Coke.

At the second store you ask – mostly in gestures – for a cold Coke. She brings out a dusty hot bottle of Coke that looks like a hold over from the last decade. Ok, so it's not cold, but it's Coke – you still have a good attitude. You fumble through the unfamiliar currency and finally give the seller what you think is plenty of money. She won't take it. You try to understand and keep pushing the bill toward her. Still she refuses. In desperation, you hold out several bills and motion for her to just take what she needs. She shakes her head, takes your Coke – your American Coke – and walks away. Your seemingly simple goal of buying a Coke has been blocked. Your adventurous spirit is gone and you are frustrated! Later your local friend explains that probably the seller wouldn't take your money because you didn't have exact change and she didn't have enough change to break your large bill.

It may not be wrong that sellers expect you to have exact change when buying something in their store, but it can be very frustrating. Especially when we come from a culture where there is little or no value on having exact change. I remember one of my first trips back to the

U.S. after living internationally. I was at Wal-Mart, and when I got to the check out I was so proud of myself for giving the cashier the exact change. It made no difference to her whatsoever. She was not impressed, and if she had any thoughts at all about my sensitivity to give exact change it was frustration that I took so long to dig it out!

A good friend reminds me often, "*If you will laugh about it later, laugh about it now.*" This is good advice in new situations where your goals will frequently get blocked and you will be frustrated. It's not a matter of if you get frustrated, but of when. Hopefully you have – or choose to have – an adventurous spirit and for the most part situations like my example of buying a Coke become a fun story and exploration of the culture. But there will be those days, I-hate-this-culture-and-everything-about-this-place-days, when you just can't muster up a good attitude. Delays, frustrations, the absence of expected things like water and electricity, language faux pas, cultural blunders, intense government scrutiny, things that aren't "fair" and things that are simply "different" are all a normal part of the cross-cultural experience.

"Our mouths were filled with laughter, our tongues with songs of joy…The Lord has done great things for us and we are filled with joy." Psalm 126:2-3

It's important – one could even say essential for longevity – that you learn to laugh at yourself in midst of these very real situations. If you'll laugh about it later, laugh about it now!

✔ LET'S GET PRACTICAL

Can you think of an example from your own life – like my trying to buy a Coke – that was frustrating? How did you respond?

It's not only important to learn to laugh at yourself when cultural blunders or frustrations happen but to also infuse your life with a good healthy dose of humor in your everyday life.

What things make you laugh? How can you incorporate those things into your regular schedule? What kinds of TV shows, comics, or other things are funny to you? Keep a few of your favorite comic strips or sitcoms around for when you need a pick me up (I had a Calvin and Hobbes book I read often during my language learning years. It made me laugh and gave my brain a rest!).

Is it difficult for you to laugh at yourself? Why? If you laugh at yourself easily how can you "contribute" that natural attitude to your team? (My roommate early on was someone who naturally laughs at herself and situations; and it was contagious! She brought humor and levity to our team that was welcomed and needed).

If you are on the more serious side, think of things that make you smile and keep those around – a picture of your dog's face up close, watching the sunrise, country music, etc. These small "happys" serve as a reminder that all is not wrong with the world no matter how frustrated, depressed, or silly you feel at some cultural mishap.

Read "The Post Office." This meditation is a real life example of a time when my adventurous spirit was lost and "different" frustrated me to the point of tears. Although I confess I did not laugh about it at the time (I cried), this is one of my favorite stories after the fact and even thinking about it now makes me laugh out loud.

THE POST OFFICE

I had my first real clash with the culture yesterday. I had ordered some pants from L.L. Bean (mistake 1 - don't order something that might not fit), so I was going to return them through the local postal system. After all, the package arrived fine through the local postal system, and I didn't think there would be a problem to send it back (mistake 2 - never assume that things will be the way you expect!). So with an American culture mindset, I searched for a good sturdy box, packaged the box securely with tape and glued the return label on the box (I had learned this lesson the hard way - my one other experience at the Post Office I had taped the seal on the envelope and they made me take my letter out and put it in a different, un-taped envelope. I knew they preferred glue over tape). I was ready for my trek to the Central Post Office.

I was meeting girls at a nearby cafe and planned what I thought was plenty of time to go by the post office beforehand to mail the box. I got to the post office and managed to find the line for international mail. There were five people in front of me so I waited patiently. When it finally was my turn the lady said - and pointed and gestured so I could understand - that I would have to have my box "packaged." That was a different line!

In Kochevnikstan they almost never send boxes. I say almost but I didn't see a single box in the post office. Everything must be wrapped in either brown craft paper and tied with string or wrapped in a muslin type material bag complete with wax seals (that's right, wax seals). And even if you send a box - it has to be wrapped. They don't use tape. Tape is a no-no on packages. They think it comes off too easily (although how it comes off easier than paper tears is beyond me!).

So I go to wait in the packaging line. There are only two people in this line but with HUGE mail outs. They weren't boxed up at all but were being wrapped in small-sized packages with brown paper, string, and wax seals. One man was sending out what looked like hundreds of thousands (literally) of insurance cards. He just handed stacks of cards to the lady wrapping and she would tie them up in brown paper. I think the theory is that lots of little packages are better than one big package. So this man had probably 30 small packages being wrapped. The second man in front of me had books and video tapes - again not boxed up at all. They were being wrapped up like Christmas packages, addressed, and mailed.

Well, I couldn't wait for all that because I had to meet these girls at the nearby cafe. So after over an hour of waiting I left, no further along than I was before. But I was undaunted with my adventurous spirit and all that. I thought, "I'll just come back after I meet the girls. It will be later (I had been there around lunch time) and there won't be so many people."

My time with the girls was wonderful. We talked about the authority of Scriptures and then all but one had to go to class. One of the girls had some free time and went back to the post office with me to help me try to mail my package.

This time I was smarter and went to the packaging line first (I was feeling proud of myself). There were only a few people in front of me so I thought, "No problem" (Hmmmm!). When it was my turn, the lady took my carefully packaged box (which was completely foreign to her) and began to tear it open and pull out the contents, strewing my necessary return receipt information all over her work space. She tells me it will be better to put the pants in two packages. I try to explain that I can't do that since they all have to be received at exactly the same time along with the return receipt. Besides, I'm thinking, "Brown paper going through the stateside system is going to get all torn up and who knows what shape my pants will be in. No, I think the box is definitely better and safer." The wrapper lady isn't too happy with my decision and tells me it will cost about $20 (instead of $5 her way). I say I'm willing to pay the extra (my friend was a great help in all of this because without her translating I would have been lost).

So the lady starts wrapping my package - but not in brown paper with string. She puts it in a muslin bag and begins to SEW it with needle and thread. Of course she stopped several times - once to help another customer with a "small package" and then in the middle of sewing up my package she decided that she needed to clean up her work space so she goes for a wet cloth and wipes everything down and sweeps. All this time, my package is sitting and waiting to be sewed! Even my local friend couldn't understand what the lady was doing.

So FINALLY I get my package wrapped up in cloth, sewed closed, and then sealed with red wax and stamped with a signet stamp. I just kept thinking, "I wish I could be a fly on the wall when the people at L.L. Bean receive this package!" I doubt they've ever seen anything like it.

So now I'm ready to mail (or so I thought) and I go stand in the line where I actually need to send the package (remember I've just been in the wrapping line!). The guy at the head of the line is sending 20 army duffle bag sized muslin-wrapped packages complete with wax seals. TWENTY of them to the States. Did I mention that while they use computers here for some things all of their record keeping is done BY HAND? The lady working has to hand write all the documentation for these packages (and an interesting note is that again no tape or staples to keep the paper together - they use glue!). The man sending the packages is nice and the woman behind the counter is working like Speedy Gonzales to get it all done, but it still looked like I would have to wait awhile so my friend left. After all, it looked like I was home free.

FINALLY after about 45 minutes, it's my turn. The lady takes my box, weighs it, makes sure all my papers are in place and shows me the price - $100!!! The packaging lady had told me $20 (my friend had translated so I know I understood that correctly). At this point, my patience failed. I had more than I could take. I'd been at the post office almost 2 hours (plus, more than one hour earlier in the day) and now they wanted me to pay $100 to send this package. I couldn't help myself. I started to cry. The lady behind the desk kept saying, "Ne plakala, ne plakala" (which means,"Don't cry, don't cry"). And she goes running off somewhere. All I could think of was how I was NEVER going to order clothes off the internet again. The lady - who really was very nice and helpful - came back with another lady who spoke English, and although she tried to explain and I tried to understand, it never did become clear to me exactly why it was so expensive (although I'm sure had I sent the package their way – small packages wrapped with brown paper – it would have been less expensive). What did become clear was that it was not worth it anymore to try to return these pants. It would have cost me MORE to send them back than they originally cost! So after almost three hours, I left with the *same package I came with and everyone staring at me, because I couldn't stop crying.*

As upset as I was, it really was a wonderful picture of learning a new culture. I expected things to be the way I'm used to (American system of postal service) and it was drastically different. It would be easy to think their system is "wrong" but really it's just different (albeit very frustrating to me!), and it's my job to adjust to those differences. I have two standard sayings for situations like this that are truths that carry me through and give me perspective:

"If you'll laugh about it later, laugh about it now."
"Nothing is all bad if it makes a good story."

I did laugh later about it as I was telling my teammates, and I think this is a great story - one I'll add to my "culture clash" repertoire.

LANGUAGE LEARNING I
It's just hard!

Journal entry at nine months:

> *Last night I was studying for my language class, and I thought to myself, "Learning language is by far one of the hardest things I've ever done in my life." I let my mind wander for a few minutes wondering, "WHY?" First of all, it's just plain hard to try to communicate – not just learn words but really communicate – in another language. Besides, it requires great time and perseverance. TIME is the key element in learning a language. Think about it – it takes children almost 2 years to even speak and then another 4-5 years to begin to read and then another 10 years (and the rest of their lives) to build vocabulary and understanding. No matter how much I study and try to cram new words, concepts, grammar rules, etc. into my head – there's only so much room in there! And it just won't all fit. IT TAKES TIME! And I want to know it NOW (yes, I come from a "microwave mentality" that craves instant gratification). But it takes PERSEVERANCE – it's a DAILY thing. If I go more than a day without speaking or listening to my new language – my mind completely shuts off! And it's a daily thing over a loooooonnnnnnnggggggg period of time. I have to just keep plugging away.*

IT'S A LIFE-LONG LEARNING PROCESS

Not all languages have the same level of difficulty – some are easier to learn than others. Regardless of how easy (or not easy) a language is to learn it's still hard – at least for the average person. I studied at a language school in the U.S. for a semester before coming to Kochevnikstan. Five hours a day of vocabulary, grammar, and conversation. Another 5-6 hours a day of homework, exercises, and memorization.

Then, my first year in country our team spent a full year focused only on language. I'm not going to sugar coat it – it was HARD! Even now, 10 years later my language (while adequate) is still not what I would call fluent. I lack vocabulary to communicate nuances of meaning; I make lots of grammar and pronunciation mistakes. I'm still learning cultural idioms and colloquial terms. Some people speak so fast and full of so much slang that I just stare at them thinking, "*I have no idea what you just said*" (to be fair I have a few friends like that in the U.S. as well). Learning language is a life-long process – in English as well as whatever second or third language you speak.

Journal entry from first year:

> *There are some days I think I will never learn the nuances of this language. I went to see a movie a few weeks ago – a movie I've seen several times in English and know by heart. I didn't understand a word of it! And the places where I knew exactly what they were saying – they didn't translate the way I thought they would. I walked out soooo discouraged. But then there are days that I think, "I'm doing really well." Like the night I held a whole conversation on the phone in my new language. I spoke. I understood. And I was elated. But once again, I must remember that language acquisition is a process.*

IT TAKES TIME

No matter how adept you are at learning language, it takes time. There's only so much you can cram into your head at one time. There is no substitute for letting what you know "simmer" in your brain and sink in over TIME. I remember my first real breakthrough in language. I had been studying intently in country for almost a year – plodding along trying to persevere. I had plateaued; no matter how hard I tried, I just couldn't seem to move forward. About that time is when I had the opportunity to spend two months in New Zealand.

Two months of NO intentional language learning, no new language, only English. I was excited about the opportunity but scared that this would be a real set back to my language acquisition. I remember getting off the plane in Kochevnikstan after those two months and being so excited that I was hearing "my language!" I actually felt like I understood what people were saying. Rather than losing the language I had, I felt like I had an even better grasp on the language than before. I could actually form sentences and remember the words I wanted to use. My "brain-break" had given me an opportunity - TIME - to let the language sink in and become a more natural part of me.[3]

DON'T LISTEN TO WHAT PEOPLE SAY

"Your language is great," said the person I had just met. Later that same day my friend said to me, *"Tammy what's happened to you? Are you losing your language?"* How good or bad your language is has as much to do with your listener as it does with your actual language level. A person who speaks good English might expect your second language to be as good as his. A person who speaks no English will probably be impressed if you can say even a few words in the language. The person who talks to you all the time and learns to "understand" your Americanized second language forgets that you aren't saying things correctly (thus making you think you are doing really well), while another friend – eager to help you improve – might correct every word you say wrong (making you feel like you are never progressing).

Bottom line: don't put stock in what other people say about your language level. If you want to objectively judge your improvement in learning the language, set some goals with your language teacher and let them be the primary person you listen to about how much (or not so much) you are improving.

DANGER OF COMPARISON

Zhanna is a natural language learner. She is what I would call fluent. When locals listen to her speak they often don't know that she's American until she tells them, and then they sometimes don't believe her. Her grammar is natural, and her pronunciation is perfect. She uses idioms and colloquialisms that she's learned from simply relating to people. Sometimes with Zhanna – especially in the early days – it was uncomfortable to speak around her. It was tempting to compare myself to her in our language levels. In my language class, it was hard to not compare myself to the other students. Either I was doing better than

---

3   You may not have the opportunity to go away to New Zealand for 2 months but the point is that it's necessary to take language breaks periodically to give your brain an opportunity to soak in all you have been learning.

them (feeling prideful) or I was doing worse (feeling insecure). Neither was an accurate measure of how my language was progressing.

The danger of comparison is great – especially for married couples when one spouses picks up the language quicker than the other or for teammates when one teammate excels and the other struggles. People learn language differently and at a different pace. Ultimately, God is our standard and we have to become comfortable being where we are in the process without comparing ourselves to others. It's humbling to learn a new language – to not be able to do something that a 5-year-old can do! Language is a primary way that God "shakes and squeezes" us in the early days of living cross-culturally.

✏ ON YOUR OWN

Spend some time meditating on how language learning is "shaking and squeezing" you. Think of 3-4 emotion words to describe how you feel about your language learning.

Now use the "4 Why" method to delve deeper into those feelings. For example:

I feel frustrated about my slow language learning.
 Why?
Because my goals of learning the language were quickly blocked.
 Why does it bother me that it's taking so long?
Because I feel incompetent.
 Why is that?
Because it makes me feel like a failure.
 Why? Failure is a normal part of learning.
Because I find significance in being able to do something well (fear of failure).

LANGUAGE LEARNING II
It takes focused intentionality

Language is NOT primarily about words and grammar (although that is the primary way it is taught in schools). Language is primarily about communication, and communication is about people understanding one another. Ultimately the goal of learning language is to be able to communicate in a way that people understand what you mean (and that you can understand them). The more you interact with people in real life settings, the more you will learn to communicate. I studied Spanish in high school and college (I even have a minor in Spanish), but I cannot communicate in Spanish. I never had any practical experience – no real life people interaction.

In addition to simply needing time for language to sink in, it takes time to learn the culture that influences all language. Grammar language and spoken language are NOT the same. Just because you literally translate something does NOT mean that you say it right. My first experience with this was asking my local friend about where I could buy batteries because my batteries had died. She started laughing at me. It sounded funny to her, because in the local language batteries don't "die" they "sit down." It's not only true of cultural idioms but also of spiritual language.

Journal entry from three months:

> *Grammar is extremely difficult (a case language) and the language in scripture is old and not widely used today. I was memorizing 2 Tim. 3:16 in my new language and as a conversation starter wanted to quote it to two of my unbelieving friends. My language isn't great, but I know I said the words correctly. They did not understand what I was saying. They were old words that they didn't know.*

PAY ATTENTION: WHAT DO PEOPLE AROUND YOU DO AND SAY?
In my opinion, the best way to learn new words or phrases is to learn from real life situations. For example, I'm on the bus and I want to

get off. How do I ask the person in front of me if they are getting off? Listen to what people say around you when they want to get off; pay attention. Even if you don't know exactly what it means, you know the context that this word or phrase is used in. You can learn the spelling and meaning later. This is the most natural way of learning things – the way children learn as they watch and listen to what their parents and siblings say and do.

The more you interact with people in real life settings, the more you will learn to communicate.

NEEDS BASED LEARNING

Keep paper with you at all times, and when you think of something you want to say but don't know how to, write it down. For example, you are meeting with a friend, and you want to talk about their beliefs. Think through what you want to say and then "test yourself." Do you know how to say those things or ask the questions you want to ask? What words do you need to learn or look up? Or let's pretend you are in a store trying to buy cell phone minutes, and you don't know how to say what you want to say. Write down the phrase in English and ask your language helper later, "*How would you say this?*" Or, "*What would you say in this situation?*" Learning language because you need to know it to accomplish something you want to do is the most motivating and lasting way to learn.

WATCH TV

Children's programs are especially helpful. I used to watch a cartoon called "Princess Sissi" every afternoon. The story line was easy as was the language. Sports events are also good. News is difficult to understand due to the use of complex sentence structures. A series – with an ongoing story line – is another great way to increase your comprehension. One woman I know learned the local language by watching the soap opera *Santa Barbara* with her host family and talking about it with them. Watching movies can be helpful if they are in the original language. You not only learn new vocabulary but cultural concepts and ideas.

KNOW YOUR LEARNING STYLE

In learning another language it's really helpful to identify your primary learning style.[4] Do you learn best by seeing? Hearing? Touching? Everyone learns well by doing, but most people have a primary way they take in information. Think about these questions:

Would you rather watch a sermon or listen to it?

Do you take notes when listening? Notes are visual and often visual learners take notes in order to supplement audial learning.

How do you recall a new word? Do you...picture the written word in your mind? Think of when you last heard the word? Think about doing the action of that word?

Pay attention to how you best take in information. You'll need to use all the learning styles to some degree, but try to utilize your primary learning style as much as you can in learning your new language.

1. Visual

If you are a visual learner, write things down so you can "picture" the new word or phrase. Read books – children's picture books or the Bible (familiar passages) are good places to start. Looking at graphs or charts of grammar rules might also help you "see" the information and remember it.

2. Audial

If you are an audial learner, make tapes (of a native speaker) and listen over and over to your vocabulary list of words and phrases. Listen to music. Folk music is a fun way to learn new words while learning some culture (folk music often embodies various values of the culture).

3. Kinesthetic

If you are a kinesthetic learner try to create opportunities for yourself to "do" your language. For example, if you are learning directions, get a map and toy car. Use your direction language to carry out commands. *"Go three blocks, turn left, turn right, etc."* Or cook a meal – using kitch-

---

4   Highlands is one of many tests to help you understand your learning style

en vocabulary talk out loud to yourself as you walk through the steps of cooking. One of my teammates – a young mom – had a house helper in her home everyday. They cooked, cleaned, and looked after kids together. My teammate's practical language and communication took off as she did the new vocabulary together with a friend.

Remember, in learning language you will make a million mistakes – so start making mistakes now! Perfection is not the goal – communication is.

✔ LET'S GET PRACTICAL

What is your primary learning style? If you aren't sure ask some friends to help you think through this. Be observant about when things you learn "stick" and when they don't. If you have access, take a test like Highlands to help you determine your learning style.

What is the hardest part for you about learning the language?

What motivates you to keep persevering?

GET OUT OF YOUR COMFORT ZONE!

We were headed to the mountains for the summer team's exposure trip: living in traditional Kochevnik homes, swimming in the glacier lake, hiking during the day and singing by the campfire at night. Everyone was looking forward to getting out of the hot city and enjoying the cool and beauty of the mountains. However, the talk on the team was not about camping. Everyone was either looking forward to or dreading (depending on your openness to adventurous eating) the traditional Kochevnik meal planned for us one night. A traditional Kochevnik meal is made with sheep meat, noodles, onions, and potatoes. It is very bland compared to some national dishes. But the kicker in a traditional Kochevnik meal is that after the meat and noodles are finished, the sheep's head is brought out and carved up. Specific pieces are handed out to guests with a blessing or exhortation. The host might say, *"May John become a man of greater vision,"* and pass him the sheep eyeball, or *"May Lisa be a woman who speaks truth,"* and hand her a piece of sheep tongue. Eyeballs and tongue are not exactly things on the menu in the average American household! In most cultures, refusing to eat food served by a gracious host is considered rude and insulting. This is definitely true in Kochevnik culture where hospitality is one of the highest values.

Alice had been very outspoken about NOT eating any part of the sheep. She was a picky eater and throughout the summer managed to quietly avoid anything that wasn't to her liking. But there would be no avoiding this traditional meal. Everyone one would be there and everyone would know it if she refused to eat.

On the trip to the mountains, I intentionally sat next to Alice. I challenged her to make a conscious decision during the weekend – and specifically during the traditional meal – to get out of her comfort zone. To eat or not eat sheep's head was not the point. Food is just food, and while not eating this meal would have been insulting to our hosts, it was not my biggest concern: my concern was for Alice. The trend of her life was to avoid anything that felt uncomfortable to her. Her habit – underneath all the excuses about food and shallow comforts – was to live in fear rather than choosing to walk by faith. My challenge to Alice was about a lot more than eating something she didn't like. It was about choosing to cultivate a lifelong habit of getting out of her comfort zone, the result of which is greater faith and authentic transformation.

Alice did eat her portion of the sheep's head. She made a choice to get out of her comfort zone. Years later I saw Alice on a visit to the U.S., and she told me how much she appreciated that conversation and how it had encouraged her in other areas of her life to not settle for being comfortable – to not settle for living in fear.

J. Hudson Taylor – a man of great faith – said, "*Unless there is an element of risk in our exploits for God, there is no need for faith.*" This truth is intricately woven into the fabric of Scripture. Hebrews 11:6 says that "*without faith it is impossible to please God.*" In Romans 14:23 Paul writes, "*…everything that does not come from faith is sin.*" We all have fears. The difference in our lives is how we meet those fears. Do we choose the safe, familiar, comfortable way? Or do we step out of our comfort zones and meet our fears with faith in the One who knows all and has the power to control all? Where fear is met with faith, there is great life change!

✏ ON YOUR OWN

Read through Hebrews 11.

What fears do you think Abraham and Moses faced in obeying God? How did their faith change their lives?

Did walking by faith make their lives more comfortable? What was their reward?

What are you fearful of in your life? How can you meet your fears with faith?

LIVING IN COMMUNITY

The principle of Scripture is community. We do not see people alone in Scripture for very long, and even then only when there is a specific purpose (Jesus in the desert - Mt. 41-11, Moses on Mt. Sinai - Ex. 34:28, Jesus with his Father - Mk. 1:35). We don't see lone rangers in Scripture (the Lone Ranger wasn't even really alone because he had his trusty sidekick Tonto). Even Jeremiah – who is perhaps the "loneliest" figure in Scripture – had a trusted companion in Baruch (Jer. 36:4-8). From Genesis in the Garden when God said, "*It is not good for man to be alone,*" to Jesus in the New Testament calling 12 men to "*be with him*" (Gen. 2:18 , Mk. 3:14); from Jethro instructing Moses, "*The work is too heavy for you; you cannot handle it alone,*" to Paul and Barnabas together being sent off by the Antioch fellowship (Ex. 18:18, Acts 13:2-3); we see the importance the Father places on living in community and working alongside others.

In addition to the specific callings of small teams of people (like the disciples sent out 2 by 2), we also see the New Testament church at large living in community. Acts 2:42-47 and Acts 4:32-36 describe what it practically looked like for believers to fellowship together. They listened to teaching together, ate together, and prayed together. They experienced the amazing things happening around them together and took care of the needs of others together. They shared their possessions and invited others into their circle of fellowship (healthy community is never exclusive but results in new people being added to the Kingdom). They met together, hung out in each others' houses, worshipped, and gave thanks together.

Paul in his teaching to the Corinthians uses the illustration of the physical body to describe the importance of each member doing it's own job and the importance of the whole body working together for the common good. (1 Cor. 12:12-30).

While living in community IS about physically living and laboring together, it is even more an attitude of our hearts. Living in community – at a very practical level – is about how we interact with and relate to others around us, especially those closest to us on a team or in a family.

It is an attitude of vulnerability, confessing our sins and humbling ourselves to one another (James 5:16, 1 Peter 5:5). It's a choice to invite counsel into our decisions and an intentionality in thinking for and encouraging our teammates toward "good labor"(Prov. 24:6, Ex.18:19, Heb. 10:24). It's an expectation that no matter how important we are, we can't get away with choosing sin because others in the body will confront us and when we are confronted with truth we choose to listen and respond (2 Sam. 12:13).

Living in community – at a very practical level – is about how we interact with and relate to others around us, especially those closest to us on a team or in a family.

📖 FOR FURTHER STUDY

Read Exodus 17:8-16.

Who were the key team members in the fight to defeat the Amalekites? Could this victory have been accomplished without these men working together? Why or why not?

Do you have a team of people to fight the battle with you? If not what will it take to put yourself in position to labor with a team?

Using the verses in this chapter as a starting point, do a topical study on teams/community. Is there a difference between "team" and "community"? If so what? What characteristics define people who live in community?

What aspects of living in community are most challenging for you? Do you want to grow in these areas? If so, how?

GOD MADE TEAMMATES MALE AND FEMALE
Part 1

Recently I was in Asia visiting a 20-something team of 5 singles (they have families on their larger team as well, but this team of 5 was sent out together for 2 years to serve alongside the long-term staff). Another co-worker and I were having lunch with one of the guys and the conversation turned to how the team was relating. He shared some encouraging stories about how he and his roommates were learning to go deeper in their relationship, being more open and vulnerable. Then we asked him how he felt the guys and girls on the team were relating. This was more difficult. He wanted there to be a greater depth of sharing and encouraging with the girls on his team. But he was honest and shared that he wasn't always sure how to do that. If he and his roommates shared too much or asked deeper questions or acted in a way that was overly protective, their actions could be misinterpreted by the girls as romantic interest instead of brotherly concern.

A few weeks later back in the U.S. at a training conference for another group being sent out, I had a similar conversation with both a guy and a girl. They longed for their team of 4 to have depth of relationship and to be mutually encouraging to one another. Both were unsure how to do that in a way that did not miscommunicate or mislead.

UNDERSTAND THAT IT'S DIFFERENT

I'm assuming that the majority of my readers came out of a campus ministry of some type whether parachurch or denominational. I worked on a U.S. campus for 10 years before going overseas, and there is a lot that is taught – even is caught – about what a "healthy dating relationship" should look like. What gets caught can range from "Neverdater" (old slang from some Navigator ministries) to only-group-dating-is-acceptable to anything goes. Whatever it was, I'd be willing to guess that your campus ministry had an "ethos of dating." That ethos combined with yours family's perspective on dating has influenced your own views more than you probably realize.

Relating with the opposite sex in a cross-cultural environment is most likely different than anything you've experienced before. You interact on a weekly (maybe daily) basis in intense situations that are often emotionally charged. You study language together, pray together, have new cultural experiences together, eat together, hang out together (who else is there to hang out with those first few months when you know no one?!?). And because you spend so much time together and there's nowhere to escape, you get frustrated with each other, tired of each other, fight with each other, and are forced to resolve conflict with each other more often and quickly than in other relationships. This generates a closeness and emotional intimacy that is not normal in the broad relational network you have in the U.S., but it is a very normal part of being on a cross-cultural team. The first step is to understand that it's different.

EMBRACE THAT IT'S AWKWARD

Not only is it different to be so intimate all the time with your opposite sex teammates, but it's awkward. Yes, intimate – while not physically intimate you are likely more socially and emotionally intimate with your teammates than what feels comfortable to you. All of this forced, up-close and personal time with opposite sex teammates is just weird. It can be weird for different reasons: maybe you don't really like your teammates. You didn't choose them but you're stuck with them (that's one way cross- cultural teams are more are like family than friends!). How am I supposed to be vulnerable and trusting of someone I don't even really like? It could be weird because you are attracted to one of your teammates or are afraid you might be. How are you supposed to act around them? You can't escape them or avoid them! Or maybe you just don't know how to relate to the opposite sex if you're not dating. How are you supposed to be "just friends"? Is that even possible? Our worldly culture of "friends with benefits" would suggest it's unlikely.

The reality is that being on a cross-cultural team of mixed gender singles is going to be awkward at times. Accept it. Embrace it. And move forward in your current reality. As in all things, there is a lot the Lord wants to teach you through this situation.

CONSIDER ONE ANOTHER

So what do you do when it gets awkward? What do you do if you don't like your teammates? Or if you feel attracted to a teammate? Or if you feel completely ill-equipped to even relate to your teammates? You consider one another. Hebrews 10:24-25 says,

> *"And let us consider [think about and ponder with effort, focus, and thought] how we may spur one another on [intentional encouragement focused on your teammate, not you] toward love and good deeds, [helping your teammate love more and labor better] not giving up meeting together, as some are in the habit of doing, [not avoiding each other because it's awkward but encouraging one another—intentionally, purposefully and Biblically] and all the more as you see the Day approaching [all the more as your team interaction reflects to your local friends how believers love and care for one another]."*

Do you know how many "one another" commands there are in Scripture? Neither do I. And I couldn't find it on Google! But there are a lot of them! And this I do know: there are more "one another" commands that are gender neutral than gender specific. That means there are more "one another" commands that apply to both men and women across gender lines than there are "one another" commands that apply just women to women or men to men. If you want to know how to consider one another – male AND female – look at what the Bible says we should be doing to, with, and for our brothers and sisters in Christ (see "One Anothering" in the Practical Resources for a place to start)!

PRACTICAL TIPS
1. Be open and honest. In addition to being honest with yourself and God, one of the best things you can do is to find a safe person to share your struggles with. By safe, I mean a same sex friend or mentor (not the guy or girl you have trouble relating to or might be interested in!). It could be your same sex teammate, your roommate, or your staff supervisor. There is some unexplained power in saying things out loud that seems to deflate the overshadowing dread that comes over us when we keep things shut up inside (remember the frogs from "The Heart of the Matter"?).

2. Invite a mature and objective perspective. It's important to have a peer friend that you can talk to about whatever you're experiencing on your team. But it's equally important to invite a mature and objective perspective to speak into your life. This could be your supervisor in country (the best choice) or a mentor in the U.S. Chances are that whatever it is you're experiencing is not "new" and talking to someone older, wiser, and not in the middle of the emotional struggle can bring fresh perspective to the situation and help you better discern what God is doing in your life.

3. Talk about the awkward as a team and agree on what is acceptable. Talk about the awkward not individually, not in detail, not inappropriately, but as a whole team: put the big issues on the table. Talk about the elephant in the room. If the guys are worried the girls will misread their intentions, then talk about that. If the girls are afraid to let the guys serve them, talk about that. As a team define what is normal, acceptable behavior for brothers and sisters in the Lord who work closely (intimately) together. Decide on boundaries you all feel comfortable with and agree upon what those boundaries mean. For instance, for safety reasons you might all agree that the guys will walk the girls home at night after your ministry events. That's the team rule so when a guy walks a girl home neither of them interpret that as romantic interest. This is an agreed upon way to "consider one another".

There are more "one another" commands that are gender neutral than gender specific.

4. Know your own boundaries and stick to them. Different individuals are tempted by different things. Maintaining physical and emotional purity, our history and weaknesses, how we give and receive love are personal issues that might not be the same for everyone. Know your own weak spots and set boundaries for yourself. Ask your same sex teammate or a roommate to hold you accountable. If appropriate, ask your opposite sex teammates to not cross that boundary. For example, it might make you uncomfortable to go to sleep while your opposite sex teammates are still in your house – even if they are hanging out with your other teammates/roommates. You might ask your teammates (male and female) to set a curfew for how late the team hangs out at your apartment. Appropriate is a subjective word. If you aren't sure if something is appropriate to share with an opposite sex teammate, then ask a more mature mentor.

5. Think brothers and sisters. I hesitate to mention this because not everyone has brothers or sisters, and even if they do that doesn't mean the relationship is a good one. But in the Kingdom of God, we are brothers and sisters in Christ. We have one Father, and until God brings the woman to the man (as he did Eve to Adam) so the two become one flesh, the person you're relating to is your sister or brother. Even if there is mutual romantic interest, the focus of your dating relationship should be to get to know one another as friends. Don't you want to marry your best friend?

In editing this essay, I asked a 20-something guy heading overseas for 2 years to give me his feedback. I specifically asked if he thought that I come across as being anti-dating. I appreciated his response:

> *No - to me it does not come across as "anti-dating" and I think a disclaimer defending your points would cheapen it and make it seem almost apologetic...instead emphasize "use that passion and energy for intimacy to develop great friendships, take yourself to the cross, put others first, learn to give and receive love, and labor well in your country." I think many young people - I've been here - are worried God's holding out on them by not giving them what they want i.e. a girlfriend or boyfriend. Baloney...when we submit to the idea that "we can only have fullness of life when we get to be married or have some significant other in our life," we exchange the glory of God for a lie. [Instead of "God alone"] it's a "God and" theology where I need "God AND a wife" to finally have all the joy and pleasure and good and rightness God has for me. ["God and" theology causes me to falsely believe] I have to suffer along wanting and desiring...that I have to stifle and stuff away till God really rewards me for bearing my cross in waiting. It's really BS, to be blunt. I played that game for part of my life and it makes sexual*

intimacy, marriage, the "one-flesh-ness" of that covenant an idol. When we submit to this mentality, that "God's not really being fully good to me until" sort of thinking, we're really signing off on letting the name of Jesus be drug through the mud. Ps. 73:25-26 "there is nothing on earth that I desire besides you!" [Jesus is enough!]

CONCLUSION - IT'S MESSY

Just recently in my time alone with God I read a Proverb that made me laugh. "*An empty stable stays clean but no income comes from an empty stable*" (Prov. 14:4 NLT). There are no "clean stables" when it comes to relationships been men and women. It's messy. But the messiness can be profitable. It's in the messiness of life that we learn to depend on God in ways we hadn't even thought of. And it's in the messiness of life that the greatest fruit is nurtured in us (think about the importance of messy manure in plant growth!). God made teammates male and female because we need each other. Even though it's messy and sometimes even painful, I believe that if you dive in and give it a try, you will find that it's worth all the messiness!

✏ ON YOUR OWN

Look back on your family upbringing and campus experience. What was the perspective of dating in each of these environments? How has this ethos affected your view of relating to opposite sex teammates?

Are there things on your team that are awkward? An elephant in the room? Would it be appropriate to bring up those awkward things with the whole team and talk about them?

Think about the opposite sex teammate that is the most difficult for you to relate to. How can you spur him/her on toward love and good deeds this week?

GOD MADE TEAMMATES MALE AND FEMALE
Part 2

My first years in Kochevnikstan, I was on a team with 2 families and 6 singles (2 women and 4 men). These 4 single guys were awesome men who loved the Lord, had a heart for the nations, and were easy to look at. Seriously, these were great guys who would be just the kind of man I'd want to marry. And here I was of marriageable age, in a foreign country with very few options for a mate, and surrounded daily by attractive, godly men. What's a girl to do? I feel awfully vulnerable writing this down, but since I try to practice what I preach about speaking things out loud (and since anyone who knows me already knows what I'm about to say), I'll just come out with it: I was seriously interested at different times in 2 of the single guys on my team (no offense to the other two guys)! As it turned out, neither of these guys were romantically interested in me. It made relating with them in the close confines of our team challenging for all of us, and yet in God's goodness He used this situation in my life to strengthen my trust in Him in ways I couldn't have imagined. And, thankfully, I'm still very good friends with both of these wonderful brothers!

So why would I share this personal story in a public book that anyone can read? Because in 25 years of working with students and young singles, I have learned that my situation is not an isolated experience. In fact, I've found that it's just the opposite: It's the norm rather than the exception (for both men and women). Living in community – whether in a cross-cultural environment or tight knit campus staff team – causes emotional attachments to develop that are easier to avoid in a "normal" situation. I could go into detail about why this happens but the important thing is what to do I do if it does happen?

CHOOSE TO LOVE

There are at least 3 words in Greek for "love." *Philio* is friendship love. *Eros* is romantic love. *Agape* is unconditional love. I'm not attempting to unpack a theological study here on the types of love and how they are used in Scripture. I'm just introducing the idea that there are different types of love and that *agape* is the highest love – godly, unconditional love. This is the type of love that God has for children and that he calls us to have for each other.

I told you that I was seriously interested in two of the single guys on my team. The first time was the hardest (as with most things). I didn't know what to do with these very real feelings. It would have been different if my teammate had been equally interested in me. Then the challenge would have been how to grow in our friendship and get to know each other in a healthy way. But my teammate gave no sign of being romantically interested in me, and when we finally did talk about it, he kindly told me that he didn't think he'd ever be interested in a romantic relationship (had I initiated that conversation years earlier it might not have been so devastating to me emotionally). So here I was with very real emotions that I could neither avoid or escape. I worked with this guy in a small team situation.[5] I saw him almost every day. What was I supposed to do with all of my romantic feelings?

Protecting our heart from loving someone who doesn't love us is not the point. Guarding our heart means protecting it from the evil of failing to love people with an unconditional, agape love.

At some point during this time, an older mentor gave me a copy of a short one-page article. I can't recall the article's title or author and I can't find my hard copy of it (unfortunately, I purged my old filing cabinet when I moved into the technological age). But this unknown author has forever impacted my life.

She wrote about these 3 types of love and posed the same question I have posed to you: what if one person has more romantic interest than the other person? What do you do with that? Her answer was surpris-

---

5   The first time I was romantically interested in a teammate was actually in the U.S. during my years on campus staff. Later, that same guy was one of the four single men on my cross-cultural team, but by then we had moved through my emotions and our long-time friendship was solid. Unreturned romantic interest in a teammate is not limited to a cross-cultural team but the likelihood does increase in a cross-cultural environment.

ing. In most cases, if someone has a romantic (*eros*) love for someone else and that romantic love is not returned, the most natural thing to do is to try to back up to friendship love (*philio*). But the challenge this article gave me, and that I pass on to you, is that rather than going backwards, the Biblical mandate is to move forward toward unconditional (*agape*) love. What does that mean? In my case, it meant loving this teammate even if he didn't return my love. It meant loving him beyond any romantic interest. It meant choosing to love him as God loves me – with no conditions. That meant that when I wanted him to pay attention to me or single me out, and he didn't, that I didn't hold that against him. I chose to love him regardless of how he did or did not relate to me. *Agape* love is a conscious choice. Our feelings grow into the truth we choose to pursue.

I'm not saying it was easy – it's the hardest thing I've ever done! It was even harder because it was difficult to "create space" and to be objective with my emotions since we continued to work closely together. But my prayer throughout that time was that the Lord would protect our friendship and help us to push through my unrequited love to a place where we could still be friends. God answered that prayer. This former teammate is still one of my very close friends. And this guy was used by God not only in the ways he intentionally taught me (I learned tons about ministry strategy from this teammate), but even more in the ways God used him to peel back layer upon layer of self protective, heart level sin in my life that hindered me from loving and receiving love. In spite of many tears and agonizing emotional heartache, I wouldn't do anything differently. This experience was one of the most personally sanctifying in my life. And in the midst of it, I experienced God's love for me in ways I had not known before.

GUARD YOUR HEART

"*Guard your heart for it is the wellspring of life*" (Prov 4:23). People quote this verse all the time as a guide for dating. I fear that most often when we say it to ourselves or others what we mean is "guard your heart from getting hurt" or "guard your heart from falling in love" or "guard your heart from getting too close to the person you are dating." I don't believe that is Solomon's intent in this proverb. It's not that we should guard our hearts from love or hurt or closeness. We are to guard our hearts from evil. And if the greatest commandment is to love the lord your God and love your neighbor as yourself (Matt 22:37-39), then it stands to reason that the greatest sin is a failure to love – both God and people. Protecting our heart from loving someone who doesn't love us is not the point. Guarding our heart means protecting it from the evil of failing to love people with an unconditional, *agape* love.

HOPE IN GOD - NOT YOUR TEAMMATE

My second experience with "unrequited love" (that's such a dramatic sounding phrase) was different. It wasn't that my emotions were any less real. But the first time around, I kept my emotions hidden for a long time before I shared them with anyone. The second time, I had learned the importance of bringing things into the light. Another big difference was the first time around my hope was in my teammates attention toward me. I couldn't have explained it that way at the time. But if he paid attention to me one day I felt great – even if my head told me it didn't mean anything. If he didn't pay special attention to me, I felt disappointed and without meaning to I held it against him. It was like he was in a hole he could never get out of because he couldn't give me what I wanted from him – his affections.

But the second time around, the Lord had done some serious work in my life. I was more mature, and from the beginning my hope was not in whether or not this teammate was romantically interested in me. My hope was in the Lord. I saw it play out most clearly in my prayers. When I prayed I felt totally surrendered to the Lord's ultimate will. If HE was in this relationship, if HE made it happen, if it was good for me, if it was good for my teammate, then it would happen. And if it didn't, I trusted that God was good in that. My hope was in God's goodness to me NOT in my teammate finally understanding how much he really liked me (which never happened).

This hope in God also played out in how I related with my teammate. We worked together in a small cross-cultural team environment. I was over keeping secrets, so I made sure a few of my closest friends knew my heart. After much prayer and objective counsel, I decided to talk to my teammate about how I felt – put it all on the table so to speak. I'm not saying that is always the right answer. In fact it's usually what I would recommend against – especially for women who tend to always want to talk about things that are better left unsaid! But I felt confident this was what I needed to do and my prior experience keeping things so secretive gave me courage to be different this time.

And it was different. This time my hope was in the Lord and there was no hidden agenda on my part. The conversation was awkward, but we both chose to embrace the awkward and keep things honest and appropriate. I suppose I was hurt when he told me he wasn't interested in the same way, but all I remember is having this unwavering confidence in the Lord that God would do what was good for both of us. My focus was not on my teammate, my feelings for him, or his lack of feeling for me. My hope was in God, and that made all the difference.

✎ ON YOUR OWN

Do a heart check – are you holding back love from an opposite sex teammate because you are fearful of what he/she might think about you. Are you "guarding your heart" from being hurt or disappointed?

Think about your current relationships with your teammates – it doesn't have to be a romantic interest. Where is your hope, your focus, in that relationship? Are you trusting that relationship to the Lord? Or do you have unconscious expectations of that teammate to relate to you in a particular way or to meet some need in your life that only God can meet?

What would it practically look like for you choose to love your teammate(s) with an agape love?

I mentioned that I would not trade all the tears and pain because of what the Lord used my circumstances to do in my life. How do you see God working in your life through your team relationships? What is He teaching you about Himself? About you?

BUILDING BRIDGES NOT WALLS

Let's play a game. Look at the list below and write down the first thing that comes to your mind. Don't think about it; just jot down a note about whatever picture, thought, or word immediately comes to your mind. After you've done the exercise yourself, ask 1-2 of your American teammates/friends to do the same thing and make a note of their responses. Finally ask 3-4 of your local friends if they will help you out with by taking this "test." Not only will it be a great way to initiate a Gospel conversation, it should be very enlightening as to what they think about these words and concepts.

What is the first word, image, or thought that comes to your mind when you see or hear these words?

Christian
Church
Missionary
Muslim
Religion
Prayer
God

Words carry meaning. Remember two big literary words you learned (or I hope you learned) in high school English: denotation and connotation? Denotation is the literal definition of a word. Connotation is a word's understood or implied meaning. In crossing cultures, we often assume that the words we use carry the same connotation to others as they do to us. This wrong assumption can be a fatal mistake in communicating the Gospel.

My teammate Dan was talking to a Muslim background student, Murat. Murat asked Dan if he was a Christian. Dan, through years of experience, had learned to answer that question with another question, "*Well, what do you think it means to be a Christian?*" Murat didn't hesitate and responded, "*Someone who worships the devil and drinks blood.*" THAT was his definition (his connotation) of a Christian. In light of this, Dan easily responded, "*Then, NO, I am not a Christian.*"

What if Dan had, out of habit, immediately answered, "*Yes, I'm a Christian.*" By Murat's definition a "Christian" is NOT someone you would want to talk to or listen to about honoring God? By clarifying the meaning of a word that we throw around and assume means the same thing to everyone, Dan was able to build a bridge that day and not a wall. Bridge-building opens rather than closes doors to discuss what being a follower of Jesus really means.

In Kochevnikstan, a nominally Muslim country, "Christian" words carry connotations that are not accurate. Some people might argue that you should still use those words and "re-educate" people of the true meaning of a word. I can understand where they are coming from – as believers we DO NOT want to water down the Gospel or any of the truths of the Scripture. However, there are enough obstacles to the Gospel. We don't want to create even more obstacles by the unnecessary use of words that automatically carry negative connotations and build protective walls around a person's mind and heart. Why not use a less offensive word if the concept can be communicated effectively and accurately in another way (e.g., using "Holy Scriptures" instead of "Bible")? We are not watering down the concept of the Scriptures – that they are inerrant and inspired by God – but simply using a name with less "baggage" attached to it.

Let me be very clear that I am NOT advocating changing words in order to avoid being offensive. For example, if you choose to use "Holy Scriptures" instead of "Bible" you want to be careful to NOT water down the content of the Holy Scriptures or to give the impression that they are a lesser book to the Qur'an (or even that the Qur'an is equal to the Scriptures). The goal is not to avoid being offensive but to give you an open door to have a discussion about the content of the Scriptures.

Let me give you an example of using words to build bridges and not walls. My teammate Mike was, and still is, good friends with a strong Muslim. This Muslim guy – we'll call him Mohammad – really liked the person of Jesus, but he could not accept that Jesus was God. At a retreat Mike, Mohammad, and another local believer sat down together and actually made a list of all the things they believed in common: God as creator, God as all powerful, God as worthy of glory, etc.

Then they made a shorter list of the things that they disagreed about. Jesus was at the top of that list. To Mohammad, Jesus was the ultimate offense against God, robbing Him of His glory by asserting that a mere man could be equal to God. Mohammad was zealous for the glory of God, but Jesus was offensive to him. Mike built a bridge with his words by identifying things they believed in common, but he did not water down the truth of Jesus' identity. To this day, Mohammad is so offended by Jesus that he and Mike don't talk much about him even if they do talk about spiritual things. But because bridges were built instead of walls, they are still friends. We continue to hope and pray that one day Jesus will break down the barriers around Mohammad's heart and that he will cross the bridge from death to life.

In building bridges and not walls the ultimate goal is NOT to avoid being offensive. The Gospel of Jesus is offensive to many, "*to one ... the smell of death but to the other, the fragrance of life...*" (2 Corinth. 2:15). The goal is to make sure you are offensive about the right things. Words can help you build bridges that open discussion so that you can begin to talk about what really matters.

✏ ON YOUR OWN

Ask 3-4 local friends about the words listed at the beginning of this chapter. What are their pre-conceived ideas about "Christians" and "Christian beliefs"?

What word changes can you make in your normal vocabulary (in English or your new language) to help you build bridges rather than walls?

Do you know anyone like Mohammad? What would happen if you sat down – as Mike and Mohammad did – and talked about what you do and don't believe the same? See "GMJGR" in the Practical Resources section to use as an outline.

CHRISTIAN TO KINGDOM

I grew up in Christian culture. As a youth, I attended a Christian church. I was known at school as a Christian girl. I was good and moral as required by Christian standards. Even before I had a real relationship with Jesus, I was immersed in "Christianity" and all the cultural trappings that go with it.

When I moved to Kochevnikstan, "Christian" became a bad word. Kochevnikstan is a Muslim background country, and although nominal in beliefs, there are still a lot of misconceptions about being a "Christian." All Americans are Christians. All Kochevniks are Muslim. It's a cultural norm. Therefore, Kochevniks can't be Christians, because religion is cultural and you cannot change your culture. Christianity is associated with the Crusades (yes, more than a century after the fact). Christians believe in three Gods. The Christian Church throughout history has been used by power hungry regimes to oppress non "Christian" religions. And the list goes on. In many places around the world "Christian" is a word that builds walls rather than bridges.

In my early years in Kochevnikstan I experienced a paradigm shift from a "Christian" mentality to a Kingdom mentality. Did you know that the word Christian only appears in Scripture 3 times (Acts 11:26, Acts 26:28, 1 Peter 4:16)? In comparison, there are 155 references to the Kingdom of God (or heaven) in the New Testament, most of them in the Gospels and most of them from the direct teaching of Jesus.

Since followers of Jesus were not called Christians in Scripture (except for 3 times, 2 of which it's a name given by non-believers), what were they called? What did they call themselves? And if these are the words 1st century followers of Jesus called themselves (and wrote down in the sacred scrolls), why wouldn't we follow suit and call ourselves by these same titles - especially in places where the cultural word "Christian" carries only cultural and negative connotations?

In Scripture, there are 4 names used more than 60 times each that believers use to refer to themselves. If you don't believe me study it for yourself – actually, even if you do believe me you should look at it yourself!

> Disciples 280x
> Brothers (or brethren) 170x
> Beloved 70x
> Saints 60x

The concept that Jesus taught was that of the Kingdom of God. He emphasizes it at the beginning of his ministry "*The time has come, the Kingdom of God is near...*" (Mark 1:14) and at the end promising he won't return until "*...this gospel of the Kingdom will be preached in the whole world as a testimony to all nations, and then the end will come*" (Matt. 24:14). Even Jesus' teaching on prayer highlights the Kingdom: "*Thy Kingdom come...*" (Luke 11:2).

There are 155 references to the Kingdom of God (or heaven) in the New Testament.

The word Christian is (or at least feels) sacred to many believers. I mean no disrespect to a beloved word, but it's important to acknowledge that "Christian" is a far more cultural word than we realize. When our paradigm shifts and we see the Kingdom emerging through Jesus' teachings in Scripture, we have new eyes – and new words – to explain the realities of Jesus and His Kingdom.

📖 FOR FURTHER STUDY

Study for yourself using the "Kingdom Of God Study" in the Practical Resources Section as a starting place.

SPIRITUAL WARFARE

"For our struggle is not against flesh and blood, but against the rulers, against the authorities, against the powers of this dark world and against the spiritual forces of evil in the heavenly realms."

Ephesians 6:12

When you live cross-culturally long enough new habits, patterns, and routines begin to form that are the result of new insights and understanding. For me, one of the most lasting "new routines" that formed was praying - room by room - through each new place I moved into (in 11 years I lived in 10 different places).

Whenever I moved into a new place I would go room to room (even the bathroom) – with my roommate if I knew who that was – and pray over that room. I prayed specifically binding the strongman with the power of Jesus and for cleansing and protection (Luke 12:29).

"In the name of Jesus, I pray that any evil that has been done here would be washed away."

"I invite Jesus to live and rule in this place and any spirits that have been invited to live here previously would be cast out by the power and name of Jesus."

"Lord, purify this room and use it now for your glory in the name of Jesus."

"Lord Jesus, set a guard around this room and this house/apt. Protect it and all in it from evil."

In addition to praying against any spirits or evil that had been there previously, I also asked God's blessing on my new home. For example:

"Holy Spirit, come and dwell in this room"

"Lord Jesus, let people feel and know your presence when they walk through the door – that they would feel safe here and at peace."

"Lord, use this house for your glory – bless it and use it to be a blessing to many."

Some of these prayers might sound "uncomfortable" to you; in North American culture we don't often talk about casting out spirits (that's for Hollywood movies). We might think to ask the Lord to make our home a "safe place" or use it to be a blessing, but we rarely consider cleansing it of any evil that might have been invited there previously. To be fair, in American culture previous owners of the places we live probably were not even knowledgeable about the spiritual realm. But you never know what evil has (or has not) taken place, and evil, like good, leaves a spiritual footprint. In spiritually dark cultures (places where the Gospel has not been preached on every corner for hundreds of years), the reality of spiritual footprints left behind becomes more and more real - more real than we are often comfortable with.

Moving into dark places that have long been held captive means that we need to re-think our methods of doing battle.

Regardless of your specific theology on spiritual warfare, I don't believe that you can read through the Scriptures and not "catch" that there is a spiritual battle going on for the souls of men (Eph. 6:12; Acts 2:26). When I first moved to Kochevnikstan, I remember that my team and I often talked about "living behind enemy lines" in terms of the spiritual battle going on around us: it was a spiritually dark place and held captive by the prince of this world (2 Tim. 2:26).

Think about being in a well lit room. Now think about lighting a match in that room. The match makes little difference in a well-lit room. It gets lost in all the light around it. Now think of being in a dark room. You light a match, and the light from that match makes all the difference in what is seen and not seen when the room is dark. A light that stands out so much will attract many things - some good things, like those who are drawn to the light for hope, and others who are drawn to the light to extinguish it because evil deeds are best done in the darkness (John 3:19-20).

When we cross cultures we are often going into spiritually dark places; that's the very reason we are drawn there because "the harvest is plentiful" and we long to see the light of the Gospel penetrate into places where it is not known. Moving into dark places that have long been held captive means that we need to re-think our methods of doing battle. The war is won – Jesus conquered death and he has overcome (Rev 17:14). But the battle is real, and we need to be prepared to fight a spiritual battle with spiritual weapons (2 Corinth. 10:4).

📖 FOR FURTHER STUDY

As you read through Scripture, pay attention to how God uses "light" and "darkness" to represent good and evil. What places in your own culture - both physical and spiritual - are "dark" (think about bars, brothels, etc.)? Are they open and full of light? What about your host culture?

In any kind of warfare, it's important to know your enemy. What does Scripture say are the characteristics of Satan (John 8:42-47, 1 Peter 5:8-9; Matt. 12:29, 2 Corinth. 11:14 - these verses are only places to start, not exhaustive).

What are the specific promises in Scripture of Jesus' power over and defeat of Satan and his schemes? Choose 1-2 of these verses to be your "spiritual shield" – a verse that you pray often and becomes the first thing you think of when faced with a spiritual attack. For example, my 2 protective verses are James 4:7 and 1 John 4:4.

Compare the number of times that the New Testament talks about the following topics:
Heaven & Hell (The Spiritual Realm)
Darkness & Light (Spiritual Warfare)
Money
Salvation

HEADLINE NEWS

At the time of this writing, my dad is 73 years old and he watches both local and world news every night. What's more, he reads his local paper from front to back EVERY SINGLE DAY! If for some reason he's out of town and misses a day, he reads through the local paper – in order – for all the days he was gone. I'm curious how many of you reading this have ever in your life read anything in a newspaper, let alone read it cover to cover.

CNN Headline News, a TV program that gives world news highlights every 30 minutes, started in 1982. Right out of college, I loved Headline News; I didn't have time to read the paper (like my Dad) or the inclination to watch local news every day, but I could get the big picture stories in under 10 minutes every hour on the half hour. Nowadays you don't even have to turn on the TV. From conflicts in the Middle East to the local Rattlesnake Rodeo in your hometown, you go to your favorite internet news website for the most recent headline news on what's happening anywhere in the world.

We live in a sound bit culture. From the advent of multi-media presentations with high-tech visual aids to the increase in video games that new generations are weaned on, many people are bored with the more traditional methods of communication like newspapers and lengthy newsletters. Not only do people want "bottom line" information on world news events, they also want bottom line information on your life and ministry (which is one reason social media is so popular).

Here are a few suggestions for writing attention-grabbing newsletters, e-mail updates, or blogs:

1. Know your audience. WHO you are writing to is an important question. Not all readers are the same. I have about 10 financial donors who don't have e-mail (I know, it's hard to believe in the 21st century, but they are all over the age of 65). For those donors, I still send out a paper newsletter 3-4 times a year. My dad WILL read a paper newsletter from cover to cover, and even for me I'll look at the pictures in a paper newsletter and maybe put it on my fridge (personally I would never print out an e-mail newsletter and put it up in my house). I am not a big fan of blogs (I know that's so old-fashioned of me!), so I rarely go check them out. The point is that different people value different styles (and frequencies) of communication. KNOW YOUR AUDIENCE and communicate to them in a way that keeps them up to date and praying for your ministry.

2. Keep your stories short. There might be a few people (like my dad or maybe your mom) who will read a long detailed story about someone you are sharing with, but most people want the highlights. As much as they may really want to know about this person you love dearly and are asking them to pray for, they don't KNOW this person and aren't as invested in him or her as you are. Most people have full lives of people they already know and are emotionally invested in. They want to know about your work and the people in it, but they generally have a limited capacity to engage with it beyond a sound bit of simple, specific information that they can pray for. It's not an issue of interest but of capacity!

3. Make it easy to read. One friend of mine would use a two-tiered approach to e-mail updates. She'd give the headlines up-front, like a table of contents, and then she would write more in the latter part of the e-mail for people who wanted more detailed information; I confess, I only ever read the headline news at the top. She knew her audience and organized her e-mail update in a way to make it easy for both to read. For me, I try to keep my e-mail updates the length of my e-mail window – something a person can open and read at a glance. If you write longer e-mails (or newsletters) use different colors, fonts, or layouts that help draw your readers' attention to the key points or draw them into a story you are sharing. Again, know your audience and think about laying out the update in a way that is easiest to read.

4. Be Creative. While there is nothing wrong with writing a long paragraph update about your ministry, it's much more interesting if you are creative in the way you present your information.

5. Use quotations. Share quotations from the person you are sharing with or from a book you are reading.

6. Make lists. List the top 10 things you wouldn't see in America, or use creative imagery to paint a word picture of the situation or person.

7. Include statistics. "Set apart" a box of some tidbit of trivia or stats. Send daily or weekly prayer calendars with your newsletter with short, specific things to pray for each day of the month or each day of the week. A Bible bookmark with prayer requests is an easy way to keep your work in front of people, making it easy for them to remember to pray for you.

8. Do a book or movie review – especially if it's relevant to your context or something you are learning personally.

9. Use song lyrics. If there is a song that has spoken to your heart or describes your field location, include it. I had one friend who wrote songs and my favorite was actually a prayer for his country "*Rain your love on the people of* _____." My current newsletter title is "Along the Road," an old song title and I often refer to the words of the song.

10. Ask a thought-provoking question. Challenge your readers to think about an issue that you might be struggling with or a statement that's given you good food for thought.

11. Include pictures. I could have included this in the "be creative" part, but pictures are so important they deserve their own point. I know one family who sends a "picture of the week". The e-mail is just the picture with a short caption under it (even though they aren't close friends, I always look at their picture). Sometimes it's a picture of their family or something their kids are doing. Sometimes it's a funny cultural picture or sometimes it's a ministry moment. Using pictures on a blog, in an e-mail update, or in a paper newsletter is a great way to capture people's attention. More is not always better, so don't feel like you always have to do a collage of pictures (sometimes that is distracting). Choose pictures that tell a story, cast vision, or simply make people laugh. After all, "*a picture is worth a 1,000 words.*"

12. Give personal updates as well as ministry updates. While people want to know about your ministry, YOU are the person they know and care about. They want to know about YOU (and your family). Share short tidbits of what you are learning, reading, studying. Tell funny stories about yourself as you are adjusting to the new culture.

KNOW YOUR AUDIENCE and communicate to them in a way that keeps them up to date and praying for your ministry.

13. Use your updates and newsletters to challenge people.
What will encourage and challenge your readers toward greater vision for the world? One of my "editorials" in a newsletter soon after I returned to the U.S. was about the sad lack of missionary biographies in my local Christian bookstore. To be honest, I was appalled that rather than Hudson Taylor and Amy Carmichael there were biographies about Sarah Palin and Justin Beiber. I challenged my newsletter readers to choose a missions biography to read and even included a list of a few of my favorites.

14. The most important things is COMMUNICATE, COMMUNICATE, COMMUNICATE.
People DO want to know about what is going on with you, especially if they have committed to financially support you or consistently pray for you. They are your TEAM in a very real way, and it's important that you communicate to them as such. If you never hear from someone or hear from them only once ever six months, it does not communicate that you are a valued team member.

Your updates and newsletters are also a way to minister to the people who are investing in you. I once shared in a newsletter that I was doing a TV fast in order to "feast" on the Lord. One friend who gets my updates shared that it was so challenging to her that she decided to do a Facebook fast, and God used it to really re-focus her attention on Him. A co-laborer shared that one of his supporters said, *"I'm so thankful for your newsletters through the years. God has really used them to disciple me."*

Communicating consistently to our team is essential for affirming the reality that we really do need them to fulfill the task that God has given us. We are a team, and it takes all of us working together to advance God's Kingdom. Here's a final closing analogy that I love to share when I speak to groups that support me. I usually ask the pastor or key leader what they had for breakfast; let's say they had coffee and a doughnut.

"So Pastor had coffee and a doughnut for breakfast. How many people do you think it took for him to eat that breakfast this morning? Let's think about it (at this point, I start to quickly rattle off all the people it took to make his breakfast to bombard my hearers with all the people they hadn't thought of before).

His coffee: someone grew those coffee beans on a coffee farm, say in South America, and then there were all the people who harvested the beans, the hundreds of people at the factory who roasted and packaged the beans to be shipped to your store, the transport people who were a part of the shipping process. Then, once the coffee is delivered to the store where Pastor bought it, there are all the people who unloaded it, stocked it on the shelf, and the cashier who sold it to him.

But what about sugar and cream? (You start all over again). *Sugar cane and dairy farms – hundreds of harvesters, factory workers, transporters, and salespeople were involved in making sure there was sugar and cream to go in Pastor's coffee.*

And his doughnut? Someone grew wheat somewhere that was then ground and packaged by hundreds of workers and shipped to the doughnut making factory. And what about the paper for the box that the doughnuts were packaged in? And if they were, say Krispy Kreme doughnuts (my favorite!), there is a bunch of corporate executives who are involved in the marketing of the Krispy Kreme doughnuts so that those doughnuts would find their way to Pastor this morning.

You get my point. It took literally hundreds of thousands of people working behind the scenes, people who Pastor never saw, in order to provide for his breakfast this morning. This is a picture of the body of Christ. YOU may not be the person sharing the Gospel with people in Kochevnikstan, but you are no less a part of the worldwide team that makes that one conversation a possibility. Thank you for your teamship. In the same way it took thousands of people to make Pastor's breakfast happen, it takes all of us doing what God has called us to in order to advance the Gospel.

✔ LET'S GET PRACTICAL!

When was the last time you sent out a newsletter or e-mail update? Do you need to send out updates more often?

Ask one of your teammates to look at your last few newsletters or e-mail updates and give you feedback or better yet ask a few trusted donors/friends who receive your update to tell you what they would like to know.

Think about your update list. WHO gets your updates? What can you do to better communicate to these people? What are ways you can minister to them? What are ways that you show your appreciation for their teamship (in more than just a standard "thank you").

Relearning What You Thought You Knew

3-6 months

WHAT IS NORMAL?

Journal entry from first 3 months:

> *What's normal in this culture? In Orchard City, especially now when it stays light until 10pm, people are out late and seem to sleep late (not like our American 8-5 days). Kids are outside my apt building until all hours talking and playing. When do they go to school? How much of this is summer schedule and how much is "normal"? Most people I know here work until 7-8pm. Is Kochevnikstan "normally" a nighttime culture? What values and practices of the people here are common across the board and which are true of only a handful of people? Because I don't know what the "norm" is in this culture, I don't know how to judge what is different from the norm.*

MAKING OBSERVATIONS

An important skill in learning a new culture – learning anything really – is making observations. What do I see? What are people doing? What isn't being done?

Journal entry from first 3 months:

> *My observations so far are that people here are laid back. American culture is a "doer" culture. One of the questions we keep asking ourselves is, "What do people 'do' here for fun? What can we go 'do' with them?" So far the answer is they sit in cafes and talk or they sit in the mountains and talk or they sit in their homes and talk or they walk in a park and talk. Well when language is a barrier, sitting and talking can only happen so much until it becomes very draining or boring.*

A great exercise the first few months is to sit in a public place and simply watch what people do and how they relate to one another. Write down your observations so that later you can validate them with other people.

VALIDATING OBSERVATIONS

The key to making good observations is to validate them. We are all hard wired to jump to conclusions based on our own cultural biases. For example, I observe that people on buses and on the street don't smile at each other. In my North American bias, I jump to the conclusion that people are unfriendly. Instead of jumping to a conclusion, how do I validate my observation? One way to validate observations is by inviting input from a variety of people - local friends, a language or culture helper, teammates and other ex-pats who have been in country longer than you. Is this an accurate observation? And if it is, what does it mean?

My first few months in Kochevnikstan, my roommate and I decided to have a party for everyone we knew, which amounted to about 8 people between both us! In addition to building relationships with us, we wanted our local friends to build relationships with each other; this was the goal. In the U.S., parties – especially among students – are a great way to create cross over. We even had a theme for the party: blue. The theme was born out a mistake in buying blue candles instead of white ones. It wasn't until later that we learned that the word "blue" in our new language is a slang word for a homosexual! But in spite of our ill-named party all our friends came – most of them in pairs. Even though we tried all night to help everyone mingle and get to know each other, the pairs who came together stuck together. In fact, at one point in the evening the pairs had literally separated themselves in different rooms. All the groups would talk to my roommate and I, but none of them were interested in talking with each other. It ended up being an exhausting party, because we ran from room to room trying to make everyone feel welcomed. So why didn't people want to talk to each other? What did our observations mean? And how were we supposed to create community and cross over if new people wouldn't even talk to each other?

Through talking with trusted friends, locals and ex-pats, we began to learn that Kochevnikstani's don't mix and mingle well with new people. While American culture tends to be more outwardly friendly and social (some would say shallow), the local culture we were living in was much more reserved externally (which also explained why people didn't smile on the street). Even the word for "friend" is a strong word that implies history and lots of relationship. Americans use the word to describe people they've just met, but most Kochevnikstani's use words like colleague, co-worker, acquaintance, or neighbor much more frequently than the word friend.

UNDERSTANDING WHAT IS NORMAL AND BEING A CATALYST FOR CHANGE

Making observations and validating them, like in the example with our "blue party," leads to a greater understanding of what is normal in our new culture. And determining what is normal is an important step in determining how much I want to be normal. How much do I want to choose to fit into the culture (contextualize) and how much do I want to change it (introduce Kingdom Culture)?

I learned from the "blue party" that while parties can be a platform for helping people who already know each other to interact, it wasn't a good idea to invite a lot of people from different walks of life. I also realized that one of the roles I play as a North American in a different culture is to be a catalyst for change. As a foreigner, I can do things that are not "normal" like smiling on the street: even if people think you are crazy they can't help but be intrigued. I don't want to infuse my own cultural biases into my host culture, but I DO want to bring Kingdom Culture into the lives of my local friends.

How much do I want to choose to fit into the culture (contextualize) and how much do I want to change it (introduce Kingdom Culture)?

SUBCULTURES

One last note about making observations and determining what is "normal" in a culture. It's important to be aware that all cultures have subcultures. A danger in learning your new culture is drawing blanket, stereotypical conclusions about a whole culture when really your observations, validations, and understanding really only apply to a subculture within that culture.

Although I have relationships with people at different stages of life, most of my time in Kochevnikstan has been spent with students. Students are a subculture. I've interacted with students on 6 different continents, and while they all have aspects of their home culture, they also share similar characteristics of student culture. Not only has most of my time in Kochevnikstan been spent with students in general, but with students attending private, costly universities where English is part of the curriculum (English-speaking students, a subculture within a subculture). I can make and validate observations in my realm of relationships that most everyone speaks some level of English, that most people have access to and frequently use the internet, and that everyone travels abroad at least once a year. These things ARE true in the subculture of my subculture – wealthy, English-speaking students. But that does not mean that those things are equally true across ALL of the culture of Kochevnikstan. Ultimately, I want to become an expert – or at least well informed – about my target group within my host culture (for me that is students). But I need to be cautious that I don't make assumptions that everyone in the culture is like my target group.

✔ LET'S GET PRACTICAL

Practice Observing. Whether you've been in the country 2 weeks, 6 months, or a year cultivate the habit of observation. As you walk through the bazaar, stroll around campus, go to a department store, sit in a café, stand at a bus stop – watch people and make observations:

How do people interact with one another?

What do people do?

For a change, choose a specific observation to focus on: people's clothes? Shoes? What signs say? Hairstyles? Food? Moms? Etc.?

3 CULTURES IN CONFLICT

Sometimes God uses small things to teach us big lessons. During my first three months, one of my constant mental struggles was what to call a waitress or store clerk. In Kochevnikstan, people yell out "girl" or "young man." To my polite southern upbringing, where we call everyone "ma'am" or "sir" it sounded SO rude to me. Even though it didn't appear to be received as rude and the girl being called didn't seem to mind, I just couldn't bring myself to call a waitress or store clerk "girl". I usually said, "*Excuse me, please*," which immediately identified me as not being from around here (as if they didn't already know!).

A constant tension in any new situation is identifying and integrating 3 conflicting cultures. There is Kingdom Culture (scriptural), Home Culture (your default preference), and Host Culture (your new norm). The mental challenge and constant tension, especially early on in the adjustment process, is sifting through which of my own values are rooted in Scripture that I want to hold on to, and which are rooted in my American culture or the subculture I grew up in (i.e., Bible belt southern culture) which I often need to hold loosely.

In my dilemma with the local waitress, I wanted to be kind and respectful (Kingdom culture), because I'm a believer and I wanted my actions and choices to set me apart. I also wanted to be culturally relevant (Host Culture), which in Kochevnikstan meant calling a waitress "girl." But no matter how much I try to leave behind my upbringing (Home Culture), I am still a product of my southern subculture where kindness and respect equal "ma'am" or "sir" but not "girl."

One of the joys for me of living in my city is that there is a large international community: Australians, Canadians, Brits, Kiwis, Koreans, etc. One of the benefits of that international community, especially as I was learning what is culturally relevant, was being able to talk to other non-American ex-pats about my observations. For example, I learned that in Australian and Canadian culture, a child calling an adult "ma'am" or "sir" was considered sassy and disrespectful. The kids on our team, who all grew up in U.S. southern culture, had to re-learn what was considered "polite" not only in the local culture but in the international community where they went to school.

Having personal values and preferences is NOT a bad thing. In fact, no matter how hard we might try, we can't rid ourselves of our own personal values or preferences that are rooted in our cultural upbringing or our family's subculture. The goal is NOT to get rid of our personal preferences, but to understand what they are, how they influence us, and to separate my personal preference from what is truly scriptural. What I want to pass on to my host culture is the truth of God's Kingdom, not my own cultural bias. But I have to diligently seek to understand the differences between the two.

SIFTING OUT YOUR AMERICAN CULTURE

Imagine that your life is a mixture of rice and flour. When you sift the mixture, the rice stays in the sifter and the flour is what comes through the sieve. The Word of God, the Scriptures, is the sifter. It is the standard of truth by which we determine Kingdom values (the flour) and our own personal or cultural application of those values (rice). When we move to a new host culture, our life gets shaken up and we must intentionally sift what we think and believe through the sieve of God's Word. What comes out of the sieve is purified Kingdom culture, and THAT is what we want to pass on to others. The chart below gives a few simple examples. You may or may not agree with me on the specific points since these are from my own personal experience. You will have different experiences to sift through.

American Culture	Kingdom Culture	Host Culture
Church is a building you go to	Church is People (Acts 20:28/Col 1:24)	Church happens in homes
Church is 1hr. Sun morn	Fellowship of Believers (Acts 2:42)	Fellowship could last hours
Easter is a religious holiday	Celebrate Jesus' death/sacrifice	Korbanite is a holiday of sacrifice (different time of year than Easter)
Being on time is important	Respect for others (Phil 2:4)	Person you are with is important

In the American Christian culture I grew up in, "Church" was viewed as a place of worship (usually a building) with a specific format (1 hour on Sunday mornings). But if we look closely at Scripture, we see that the principle of church isn't about a building but about the body of believers, and the format isn't limited to a 1-hour service but is about fellowshipping with one another in homes, over meals, through teaching and prayer, etc. (Acts 2). I'm not saying that our cultural choices like our church styles, formats, or preferences are bad, but there is great danger in passing on our cultural applications as absolute Biblical truth rather than the principles from Scripture (which can be applied in multiple ways). In fact, adhering to the man-made interpretation of the law, which we call legalism, was what the Pharisees did, and Jesus called them out on it (Matt. 15:1-20).

In Kochevnikstan, Easter is associated with the Orthodox church: it is an Orthodox holiday that Kochevniks and regional people groups want nothing to do with. However, Kochevnik culture has a holiday called Korbanite. As part of this holiday celebration, a family will sacrifice a sheep to pay for the sins of the family throughout the year and share the cooked meat of the sheep with their family and neighbors. Korbanite is a much more culturally relevant way than "Easter" for Kochevnik believers to celebrate the death and resurrection of Jesus , the lamb of God slain for the sins of the world.

Another example of sifting through these three cultures is punctuality. Very few cultures in the world value time and punctuality as much as North Americans do. It's my personal preference to be on time, and even after 10 years living in a non-punctual culture, I still hold on to my personal preference. HOWEVER, I recognize that punctuality is NOT a Kingdom value. I don't think Jesus wore a watch, and in Scripture I never see him rebuke anyone for being late. The Kingdom value I DO see is showing respect to people (Phil. 2:4). In American culture, being on time is a way to show respect, but in Kochevnik culture the person you are with is more important than the person you are going to meet. So if you are late, it's not disrespectful but it's showing respect to the person you are with. There's nothing wrong with maintaining our own values (I still try to be punctual and my local friends know that it's important to me), but I cannot force my personal values on others as absolute truth.

THINK ABOUT YOUR PERSONAL AND CULTURAL VALUES

The point of the examples above is to challenge you to think about your own values and preferences. What values do you hold as absolute Bible truth that are really just rooted in your cultures application of truth? What are the values, the non-negotiables, that are rooted in Kingdom Culture (Scripture)? Some will be the same, but you'll be surprised at how many are not.

When I came to Kochevnikstan my list of non-negotiables was long. Over the years, it's gotten shorter and shorter as my view of God has gotten bigger and bigger. At the end of the day, I can sum up my entire list of absolutes in one phrase, *"God is God and I am not!"*

If we don't intentionally sift through our own cultural values, then we will unintentionally pass them on as the absolute, biblical rule of life to the people we invest in. That's legalism like the Pharisees, not the freedom of the Gospel.

✎ ON YOUR OWN

What is something culturally that has been hard for you to accept or do? Use this as a starting point to sift through what is really going on. Why is it hard for you to embrace this culture point?

Can you think of any situations in your life or culture where the application has become more important than the principle behind it?

What are specific ways you can train yourself to recognize the principles behind observations or the application (it's the principles we want to live by and pass on to people)? Discuss this with your teammates and/or mentor.

INSIGHTS INTO AMERICAN CULTURE I
American culture for dummies

When I was in language school, one of the things they recommend-ed that we read, or at least skim, was the book *English Grammar for Dummies*. In order to learn a new language, especially the grammatical structures of a new language, it's important to understand some of the basics of your own language. For example, in the language I was learn-ing there is a whole case dedicated to the direct object. If you don't know what a direct object is, it's kind of hard to apply the correct case to that part of speech!

In a similar way, it is helpful to understand some basics about your own culture in order to gain insight into your new host culture. The obser-vations below are not empirical study findings, and I'm not claiming to be the expert on American culture. These are simply my own thoughts on American Culture learned through personal experience.

FOUNDED ON CHRISTIAN VALUES AND ETHICS
On one of my first home assignments back to the U.S., I was getting gas at a local gas station. This was before the days of "pay at the pump" with a credit card. I pumped my gas, then went inside to pay. As I was walking into the store, it occurred to me that it would be so easy to just pump my gas then drive away without paying, which is exactly what would've happened in Kochevnikstan. In Kochevnikstan, you have to pay FIRST and then pump your gas (the pump is controlled by the cashier and will only pump to the amount you have pre-paid). But in America, there is a foundational belief that people will do the right thing (or at least fear the punishment of doing the wrong thing), and pay for the gas.

You might argue that America is changing, and that "nowadays" you can't trust people to do the right thing. I agree that since the 1960s American culture has become less and less "Christian." I get that. Yet the reality is that the very foundation of American culture is rooted in and built on Christian values and ethics.

It's not my intent to go into an extensive history lesson; I'm not an expert on American or World history. I do want to point out that America is a country that was founded by people seeking religious freedom.[1] The original pilgrims, the Puritans, brought their beliefs with them and infused them into the fabric of our American culture.

Think about these Christian values played out in our culture:

1. Honesty: In his book *Peace Child,* Don Richardson tells his story of working with the Sawi people. In Sawi culture, betrayal and trickery were highly valued. The better you were able to deceive your friends, the more respected you were. While not all Americans are honest, the foundational value taught in schools from Kindergarten on is, *"Honesty is the best policy."* Even if honesty is not always practiced, it's still valued.

2. Giving: In 2009, American individuals gave over $200 BILLION to charity. American culture may be more and more materialistic, but there is still a fundamental value of generosity and a sense of responsibility for helping the less fortunate. And that is not limited to Christian culture, it's becoming more and more "popular" among secular wealthy companies and individuals to find a "cause" they can financially give to

---

1   The early cultures that developed after Adam and Eve sinned in the Garden of Eden were pagan; God called Abraham out of a pagan culture to establish a new culture of God followers. Egyptian culture worshipped Pharaoh and other gods. Early Chinese culture was rooted in Taoism and philosophy. Early African and South American cultures were tribal and inundated with animism and ancestral worship; Australia was originally a penal colony. The Pagan Roman Empire spread across Europe, and although Germany and France were the home of the Reformation their foundational cultures were barbaric and pagan. Even the isles of Great Britain – a sending nation for countless missionaries in the 19th and 20th centuries – are rooted in Celtic, pagan culture. Israel is the only other nation state established in a pursuit of religious freedom and it is not Christian. There were Native Americans in North America committed to the same idea of ancestral worship that was present in South America and Africa. The Catholics and Jesuits took over South America and conquered in the name of the church. So if you compare South America and North America, they have the same foundational beginnings. What made the difference? Priests came to South America alone or in a small group of monks. The Puritans, however, brought their wives and their families. When families pass on their values to their children, it begins to have an impact. As families reproduced and expanded, Puritan values were passed on to the next generation. By 1776, when our Declaration of Independence was written, we had three generations of Puritan families that had called this place home and they influenced the founding principles of "life, liberty and the pursuit of happiness," which translates as a freedom to decide your own course.

and personally invest in helping.

3. Stealing: I had a significant amount of money stolen from my apartment in Kochevnikstan. Not long after that, my teammates also had money stolen from their house – twice. In all three cases, the primary suspect was a trusted friend, and in two instances the suspected culprits were believers. As my teammates and I discussed these situations, we realized that our own commitment to not steal was rooted as much in our upbringing as in our relationship with God. Growing up, my momma would've skinned my hide if she found out I stole something! "*Thou shall not steal*" is a basic belief taught to all children and upheld by the laws of our country. But in Kochevnikstan's heavily communist-influenced culture, there is a "Robin Hood" mentality: it's not really stealing if the person you take from has more than you. One of the most famous and most read Kochevnik children's story is *Aldar Kaisar*; he is honored and respected for his shrewd deception.

4. Language: English language, which is not uniquely American, is full of biblical metaphors ranking second only to Shakespeare as one of the cornerstones of the recorded language.[2] We talk about being a "scapegoat" or "slaying the giant(s)," "fighting the good fight" or "from the mouths of babes," or dozens of other words, idioms, or metaphors rooted in our Puritan-biblical foundation and history.

The original pilgrims, the Puritans, brought their beliefs with them and infused them into the fabric of our American culture.

These are just a few of the Judeo-Christian values that permeate American culture. I'm definitely not saying that America or Americans are all true followers of Jesus. This discussion is not about relationship with God but about the foundational values that have influenced our culture.

---

2   From www.phrases.org.uk/meanings/bible-phrases-sayings

🖊 ON YOUR OWN

Think about your childhood. What values did your parents instill in you? What values did you learn (or were reinforced) in your education from elementary school through college?

What are the culturally ingrained values you see in your host culture? What kind of history does your host culture have that influences their value system?

Find out more about your host culture's history: choose a book to read, ask questions of knowledgeable local friends about their history, ask about what children's stories they hear as a child (children's books provide great insight into the values of the culture passed on to the children).

INSIGHTS INTO AMERICAN CULTURE II
American culture for dummies

THE LAND OF OPPORTUNITY

"The idea of the self-made man is inextricably tied up with that of the American dream. It is his image that has lured thousands of immigrants to our shores, all hoping for the chance to turn a handful of beans into a vast fortune. The self-made man is he who comes from unpromising circumstances, who is not born into privilege and wealth, and yet by his own efforts, by pulling himself up by the bootstraps, manages to become a great success in life."[3]

Consider these self-made American men:
- J.D. Rockefeller was the child of an absent father
- Frederick Douglas was an African slave
- Ralph Lauren was a Jewish immigrant
- Ray Kroc (McDonald's) was a high school drop out
- Thomas Edison was kicked out of school and practically deaf
- Abraham Lincoln was the son of an uneducated farmer
- Clarence Thomas (Supreme Court Judge) was abandoned by his father
- Walt Disney and Milton Hershey had multiple failed businesses before they achieved success
- Arnold Schwarzenegger is an Austrian immigrant turned bodybuilder turned actor turned politician

American Culture is riddled with the success stories of self-made men. It's ingrained in our culture, and because of that we are inspired to make something of our own lives. Because of these models, we believe that we **can** achieve success! This value that anyone can become anything is not common. Many cultures of the world are much more fatalistic in their outlook: *"One person can't make a difference. Why should we even try to change our status or state in life – we are who are we are."* In Kochevnikstan, like many cultures, there is no ingrained value of the "self-made man" and no opportunity to change your "fate" in life.

---

3   *Strive and Succeed* by Horatio Alger Jr. (from website artofmanliness.com)

In fact, the very opposite is true.

Consider growing up as an orphan in a culture where relationships and connections are the most important thing. In our American mentality (based on our value of self-made people), that orphan can just decide to "make something" of his life. From our American perspective, it's easy to become critical and judgmental if he doesn't "try harder." But in a fatalistic world view that says you have to have family connections to be something, that orphan's cultural foundation works against him and tells him, "*Why try? It won't make a difference.*"

Or consider living in a caste culture. It doesn't matter how smart you are or how hard you work or how much money you make, you will never be accepted into society in a different class from the one you were born into. No J.D. Rockefellers here. The cultural norm – the caste system – defines your state in life, not your own efforts.

America is the "Land of Opportunity;" it's ingrained in our culture, our history, and our mentality. We can't change who we are or the cultural influences we've experienced since childhood, but we can become more aware of how those cultural norms impact how we think about, minister to, and love people who have a very different cultural upbringing.

VIEW OF GOVERNMENT - "NO ONE'S COMING AFTER US"
When I was teaching at a local university I would try to do activities that created discussion, especially since my English class was focused on conversation. One day in class, I had my students do one of those survival exercises, the kind where your airplane crashes and your group has to decide which items are the most important to keep and rank them accordingly. Then you "grade" your answers based on what the "experts" say are most important to have. In this particular exercise, the expert advice was that the victims should stay where they are and wait for help to arrive. One of my more astute students raised his hand and said, "*You are an American so maybe help will come for you, but no one is coming for us!*"

In American culture, we have a basic belief that the Government will look out for its citizens – at least we believe that is what government is supposed to do. We may not trust what politicians are doing or saying, but there is a foundational belief that government is *"of the people, by the people, for the people,"*[4] and that one of its primary functions is the protection of its citizens. If the government ceases to fulfill its constitutional function, then the people have a right to complain and even to change the government. This concept is at the very core of America's birth as a nation.[5] The basic idea of "rights" that is so ingrained in the American mentality is foreign to many cultures. They distrust their governments and with good reason. They do not believe they are empowered to orchestrate change. Their governments have a long history of dictatorial leaders whose only in interest is gaining power, controlling the people, and lining their own pockets.

FREEDOM VS. SECURITY

A few years ago, Russian president Vladimir Putin was *Time Magazine's* Man of the Year. I remember reading the article and wondering how the Russian people could put up with such restrictions of their individual rights after having experienced such freedom when Communism first fell. As one of my teammates and I were discussing this, she said something that gave me new perspective. She commented, *"Russians value security more than freedom."*

Could that really be true? I cannot imagine valuing security more than freedom. American culture is built on the foundational belief that all men should be free. Puritans sought religious freedom. The Founding Fathers rebelled against an oppressive government for the freedom to govern themselves. The Civil War boiled down to freedom for slaves (Union) and freedom to secede (Confederacy). WWII raged for years in Europe before the "sleeping giant" entered the war because of an attack on our homeland – an attack on our freedom. *"The land of the free..."* expressed in America's national anthem is woven into the fabric of our culture.

---

4   From "The Gettysburg Address" by Abraham Lincoln 1863
5   If you think I'm totally off base in my comments about our government, and it has set you off on how the government doesn't do what it's supposed to, then you've really just proved my point. As an American citizen you believe you have the right to complain about how the politicians run things and that our government should - even if they don't - listen to what the people have to say.

Yet my friend's comment made complete sense to me. I thought of all the over-40 taxi drivers I had talked with who all agreed that times were better under the old regime. Why? Because they had security. There was food in the stores, and their money had value. The fall of the regime might have brought some freedom with it, but it also brought a lot of instability, insecurity, and an influx of western culture – the bad along with the good. These older men didn't so much remember the limitations on their personal freedom, but they longed for the days when they felt more secure. Though I doubt they could have expressed it, their value for security was greater than their value of freedom.

I'm not saying that one value is more "right" than the other, or even that they are in conflict (although often they are). I'm simply pointing out that the foundational values of nations are different. If we are going to learn to love people where they are, then we need to begin to understand what values – rooted in their history and culture – most influence them.

WIDE OPEN SPACES

One summer we brought a group of six Kochevnikstani students to the U.S. for a training program in Florida. At the end of the project, we road-tripped from Florida to Colorado. One of the students was dying to see the "big city" and kept asking where the skyscrapers were (the largest city we actually drove through was St. Louis). What most non-Americans know about America is what they see in Hollywood films, and many movies take place in big cities like New York, L.A., or Chicago (did you know there are only 9 cities in the U.S. with over 1 million people?).[6] Most of America consists of cities under 500,000 and lots of wide open spaces. In fact, the "American Cowboy" is iconic and synonymous with wide-open spaces.

The westward expansion period of American history is as much a part of our cultural influence as fighting for freedom or the self-made man. In the same way that Americans value freedom, we also value space.

---

6   New York City, Los Angeles, Chicago, Houston, Philadelphia, Phoenix, San Antonio, San Diego, Dallas. From: http://www.infoplease.com/ipa/A0763098.html 2012 population estimate.

And it's not limited to spacious farmlands, cattle ranches, or National Parks. Our houses are large, and there's always a dedicated living room and often a dedicated dining room (dedicated meaning no one sleeps there on a regular basis). We have large parking lots with wide parking spaces.[7] In our relationships, we want "personal space" – an unspoken circle of space that people should not invade when talking to us. Even our washing machines are huge![8]

> ## Cultures are made by men, influenced by history, and reinforced by traditions. Cultures themselves are neither right nor wrong but simply reflect the values of the people.

In many cultures it would be strange for family members not to live together. It's not uncommon for multi-generational families to all live together in the same 2-3 room apartment (not 2-3 bedrooms, but 2-3 rooms with each room serving as a sleeping space for someone – no dedicated living room). This isn't true just in large cities where land is scarce but it's also true for many village cultures. The need for personal space simply is not as valued by most cultures the way it is in American culture. The desire for wide-open spaces is woven into the fabric of our cultural history.

CULTURES ARE MADE BY MEN

Cultures are made by men, influenced by history, and reinforced by traditions. Cultures themselves are neither right nor wrong but simply reflect the values of the people. In advancing the Gospel into a new culture (our host culture), it's important to grow in understanding not only of the host culture but also of the cultural values we bring with us (our home culture). Even more importantly, consistently be sifting

---

7   On one of my home assignments just after I had started driving in Kochevnikstan I was amazed at how BIG American parking spaces were – they were 1.5x wider than the parking spaces in Kochevnikstan.

8   This was another of my "wow" moments on a home assignment. My sister-in-law's washing machine was HUGE! One of my first washing machines in Kochevnikstan was big enough for one pair of jeans, a t-shirt and underwear. There was not space in my apartment for a bigger machine.

both our host and home cultural values through the Kingdom Culture of Scripture. Kingdom values are the ones we want to pass on and infuse into the lives of people to whom we minister.

✎ ON YOUR OWN

Think about 1-2 people you know in your host culture with whom you can have honest conversation? Ask them what they think are high values in their culture. Do you see this? Do you see values in their culture that they don't? (Keep in mind that often we do not see our own cultural values. It might take talking to a few different people to get below the surface answers about the culture.)

Do the "Kingdom Culture Values Study" in the Practical Resources section. What Kingdom Culture values do you see in American culture? In your host culture? What Kingdom Culture values are missing in each of these cultures?

BE A LEARNER

Journal entry:

> *There must be a high value on learning when crossing cultures. "Investigation" must happen if we are to be successful in penetrating this people group. Not only must there be a high value on learning, but a high value on learning for a LONG time. I must avoid the danger of jumping to conclusions or stopping at a surface level understanding of the people and culture.*

In Acts 17, Paul models this commitment to observation and learning when he's in Athens. Acts 17:23 says, *"for as I walked around and looked carefully at your objects of worship…."* Paul was a learner of his host culture. He looked and saw what was present in the culture and started his discussion with the familiar.

CULTIVATE CURIOSITY

In my current job, one of the privileges I have is getting to visit teams of 20-somethings in different countries who are serving alongside long-term laborers. It's always fun for the team to show me around their new city and, as a naturally curious person, I am full of questions about everything from the culture, to their adjustment, to how they relate with one another and with their local friends. The most common response to my curiosity is, *"I don't know,"* which is not so surprising. Most of the teams have been in-country only a short period of time when I visit. What is very surprising to me is that they don't seem to have any of the same curiosity that I do.

It's not my intent to be critical of a young generation, simply to point out an observation I've made time and time again. This current generation lacks curiosity. Perhaps it's the availability of Google to answer any and all questions at the touch of a finger that trains people to not cultivate curiosity beyond what they can find out online. Or perhaps the world of 20-somethings is so full of an over-abundance of unused knowledge that more information feels unnecessary. Regardless of the reason, there is a need for cross-cultural workers of any age to cultivate curiosity; to learn to ask questions of what, why, and how; to practice the habit of making observations and being learners of the culture and the people around them.

IDENTIFY REDEMPTIVE ANALOGIES

Don Richardson's experience with the Sawi people demonstrates the value of learning and identifying cultural clues to the Gospel. He relates his experience in the book *Peace Child*. In Sawi culture, deception and manipulation were highly valued character traits. When they heard the story of the Gospel, Judas was the hero to them. Finally, Don Richardson observed in Sawi culture what he later termed a "redemptive analogy."[9] If two tribes were warring, there was only one way to make lasting peace. The chief of one tribe would give his newborn son to the enemy tribe. As long as that son lived, the tribes would be at peace because the chief would not chance killing his own son in a tribal war. The Sawi people came to understand that Jesus is God's "peace child," and he lives eternally so that God is no longer at war with mankind.

Intentional learning is not only of benefit as it opens up greater understanding of how to present the Gospel in your new culture, it's also a way to connect and build rapport with your friends. I have a picture at a park of me with "Crodila Gena," a favorite children's cartoon character (I watched this cartoon in my early days to help me learn language). Crodila Gena sings a famous birthday song that is woven into the childhood culture of most of my friends. Even to this day, when I mention Crodila Gena they love that I know who he is.

EXPRESSING WHAT YOU ARE LEARNING

One of the best ways to process what we are learning about our new culture is to find creative ways to express it. My first year in Kochevnikstan, I set aside one day a month to go on a photography treasure hunt. I would choose a place or perhaps an event and go take pictures. The goal was to try to capture pictures that told a story or revealed some cultural insight. Another way to express what you are learning is short essays. Much of this book is a collection of cultural essays I wrote in my early years of living in Kochevnikstan. Writing

---

9   In *Eternity in their Hearts* Don Richardson unpacks more fully this idea of redemptive analogies.

helped me to express the things I was learning and gave friends and family back home a "picture" of what life was like in this new culture. If you are artistic, you can draw (I tried having a "drawing" journal, but my artistic ability is limited to stick people). If you are musical, try writing songs or jingles; it's a great outlet for expressing your frustration about aspects of the culture. Try writing a beautiful song as a prayer for the people of your country.

Whether you write essays, take pictures, draw, paint, write songs, or make statues out of recycled materials – find a way to creatively express what you are learning in your new culture. Set aside time as a team to share your different creative expressions of your cultural learning.

📖 FOR FURTHER STUDY

Read through Acts 17, making observations about how Paul interacted with the culture. What was the result of his study of the culture?

Asking good questions is a way to become a learner and practice curiosity. Read through the Gospels making note of all the questions Jesus asked. What types of questions did he ask and for what purpose? From your study, make a list of 5-10 questions that you can ask people to be a learner.

Personal Reflection: Do you consider yourself a curious person? What motivates your curiosity (or lack of it)? How can you cultivate curiosity in your life?

GRAY MATTERS

My first time overseas as a believer was a summer spent in Thailand. We spent most of the time in Bangkok, working on a college campus. However, near the end of the summer we did an evangelistic trip in the south, showing the Jesus film in several different villages. I had just graduated from college and was passionate about reaching the world for Christ. My life was full of non-negotiables and absolutes.

We arrived in a small village, and the pastor met our team and helped us get settled in the homes where we were staying. The girls all stayed at the pastor's house. The guys also stayed at the pastor's house – the pastor's second wife's house. The pastor in this small village had TWO wives. For my American-Southern-Bible-belt-conservative cultural mind, this was a stretch. It was messy. What was I supposed to do with this? Polygamy isn't "right," but what do you do? Advise divorce? That's not "right" either. One of the guys on our team – a "right is right" prophet type – wanted to confront the pastor. Can you imagine a young guy of barely 21 confronting a 40-something established and respected elder in the Thai believing community? Take that to heart – 20-something years of life experience and a few months in your country does not make one an expert. James 1:19 is a good rule of thumb when you encounter these messy situations. Be *"quick to listen and slow to speak...."*

Fortunately, my teammate restrained his urge to confront the pastor about his polygamy, and the more we watched and observed, the more we saw what a GOOD testimony the pastor and his family was to this small village. The two wives didn't fight, which apparently (and understandably) was not normal. The fact that they didn't fight set them apart from the other wives in the village and was a testimony to the power of Jesus.

Since that time, I've encountered many other situations that don't have clear-cut answers. I've learned through experience that while there is absolute truth, there is a lot less of it than I used to think. And while I really love things that are black and white, most of the world lives it's daily life in the "gray."

What do you do with a situation like the one I described? How do you think about and process something that doesn't have a clear-cut "right" answer? Paul addresses gray matters in Romans 14 and 15:13. Read through this passage, asking the Lord to give you insight, wisdom, and understanding. Below are some of my own personal meditations. I am not saying that my questions or answers are the right ones, but they are honest food for thought. Dialogue over these thoughts with the Lord and with your teammates.

> *Accept him whose faith is weak, without passing judgment on disputable matters.* (14:1)

"Disputable matters." What exactly are disputable matters? What is essential to the Gospel – the absolute musts to enter the Kingdom of God? What things do I make the issue? What things are appropriate to a particular culture (like southern culture or Kochevnik culture)? What things are my own personal convictions?

> *Each one should be fully convinced in his own mind.* (14:5)

What is the difference between what I am fully convinced of and what is absolutely true of the Gospel? I'm fully convinced that lying is wrong – for me to lie consistently or even once would be absolute sin for me as it would be an offense against my own conscious. Does that mean the same is true for everyone? Can someone be a believer – a child of God – if he lies? What about theological differences – pre-destination vs. free will? Suffering and perseverance vs. health, wealth, and prosperity? Where do I personally stand on these (and other) issues? If I know what I believe and am convinced of it in my own mind, then I think it's easier to see things from another's perspective.

> *So then, each of us will give an account of himself to God. Therefore let us stop passing judgment on one another.* (14:12-13)

"*Live your life for an audience of One.*" I learned this phrase years ago and it applies more and more the older I get. Ultimately, when I stand before God, He will not ask me how Sarah lived or what John believed. I will give account of my beliefs and actions to the Lord and to Him alone. Therefore, I must be certain (fully convinced) BEFORE GOD that the choices I make are pleasing to Him and in obedience to His leading in my life – even if other people don't understand them. And I must stop being judgmental of others who do not choose to apply the Word of God in the same way I do. They may be wrong, or they may be right; either way they do not answer to me. They too will answer to the Lord and to the Lord alone. I am responsible to speak the truth as best as I understand it, but I am not responsible for anyone else's choices.

> *For the Kingdom of God is not a matter of eating and drinking, but of righteousness, peace, and joy in the Holy Spirit because anyone who serves Christ in this way is pleasing to God and approved by men. Let us therefore make every effort to do what leads to peace and mutual edification.* (14:18-19)

The Kingdom of God is not about a set of rules, a list of dos and don'ts. It's about the intangibles of life like righteousness, peace, and joy. So how do I make peace with a fellow Kingdom citizen who has vastly different convictions than I do? How I do I build up a brother or sister who is making decisions I would not choose? How do I pursue peace with other believers without compromising my own beliefs, values and convictions? How do I disagree in a way that honors God?

> *Everything that does not come from faith is sin.* (14:23)

Obedience is doing what God says. God says it. I do it. That's not so hard. But faith is doing something when I'm not sure what is "beyond," when the way in front of me is not clear, when I'm not sure what is "right." Faith, more than obedience, is required in the gray areas.

> *May the God who gives endurance and encouragement give you a spirit of unity among yourselves as you follow Christ Jesus so that with one heart and mouth you may glorify the God and Father of our Lord Jesus Christ. Accept one another, then, just as Christ accepted you.* (15:6-7)

Lord, give me a spirit of unity with other believers even if we disagree about various applications of truth. Give me eyes to see beyond the differences to the heart of the matter. In all things, let me glorify you. Give me the grace to accept and love others thus fulfilling Jesus' command and promise "Love one another as I have loved you...by this all men will know you are my disciples, if you love one another" (John 13:34).

✎ ON YOUR OWN

What are the "gray matters" you are facing in your new culture? What is your natural response to these circumstances? Ask the Lord to give you insight and understanding in these areas.

What is your own matrix – your grid – for thinking through "gray matters"? How do you process through things that are not clearly "right and wrong"? If you don't have a clear way that you think through gray matters, ask the Lord to begin to develop this in you. Talk with teammates and other expats about how they think through issues that are not clear cut.

THE LIBERTY OF OBEDIENCE

As you move outside the safety of the familiar and into a world full of conflicting ideas, philosophies, and belief systems, the greatest challenge you face won't be sifting through truth and untruth – but between varying applications of truth. In crossing to another culture you will face many questions that don't have clear-cut right and wrong answers. You must decide for yourself how you will respond. For example:

When a policemen expects you to pay a bribe or he'll take your drivers license

When your friend asks you to loan her money (not a few dollars but several hundred dollars)

When a beggar comes knocking on your door

When your house help or roommate (or trusted friend) steals money from you

When your colleague is falsely accused of embezzlement and faces jail time because of it

When your drunk neighbor comes home and hits his wife and kids

When the only way to "expedite" your visa is to pay the lawyer $200 under the table

How do you know what to do when what's "right" and "wrong" seems to be redefined by the new culture you live in or thrown into confusion by the expats around you who don't seem to agree on a "SOP" (standard operation procedure)?

What sets Christianity apart from other belief systems is that as Christians we are called first and foremost to a relationship. We are called to follow and obey a person not a set of rules.[10] Even in Christian circles "rules" (applications of truth) change. How do you know what you should do? Jesus promises us the Holy Spirit whose job is to "*convict us of all righteousness*" (John 16:18). As we quiet our lives long enough to hear his still small voice we hear him say "*this is the way, walk in it*" and then we obey (Isaiah 30:21).

In *The Pursuit of God*, A.W. Tozer asks the question, "*What makes a saint?*" His answer:

> "*Prying into [the mysteries of election, predestination and divine sovereignty] may make us theologians but it will never make us saints...the one vital quality which they [Luther, Finney, Moses, Isaiah, Paul, St. Francis, etc.] had in common was spiritual receptivity...they had spiritual awareness...and they went on to cultivate it until it became the biggest thing in their lives. They differed from the average person in that when they felt the inward longing they did something about it. They acquired a lifelong habit of spiritual response.*"[11]

Spiritual receptivity – the liberty of obedience – is cultivated as we learn to listen to His voice and obey it. Imagine Hosea's surprise when God told him to marry a prostitute – not common advice for a Christian. Or what about Noah being told to build an ark (remember it had never rained up to this point)? His peers didn't understand, but he chose to obey although the plan was very unorthodox. It's unlikely that God will ask you to do what he asked Hosea or Noah, but chances are that you will be faced with your own circumstances in which God asks you to make unorthodox choices.

In her book *The Liberty of Obedience*,[12] Elisabeth Elliot poses a ques-

---

10   Certainly as believers we are to obey the Scriptures, but Jesus' call to his followers in Matt 4:19 is "Come follow me..." not "come follow all the rules of the Pharisees..." The call is first and foremost to a relationship rather than to a religion (a set of rules).

11   *The Pursuit of God* by A.W. Tozer p. 64-65

12   For many years *The Liberty of Obedience* was my standard gift for all graduating college seniors. It's a small book with very thought provoking concepts that challenged me to live freely in obedience to Christ and helped prepare me for cross-cultural living by encouraging me to learn to identify principles vs. applications.

tion about modesty as an example of principles and applications. She asks, *"How do you teach modesty to a tribe of people who don't wear clothes?"* Paul says, *"I also want women to dress modestly, with decency and propriety, not with braided hair or gold or pearls or expensive clothes..."* (1 Timothy 2:9). So does that mean if I braid my hair in 2012 that I am being indecent? Or if I wear my grandmother's pearls I am a harlot? What does it mean to dress modestly? In 1900, it would have been immodest to swim in anything less that a bathing costume that covered practically all of your arms and legs. In many African cultures the women are completely topless, but they would never wear shorts revealing their thighs – that would be considered immodest. Scripture teaches women to dress modestly – a principle – but what does that mean in application?

Let's be clear. We are NOT talking about pluralism (all things are acceptable) or relativism (whatever you think is ok). Everyone doing what is right in his own eyes is not acceptable (Judges 21:25). However, it is equally true that God does not call us all to do exactly the same things or to respond to the same situation in exactly the same way. He's given us different gifts, talents, bents, personalities, and perspectives, and these differences allow us to make different decisions (applications) while still holding on to the same principles. Paul and Barnabas responded differently to John Mark's desertion of them in Pamphylia, and thus made different decisions about how to proceed with God's unique calling to them (Acts 15:37-40).

Flour is a simple illustration of the difference between principles and applications. Flour is a basic ingredient in a lot of different foods. Mix with butter and sugar and you have the makings of a sweet cake. Add chocolate or other flavors, and the cake becomes even more specialized. Mix flour with some bacon grease and sausage, and you get white gravy – a savory southern favorite. The same basic ingredient used in the same basic way results in two very different foods. Likewise, it's essential that we learn to recognize the basic principles of Scriptures while allowing ourselves and others the freedom to apply those principles in a variety of ways.

As you become more and more immersed in your new host culture you will find a lot of things that at first glance seem "wrong" – and maybe they are. But take the time to look deeper, to discover the principles behind the actions. In the same way, make time to evaluate your own "non-negotiables" in life. How much of what you believe to be absolutely true is really just an application of truth that, through your own cultural tradition, has become truth itself. That's what the Pharisees did, and Jesus called them out on it (Matt. 23).

In your new culture, you will face situations far outside the realm of your own cultural experiences. You must learn to decide for yourself, before the Lord, how you will respond. How do you apply kindness, justice, joy, forgiveness, righteousness, generosity – principles of God's Kingdom – in your own unique circumstances? And how do you stand firm in those decisions when others around you choose to respond (apply) these truths differently. (See "On Money" for examples.)

Remember that while God has given us standards (principles) in His Word, he has first called us into relationship with him. Don't seek to be perfect at keeping all the "rules," but seek to know the One who made the rules in the first place. Cultivate the habit of spiritual receptivity. Learn to listen for His voice (through His word, His Spirit, and His people) and obey it. This is the liberty of obedience.

✎ ON YOUR OWN

Read John 10. What does Jesus say about learning to listen to his voice? How can you practically cultivate a habit of spiritual receptivity?

Think about the relationship between the law, obedience, and relationship with Jesus. How do these three things go together? How do they not go together?

Take some time to evaluate your own "non-negotiables" in life. Test them against Scripture. Are they principles or applications you've learned through your cultural heritage?

ON MONEY

Did you know that Scripture has more to say about money than about heaven and hell? *"The love of money is the root of all kinds of evil"* (1 Tim 6:10); *"You cannot serve both God and money"* (Matt 6:24); *"Give to everyone who asks..."*(Luke 6:30) are just a few of the verses that come to mind about money.

One of the areas in which you will need to decide how you will personally respond is in regard to money. Giving it, lending it, having it stolen, and expectations of you as a rich American.

For one of my teammates, Peter's words to a beggar in Acts were the voice of conviction: *"Silver and gold I have none,"* Peter said. And yet my teammate couldn't say that – she DID have "silver and gold" in much greater abundance than her neighbors. What did that mean for her in how she responded to the financial needs of the people around her?

Another teammate wrestled over Jesus' words in Luke 6: *"Give to everyone who asks."* He was convicted of his own sin of omission in not giving when asked. And yet, what does it mean to truly obey Jesus' word in this? What do I give? How much? Do I give everything that is asked for? (Jesus didn't say that.) What if what's asked for is to be used on things that aren't good for the person (like alcohol or an abortion)? How do I keep this command of Jesus?

Depending on the culture that you live in, you will be viewed as rich – America and thus Americans are generally viewed as rich. And compared to the majority of the rest of the world, it's true. The U.S. Bureau of Census lists a single person at poverty level if he makes $11,491 a year and for a family of 4 the number is $23,018.[13] Did you know that in the 48 contiguous states, a family of 4 can qualify for free government food if their income is $41,000 a year or less ($20,000 for a single person)?[14] $41k is considered poor enough in the U.S. to receive

---

13   From the U.S. Census Bureau website at www.census.gov/hhes/www/poverty/data/threshld/index.html
14   Statistics from USDA Food and Nutrition service at www.fns.usda.gov/wic

free government aid. What's the average income of the people you live alongside?

In some cultures being viewed as "rich" is enough reason to take advantage of you. When I was visiting in East Asia, a long time friend told me that the bazaar vendors believed it was their right to take advantage of the rich Americans who bought their goods. Their starting price was always 3-4 times more than the price they would actually sell it. If the American (or foreigner) would pay that amount, he deserved to be cheated. Before you go getting indignant, think about your own view of the rich in America. I confess that I've often thought, "*Well he can afford to pay that much, so he should.*"

The point is that as an American (and I apologize to all non-Americans reading this, but if you are from a developed culture the same probably applies to you), you will be viewed as rich and you will need to make decisions about how you will respond to the requests for money that will inevitably come your way from friends, neighbors, beggars, etc.

Even if you don't have a lot of money, you are still called to be a wise steward of what you do have. How you choose to spend it, invest it, and save it will set a precedence for years to come.

Here are just a few examples from my own personal experience and the decisions that each event led to:

1. A student in my English class asked for several hundred dollars but wouldn't tell me why she needed it. I was convinced the money was for an abortion, but the student wouldn't say. This was my first year in the country, and I was conflicted. After much prayer and wrestling, I said "no" to the student. I would not fund an abortion, and even if the money was for something other than that, I did not want to set a precedence. I decided that my "standard"[15] rule

---

15   In all these cases I decided on a "standard" procedure, but as in all things, "standard" can be trumped by a specific leading of the Holy Spirit.

would be that I would not give or loan money to students in my class.

2. A disciple asked to borrow money to buy a train ticket home.
I had decided that I wouldn't loan students money. But this was not a student in my class, this was a girl I discipled. I knew she didn't have money to get home but also was convinced that she would be able to repay the money if I loaned it to her. This led to another "standard" – if I ever felt led to give money to someone, I would give it with no expectation of being repaid even if the money was a "loan" in the receiver's mind. Sometimes I made it clear that I didn't want to be repaid, and sometimes I let the person take the money as a loan. But either way, my expectation was that I would not see this money again. This was to protect me from becoming frustrated with friends who "borrowed" money and didn't pay it back.

3. $1,000 was stolen out of my apartment with my only "suspect" being a close friend.
This was one of the hardest things that ever happened. To give money willingly without expecting it to be re-paid was one thing. But to have money stolen from me by someone I trusted – this grieved my spirit and betrayed my trust in people. I knew, or thought I knew, who had taken the money. Because I had no real proof, I did not confront the person. Confronting her would have only caused more deception (I was pretty sure she would lie to me even if she had taken the money), and while I hated not knowing for sure what happened, I hated even worse the idea that she would lie to me about it. I continued to relate to this friend (a believer and girl I had discipled), but I never trusted her in the same way again. The reality check for me in this situation (and a few other similar ones with team-mates), is that entering the Kingdom of God does not immediately undo a lifetime of influence by a corrupt culture or our own depraved nature. I need to change my expectations of people. The fact that I would not steal has much less to do with my being a believer than it has to do with growing up with parents who taught me that stealing is wrong. My expectations of the people in my host culture needed to change. The standard I set from this situation was to not keep cash in my apartment for any extended period of time, and if I did need to keep cash on hand I tried to move it around so it wouldn't always be in the same place.

4. Newly hired local staff asked for support from all the ex-pats in the community. Depending on where you are laboring there will be locals who, like you, raise support to pay for all or part of their expenses. Since they likely view you as the rich Americans, you will be the first people they ask for support. And not just your friends – even those people who don't know you. We had a summer team and some new staff from another organization come to one of our sports day activities with the sole purpose of talking to all the visiting Americans to ask them for support. I believe you need to be giving and investing in building the Kingdom (in the same way your supporters invest in you). But you need to know what, how, and who you will give to. Think through your own giving strategy – where will you invest your own finances? I've decided that my personal giving needs to meet one of three criteria:

Strategic (e.g., working with Muslims in Southern Europe)

An area that I don't personally minister (e.g., African Americans or inner city works)

Respect for the person/family's walk with God

5. Because I felt that I had more money than my local friends, I paid for everything all of the time. This is a subtle situation that sneaks up on you. If you find that you are richer than all your local friends, one of the responses could be to start paying for everything you and your local friends do together. But paying for everything and reinforcing the idea of the "sugardaddy" is not the answer. I worked with students who were poor by every country's standard, and I was a lot older than them, so I often fed them at my house. When we went out, I let them choose the place (in their price range) and let them pay for themselves. Helping isn't always helping – sometimes it hurts more than we know.[16] People want and need to contribute, so I also learned ways to ask for and receive real help from my local friends that wasn't necessarily monetary.

6. Homeless, drunks, grandmothers, disabled, gypsies, or

---

16   I recommend a book called *When Helping Hurts* that offers a great perspective on working in undeveloped and poor cultures.

kids begged for money on the street. Depending on your location, this will be much more prevalent than you are used to in your American suburb culture. To be honest – I'm ashamed to admit this, but I'm being honest – it's not hard for me to walk by a beggar. After being exposed to teammates and friends with a genuine heart for the poor and being challenged by Jesus' mandate to *"give to everyone who asks,"* I began to wrestle with the question, *"What do I do when I see people on the street?"* This is still an ongoing question for me, but I have landed on a few things as "standard." Except for grandmothers (who usually have homes and are not alcoholics), I don't give out money. Often gypsies and kids have a "pimp" and don't even keep any money they are given but pass it on to their "protector". If a beggar asks me for something, I will go with him, if possible, to buy a meal at the closest store or restaurant or bring something back to him. I even started keeping Wal-Mart bags of non-perishable goods in my car to hand out to a beggar at a red light. If someone only wants money and won't take food, that is their choice. I usually take this as a clear sign that they either aren't as desperate as they seem or they want money for something I wouldn't approve of.

These are just a few examples of decisions you will have to make in relation to money. Similar to the issue of corruption, the responses are as varied as the people deciding. The "right" answer is to wrestle with the question, asking God what you should do and obeying what he shows you. *"So then each of us will give account of himself to God"* (Rom. 14:12).

One final note, especially for those readers who have recently graduated from college. Money – how you use it, how you think about it, how you long for it, or run from it – will be a major area in which you will need to lay down foundational values at this stage of life. If you just graduated from college, you probably have not had a lot of money up to this point (unless you are a trust fund baby). I expect you've had part-time jobs, maybe even full time jobs to pay for school or expenses. But you are embarking on a career now. From this point forward, you will join the work force and earn more money than you ever have before (I mean after all, isn't that the reason you spent all that money on college?). Even if you don't have a lot of money, you are still called to be a wise steward of what you do have. How you choose to spend it, invest it, and save it will set a precedence for years to come. If you've never done a Bible Study on money or a practical course on budgeting and financial planning principles, I suggest you use some of your personal development time while overseas to do just that.

"The real value of money is it's potential to do something that will outlast time."

📖 FOR FURTHER STUDY

Using a concordance (biblegateway.com is an online one I often use) look up all the references in Scripture about money. Summarize your study into a one page outline that has practical application in your own life.

Ask a financial mentor to recommend a book about money that contains both a biblical foundation as well as practical principles for managing money.

3 WORLD VIEWS

During my second year in Kochevnikstan, we took a team retreat to the mountains. We invited a good friend from a different organization to come and share with us about his experiences living and laboring in this culture. It was during this time that I was introduced to 3 different world views. The concept was a complete paradigm shift for me, and since then it has influenced the way I read the Scriptures and observe cultures. I want to share these 3 world views with you in hope that – like me – God will use this to open your eyes to see your new world in a different way.

GUILT VS. RIGHTEOUSNESS

In western cultures (North America, Europe, and countries with European roots), we embrace a guilt vs. righteousness world view. America was founded on a desire for religious freedom, and much of our mentality, laws, history, and world view are heavily influenced by the Puritans. We view Scripture through a clearly defined sense of right and wrong. If you do something "wrong," you are guilty. Even in our post-modern culture that tolerates every person making his own standard, if we do "wrong" by that standard, we are guilty. Our legal system is based on a world view of guilt vs. righteousness with government-made laws as the standard. If you break the law, you are "guilty," and if you are guilty, you must be punished. This western world view influences how we live and disciple among the lost.

Before coming to Kochevnikstan, I worked on a U.S. college campus. When I shared the Gospel with someone, my first step was to help them understand that they are guilty before God – guilty of sin – and in need of forgiveness from God to be made righteous before him. Think about the Gospel tools you've learned to use or the first verses you normally take someone to when sharing with them. Most likely, they are verses that point out our guilt before a righteous God.

I'm not saying that these tools are not useful, and I am certainly NOT saying that people are not sinful. Scripture is clear that "*all have sinned and fall short of the glory of God*" (Rom. 3:23). My point is that in our western cultural world view, sin = guilt and the opposite of sin is righteousness. Guilt and righteousness are emotional responses to sin. But there are two other major world views where sin and its opposite take a different emotional form.

> ## We all feel guilt, shame, and fear, which are responses to our own sinful nature to some extent. But at a cultural level, one of these world views usually becomes dominant.

SHAME VS. HONOR

It's common knowledge that Asians are a "save face" culture. Shame is the most powerful emotion that an Asian man or woman can feel and certainly one he or she wants to avoid. In this world view, the emotional response to sin is shame (rather than guilt) and the opposite of shame is honor (rather than righteousness).

It doesn't matter so much to an Asian person if you are guilty or not, but whether your actions bring shame on yourself or your family. It's one explanation for why corruption is often prevalent in Asian cultures – if you are guilty of breaking the law (for instance by taking a bribe) it doesn't matter as long as it doesn't shame your family. And if it provides money for your family so that they "look good" to their relatives and friends, then the dishonesty actually brings honor to the family, and honor is more important than righteousness.

Since as North Americans, we come to Scripture with a bias of guilt and righteousness, we often don't see the other two world views at first. But Scripture is full of examples of both of these other world views. Even as early as the Garden of Eden, we see both shame and fear before guilt. Before Adam and Eve sin, they are naked but not ashamed. After they sin, and God comes looking for them, what is Adam's response to why he hid? Because he felt guilty? No. Because he was naked (inferring shame) and afraid.

In numerous stories, God takes away the shame of his people and bestows honor on them. David fights Goliath in order to *"remove the dis-*

grace of Israel" (1 Sam. 17:26). In dealing with the adulterous woman who is being stoned, Jesus does not address her guilt but her shame; he "covers" her with honor, exhorting her to go and leave her life of sin and shame (John 8:1-11).

This paradigm shift affects the way we approach shame-based cultures with the Gospel. Approaching shame-based cultures with a strong guilt vs. righteousness perspective will not be very effective. Righteousness is not as highly valued as honor. When we break God's law, we bring dishonor to his name – the name of our heavenly Father and creator. We are ashamed (sinful) before God and cannot be reconciled to Him, because we do nothing to bring him honor on our own. It is only through Jesus – who brought perfect honor to his father – that we can be made right with God.

FEAR VS. POWER
The third world view is fear vs. power. This world view is held by mostly tribal cultures although it is also common in Folk Islam where true adherence to the Qur'an is diluted with ancestor worship and forms of animism. It can also be an element of New Age culture where things like horoscopes, fortune tellers, crystals, etc. are believed to have real power over our lives. People live in fear that this power – whether a witch doctor in their village, the spirits of their ancestors, or a fortune teller – will consume them if they do not obey them. Sin in this world view takes the form of fear that pushes someone to worship created things to which they attribute power.

We see this world view played out in Elijah's power struggle with the priests of Baal. God reveals his supremacy, showing himself to be far more powerful than the false god Baal (1 Kings 18:38-39). In Luke 8, Jesus displays his power over the weather (v. 22-25), demons (v. 26-38), sickness (vs. 43-48), and death (v. 440-41, 49-56). I've found this to be a convincing passage when talking with people about the false power of horoscopes and fortune tellers. If you want REAL power over the everyday worries of life – look to Jesus.

CONCLUSION
It's not that one of these world views is right and the others are wrong

– they are all an integral part of humanity. We all feel guilt, shame, and fear which are responses to our own sinful nature to some extent. But at a cultural level, one of these world views usually becomes dominant. For me, the application of this paradigm shift, this realization that there is more than one way to view the world, opened my eyes to better understand how to help people deal with their sin as guilt, shame, or fear, and how to introduce God's righteousness, honor, and power through the person of Jesus. Understanding where people are coming from, their world view, will help us better understand how to move them toward a real relationship with the Living God.

But don't take my word for it – get into the Scriptures yourself! Ask the Lord to give you new eyes to see His truths from these other world views, eyes to see and hear God's truth in the way your new friends will be able to hear it.

📖 FOR FURTHER STUDY

Read through these familiar Bible stories. How do you see these 3 different world views play out in each? How can you use these Bible stories to share truth with your new culture?

Genesis 3, 1 Samuel 17, 1 Kings 18, Luke 8, John 8

DREAMS AND VISIONS

"I'm Kochevnik; I will never become a Christian," said Aizhan to the camera filming her. A short-term team was filming stories of people they had met during the summer and Aizhan, one of my first friends in Kochevnikstan, was telling her story. I met Aizhan my first year, her freshmen year, and we hung out, shared our lives and beliefs, and talked about God. At times, she showed interest, and I saw her move towards God. Yet after 3 years, Aizhan's comment was that she was Kochevnik and would never become a follower of Jesus.

Fast forward one week. We were having a cookout with lots of our local friends. When Aizhan arrived, she pulled me aside along with one of the girls she'd spent a lot of time with that summer. She was bursting with excitement, *"I've become a believer!"* Amazed and a little skeptical, we asked what had changed her mind, and she began to tell us about a dream. She was in her dorm room when she smelled smoke. There was a fire, and she was trapped. She tried to escape but couldn't. She knew she was going to die. But then she vaguely saw someone beckoning her to follow him. He led her out of the dorm and saved her from the fire. Aizhan instinctively knew that person was Jesus. Her dream – that touch point with Jesus – was what she needed to finally choose to believe what she'd heard me and others tell her so often.

Aizhan's story is not unique. Another friend finally surrendered to Jesus after a fearful dream where she cried out for help to Jesus. One of my language teachers, though she never trusted Jesus as her Lord, dreamed on several occasions that Jesus came to her. An orphan boy who'd been hit by a car, unconscious and near death, saw a man in white who told him not to worry because he was going to live and that he (the man in white) would be with him.

I've heard stories of Jesus appearing in the dreams of unreached peoples, however, in my own experiences in Kochevnikstan, the dreams were the final event that gave a superstitious person the courage to follow Jesus in the face of cultural rejection. These people had heard truth from a real person, like me. They knew the truth in their head, but it took dreams and visions to finally bring them into the Kingdom.

In the Western World, we don't put much stock in dreams and visions. That's superstitious, ridiculous, and something Hollywood dreamed up. The devil is a little red man with horns and a tail, a fictional character of our imagination. But Scripture says something very different. Scripture has a lot to say about spiritual warfare, the reality of our enemy Satan, and about how God uses dreams and visions to speak to his people. My goal in this short essay is not to debate the theology of these things in the 21st century, but to make the point that living in another culture will challenge you out of your comfort zone in many ways – specifically in regard to our beliefs about the supernatural. Everything we thought we knew for sure will be challenged and we will be forced to re-evaluate, *"Do I believe this because it's what I've always been taught?"* OR *"Do I believe this because this is really what Scripture teaches?"*

Asking God to give people "dreams and visions" became a standard prayer for my team in Kochevnikstan. We still prayed that they would know and trust God's word, but we added to those prayers that God would touch their hearts and speak to them in a way that they would understand. Even for my well-educated, logical friends, dreams and visions were a means God used to open their eyes and hearts to the reality of Jesus.

📖 FOR FURTHER STUDY

Study dreams and visions in Scripture (e.g., Joseph, Daniel, Peter, Paul). To whom was the vision given? Why? What was the result?

Read Isaiah 55:8-9. Can you think of examples in Scripture where God does things or tells his people to do things that are "unconventional" and "uncomfortable"? (Joshua, Samson, Hosea, Jesus)

DEVELOPING COMMUNITY

I am committed to fellowship. I know it is not good to be alone. I feel weak and tired and lonely when there isn't someone there to support and encourage me to keep running the race with perseverance. I long for meaningful and deep friendships. Whether you are male or female, we all need people who will sharpen and challenge us – people who will ask us the tough questions and encourage us with truth. Perhaps as you read this you are thinking, *"Yes, that's exactly what I want. But there isn't anyone like that in my life. There isn't anyone who will ask me the tough questions (or anyone I trust with the answers to the tough questions). I want the kind of friend and fellowship you are writing about, but I don't know where to find it."* Let me encourage you: God is faithful to provide what you need!

Michele was a tangible display of God's faithfulness to provide a "kindred spirit" for a specific time and place in my life. I met Michele when I was in language school even though she wasn't in language school. I was in class all day and studied all night. I'm not a super relational person, but I was starved for deep, meaningful interaction. Several of my teammates were studying with me at the same time, and while I had good fellowship with them, I felt like I needed another "outlet" – a non-teammate friend with whom I could talk about the deep things of my heart. I began to pray for such a friend. I had made a decision to eat in the campus café so I would have an opportunity to meet a greater variety of people. That's where I met Michele. We hit it off immediately. We both had a heart for the world (Michele was a nurse and had worked in Nepal); we both loved to walk; and most of all, we both loved to talk about deep things in Scripture. Michele and I did not stay in touch after I finished language school. As our physical locations changed, so did our relationship. But Michele was an answered prayer in my life, an example of God's faithfulness to provide a specific need at a specific time.

For my male readers, don't tune me out just yet. The idea of a "kindred spirit" might not strike a cord with you, but maybe the idea of locking arms will. One of my favorite "man books"[17] is called *Locking Arms* by Stu Weber. In it, he talks to men about the importance of men locking arms with one another in their fight toward righteousness and right relationship with people (think of the wildly popular *Band of Brothers* mini-series). One of the things I took away from that book is the idea of having lifelong covenant relationships – men and women you might not see on a daily or even yearly basis but with whom you have chosen to lock arms with throughout your lifetime. These lifelong mentors and friends are people that you consistently go to for counsel about big life decisions and to share the hardships, hurts, and joys of life's journey. Stu's admonishment to develop covenant relationships influenced me, and as I've aged, I've made conscious decisions to stay connected to a handful of men and women who continue to be mentors, counselors, and friends in my life.

> ## Ultimately, only God can give us a deep connection with other people (so don't forget to ask Him). But there are a few simple and intentional things we can do to cultivate deep relationships, whether short or long-term.

Both types of relationships – short-term ones like Michele and lifelong covenant relationships – are important to develop. Ultimately, only God can give us a deep connection with other people (so don't forget to ask Him). But there are a few simple and intentional things we can do to cultivate deep relationships, whether short or long-term.

Be vulnerable and choose to share your life with others.

It's hard to become deep friends with someone who does not volunteer information about themselves. If it's hard for you to share about yourself, set some tangible goals each week to choose to volunteer

---

17   During one season of my life I was eager to read all kinds of "man" books. I work with men (more men than women) and as much as is possible, I want to understand how men think. I have to be honest and say that, in my opinion, you men have the harder job. Women are much more complicated than men are to understand. On behalf of my sex, I say "thank you" for your efforts to try to understand us no matter how fruitless your efforts might seem at times!

something personal that your friends haven't asked about (I did this in college and it radically changed my relationships).

Invite others to ask you tough questions. Do you get upset or angry when people ask you personal questions? Do you feel like they are "prying" into your life? How do you receive correction? Do you invite this type of genuine accountability? Proverbs has much to say about a wise man accepting and inviting counsel, rebuke, and correction. In some cases, you might need to help your friends know what tough questions to ask you – that means sharing with them the things you struggle with. I have a personal commitment with one of my closest friends to tell her anything that becomes a struggle for me – whether she asks or not (and the more foolish it feels to tell her, the more certain I am that I need to tell her).

Ask your friends tough questions. To have a good friend you also have to be a good friend. Confrontation is hard, but it is a test of true love for a person. To never ask the tough questions is to basically say, "*I care more about what you think of me – if you like me or are mad at me – than of what is good for you,*" and that is NOT love. "*He who rebukes a man will in the end gain more favor than he who has a flattering tongue*" (Proverbs 28:23). Another reason we neglect asking our friends tough questions is that we are afraid they might actually answer them. Sometimes I just don't want to know what is really going on with someone. I'm overwhelmed enough with my own life, how can I handle the issues in someone else's? And yet, Scripture tells us to bear one another's burdens (Gal. 6:2). It's not our job to fix things, but anyone can listen and help a friend take his burdens to the Father.

Pray together. Several years ago two of my friends, who live on different continents, went on vacation together to Hawaii. Later as I was talking to one of the girls, she told me that while the trip was great, the thing she most regretted was that she and my other friend had not spent any time praying together. It's difficult to keep up pretenses when you are on your knees before the creator of the universe. Commit to pray together often with your friends, and commit that you will be completely honest in what you say – talking to the Father and not to each other. Few things will develop intimacy in your friendships quicker than this.

Kindred spirits and covenant relationships are gifts from the Father. The more I grow and the closer I draw to the Father, the harder it is to "find" a friend who can go to the deep places with me. But God knows what is good for us and I believe that he will give us this gift of covenant relationships if we will ask him for it. After all, it's His idea – community os the principle of Scripture.

"...ask whatever you wish and it will be given unto you" (John 15:7). If we ask but do not receive there are two possible reasons. One is that *"you ask with wrong motives that you may spend what you get on your pleasures"* (James 4:2-3). In other words, we are asking for something out of a motivation that isn't pleasing to the Father. The second reason we might ask and not receive is we are asking for something that isn't good for us. God's promise is that *"no good thing does he withhold from those whose walk is blameless"* (Ps. 84:11). If I ask and if I am obedient to do my part and still don't have the kind of deep friendship that I long for, it's because it's not good for me. I may not understand the reason it isn't good, but I can trust that God has something else in mind – something that it is ultimately for my good.

✔ LET'S GET PRACTICAL

This week, choose to share a struggle with a friend (even if they haven't asked) and/or ask one of your friends a "below the surface" question. Be willing to listen to them, even if what they share overwhelms you (it's not your job to fix anything – just ask, listen, and pray together).

If you don't have a close friend or are in need of a friend to meet a specific need in your life, begin today asking God to provide what you need. He knows your needs even better than you do and will provide accordingly.

SUPERLATIVES OF COMMUNICATION

Superlatives. If you teach English, or if you loved English in school you might recognize the term. You know what superlatives are – you just might not know they are called that. Kind, kinder, kindest. Blue, bluer, bluest. These are superlatives. The superlatives of communication are hard, harder, hardest.

COMMUNICATION IS HARD

Let's be honest, communication is hard. If you are a quiet person, maybe it's difficult for you to formulate what you want to say when you want to say it. You just can't get out what you want to communicate. Even if you are a natural talker, that doesn't ensure that you are communicating. In fact, sometimes if a person is talking a whole lot (you are probably thinking of a specific person right now), you can sort of tune them out and not really listen, and communication doesn't happen.

COMMUNICATING IN A WAY THAT IS UNDERSTOOD IS HARDER

Communication is a two-way street. Just because you say something, does not mean that you have communicated. You have to say what you mean in a way that is understood by your listener. If your listener doesn't get the point (both content and tone), then you haven't communicated.

Just this week I had a conversation with a teammate trying to understand his specific communication style. Mark and Ben had been dialoguing about an upcoming conference. Ben was asking Mark to give the green light on the event. Mark was all for the event but wanted to be careful to not commit himself (or his team) to something that he couldn't fulfill. Both wanted the conference to happen, but Ben's direct communication style and Mark's more diplomatic (and less direct) style hindered understanding. Each thought the other was saying something they weren't.

It's important that we make an effort to not only understand our natural style of communicating but also to be learners of how our teammates, friends, and family both communicate and hear things that are communicated to them (Mark heard Ben asking him to commit to something he wasn't sure he could commit to. Ben only wanted to know if they could move forward to pursue this event). The key is adjusting our natural style of communication in order to increase the chances that what we say is understood.

COMMUNICATING IN A WAY THAT CANNOT BE MISUNDERSTOOD IS HARDEST

It's hard to communicate in a way that is understood but not nearly as hard as communicating in a way that cannot be misunderstood. Misunderstandings happen all the time, and no matter how committed you are to effective communication, no one does it perfectly all the time. But as much as possible, the goal is to think about how we can say things in a way that cannot be misunderstood. That means thinking not only about how you want to say something but how what you say will be received.

✔ LET'S GET PRACTICAL!

Initiate a conversation with at least one teammate about what "effective communication" looks like for them. Do they like direct, bottom lines up front? Do they prefer to have all the information first? Do they need some "relational" talk before getting down to business? Think of times when the two you have communicated effectively. Are there times where you felt like communication was misunderstood? Why?

Think about your own communication style? Is communication important to you? (It's not a high value for everyone and there isn't anything wrong with that). How do you like to receive information? How do you naturally give information? It's important to understand your own style of communication so that you can choose to adjust it as needed to effectively communicate with others.

REALITY CHECK

Have you ever read the book *Bruchko* by Bruce Olson? In my mind, this book is the epitome of someone (other than Jesus) becoming like the people they minister to. However, few people will ever become as much like who they minister to as Bruchko did. In my own experience in Kochevnikstan, as much as I loved and thrived in the culture, I never became Kochevnik. In fact, I often wondered what kind of joke the Lord was playing on me to send me to a culture so drastically different than my natural personality (looking back - no doubt it was the refiner's fire!). For instance, consider lying. American culture discourages lying, but my personal upbringing made it a sin above all sins. So why would God send me to a culture where lying is accepted and even an art form? Or what about planning, organization, and structure? In one personality test I rate in the 90th percentile of people who need organization and structure to function. And yet, God sent me to an unplanned, live-in-the-moment culture. I'm sure my repeated but futile attempts to organize and plan the totally unplanned must have made God smile!

In living cross-culturally, we all at some point come face to face with the reality that we will never be completely local, never truly an insider. I have a friend who is the most incarnational North American I know. She speaks 2 of the local languages fluently. She lives with a local family and is considered their daughter. People who meet her are sometimes even surprised she isn't local. But no matter how well she blends into the culture, understands it, and is loved by the people there, she will never BE a local. This became clear to her when her host family began putting pressure on her to marry a relative – a local who wasn't a believer. In that culture, if she were really their daughter, my friend would have had to submit to the wishes of the family. But as much as she looked and talked and sometimes acted local, in the end she was still an American (it wasn't until her American parents came to visit that the local family stopped pressuring her to marry their relative).

After living in Kochevnikstan for about 8 months God gave me a "reality check" about what he wanted from me as I lived and labored among the lost of my host culture. Here is an excerpt from my journal that first year:

> *One great perspective switch has been the reality that I will never be a local. I came…gung ho and passionate about being all here. Now after 8 months I realize that 20 years of living here would not make me a local. I went through a time when I felt really defeated…In my black and white mind, it's either I am a local or I am an outsider. But, I am finally getting to a place where I see that there IS a middle ground. I can be here and find my "niche" in this culture without being "local". And in some ways that's more helpful than if I were a local. This perspective has changed how I think about "living" here. I'm not really sure what that practically means - I'm still thinking on that one.*

At a conference several years after this journal entry I heard a veteran laborer sum up these thoughts in one simple phrase. He said, *"I don't need to become African, just be a Brit who loves Africans."*

✏ ON YOUR OWN

Read 1 Thessalonians 2:8 and look at Paul's interactions with the people he ministered to. How (specifically) does he express genuine love and concern for them?

Who are you more like: me with my drastic personality differences from the local culture or my friend who easily melded into the local culture? How do either of these realities affect your ability to minister to the people you care about?

How do you think God can and is using your personality differences (different from the local culture) to influence your friends and host country?

WHAT DO YOU DO FOR FUN?

What do you do for fun? My friend in the U.S. was asking a general question, inquiring about my life in this new culture. But her simple question hit a cord with me. What DID I do for fun?

So many of the things that were fun for me, I couldn't do in this new culture. I love to mow the grass (my brother says it's because I don't have to do it all the time), but I had no yard and certainly no grass. I like to do little household projects: repaint a room, refinish a table, hang pictures. But in Kochevnikstan, my apartment walls were wallpapered and hanging pictures required drilling through concrete (I tried to do it myself once, but it was a disaster!). I love movies and as it turned out, I watched a LOT of movies over the years. But while that was a pleasant escape, I wondered what other "fun" outlets I could do or learn.

Depending on where you are laboring, chances are that your country is a "dark" place, spiritually speaking. Life is intense and heavy. The spiritual battle is felt more readily. There are advantages to this – often times I felt like my life in Kochevnikstan was more "real". I felt sharper (spiritually) and more alert than when I was in America, because I had to be! But the intensity can only be maintained for so long before we need a break. When I read through the Gospels or Acts, I often wonder what Jesus, the disciples, or Paul and his travelers talked about walking along the road. Did they tell jokes? Laugh? Tease one another? Laugh at one another's childhood stories? I think they must have. I think they enjoyed life, as it was, without expecting it to be more satisfying than it can be. I think they had, in the words of an old song, *"moments of rest and glimpses of laughter…treasured along the road."*[18]

William Wilberforce, the 18th century British abolitionist brought to life in the movie *Amazing Grace*, was a man under great pressure because of his passionate pursuit to rid Britain of slavery. So much so, that he found it absolutely necessary to take time every week (his Sabbath) to be with the Lord and enjoy the simple pleasures of life. In the

---

18   "Along the Road" Susan Ashton, Margaret Becker & Christine Dente

book *Amazing Grace in the Life of William Wilberforce* John Piper says of Wilberforce that he possessed "*a joyful ability to see all the good in the world instead of being consumed by one's own problems even if those problems were huge...for Wilberforce, joy was both a means of survival and perseverance on the one hand, and a deep act of submission, obedience and worship on the other hand. Joy in Christ was commanded. And joy in Christ was the only way to flourish fruitfully through decades of temporary defeat.*"[19]

The Teacher writes in Ecclesiastes that "*a man can do nothing better than to eat and drink and find satisfaction in his work. This too, I see, is from the hand of God, for without him who can eat or find enjoyment*" (Eccl. 2:24-25).

📖 FOR FURTHER STUDY

Do a topical study on joy. What are the differences between joy, happiness, and fun? Are all three legitimate desires/goals?

Do a character study on Jesus' life (or Paul's), focusing specifically on how they handled the stresses and intensity of their lives/calling. Do you think Jesus/Paul had "fun"? If so, in what ways?

In the midst of spiritual darkness and heaviness, what do you do for "fun"? What are the ways you find "moments of rest and glimpses of laughter...along the road"?

---

19   *Amazing Grace in the Life of William Wilberforce* p. 60, 63

PORN AND OTHER PITFALLS

It was everywhere I turned. TV channels that played cartoons during the day would turn to hard core porn after a certain time at night. In Kiosks (at a child's eye level), were baseball card style trading cards that instead of sports stars, sported pictures of naked women. The local Swap and Shop (newspaper for sellers), opened up to nude women right next to an ad for a plumber and electrician. And porn videos on the shelf in stores were often right next to kid's programs. Local people were so desensitized to porn that they didn't think twice about it. In fact, one neighbor told my teammate that she used porn videos to teach her kids about sex!

There is oodles of literature out there nowadays about the dangers of pornography, how to avoid it, how to overcome an addiction to it, etc. My goal in this short section is not to reiterate all that is already out there (hopefully your sending organization has built in accountability to help you be aware of this pitfall). I simply want to say that pornography is one pitfall that will slowly creep up on you, desensitize you, and eventually take you out of the race.

Before I ever went overseas, one of my friends told me that there are two places that Satan always attacks – the place you always struggle and the place you never thought you would. If you have struggled with pornography before, chances are it will come up again. Whatever struggles you have, porn or otherwise, will only be intensified in the uncomfortableness of adjusting to your new culture. Satan will tempt in the tried and true places of our lives. But even if pornography is not something you've struggled with before going overseas, it doesn't mean it won't become a pitfall for you once immersed in a desensitized, amoral, or immoral culture. Satan loves to find new ways to attack that we never thought would be a pitfall.

Two single guys I worked with in Kochevnikstan were always being pressured by local guys about sexual issues. Porn was not something they had struggled with before, but it was always in their face in this new culture. They had to learn to take extra precautions and intentionally pursue open accountability with each other. In one extreme situation, a group of local guys, in an effort to "help" their American friend, set him up with a prostitute. Don't be fooled into thinking you are immune. It's important to be *self controlled and alert [because] your enemy prowls around like a roaring lion looking for someone to devour*" (1 Peter 5:8).

While pornography is usually associated with men, women are not immune, especially in an age of increasing sexual freedom. Internet websites are not just targeting men anymore. Masturbation among women as well as men is more prevalent (or at least talked about) than ever before. It's promoted as a way for women to have control over their sexual needs (rather than needing a man). Both pornography and masturbation are things done in secret – you can pretty easily keep these "self satisfying" habits compartmentalized from the rest of your life and secret from your co-workers or even roommates and spouses.

Pornography is not the only pitfall you'll encounter overseas. At the heart of it, porn is just a way that a person seeks satisfaction when their life feels unsatisfying. Living cross-culturally heightens the temptation not only because porn is so "in your face," but also because you are more likely to feel alone, insecure, depressed, unsatisfied, or disconnected. You are vulnerable in ways you haven't been before.

While you might not be tempted by pornography, there are other pitfalls you might turn to for satisfaction. A few examples include (but are not limited to): unhealthy attachments to and expectations of your teammates, emotionally heightened relationships with locals (you feel alive because this local guy or girl pays you so much attention and dotes on you), food (over or under eating), or excessive exercise (a common comfort substitute). Relationships, food, and exercise are not wrong in themselves – in fact they are all good, just as sex is a good thing – but when we begin to seek satisfaction in these good gifts of the Father rather than in the Father himself, we've sinned against God. Jeremiah 2:13 says, "*My people have committed two sins; they have forsaken me the spring of living water, and have dug their own cisterns, broken cisterns that cannot hold water.*" At the heart of pornography (and the many other places we seek comfort or satisfaction), is a turning away from the one source that can truly satisfy our desires, the spring of living water, and seeking satisfaction in broken places that will never truly satisfy.

Living in another culture does not create this "forsaking and digging" that Jeremiah 2 talks about; it's inherent in all of us as a result of the fall. As St. Augustine says, *We are not sinful because we sin, we sin because we are sinful.* But the pressure cooker of living in another culture does heighten and intensify our natural bent toward whatever satisfaction substitute we seek.

So beware of porn and other pitfalls that will take you out of the race. Be on your guard (1 Peter 5:8). Invite and offer real accountability without judgment (James 5:16, Rom. 14:1,13). Commit to openness rather than secrecy. Know your limits and set boundaries for yourself.[20]

✎ ON YOUR OWN

Think about your own life. What are the places you have always struggled? What are the places you never thought you would struggle? Do you see Satan tempting/attacking you in either of these places?

What are boundaries you can set up for yourself (with accountability) to help you combat your areas of weakness?

What would it look like practically for you to forsake the broken cisterns in your life and begin to drink deeply from the spring of living water (Jer. 2:11-13)? How can you tell if you are drinking from a broken cistern or spring of living water?

---

20   Covenant Eyes is an internet accountability tool but can't be replaced by personal openness and sharing.

YOU ARE NOT AS IMPORTANT AS YOU THINK!

I was having coffee with my campus director, talking through current ministry situations. I was feeling an overwhelming sense of responsibility for something that I could not fix or control. After kindly listening to my venting for a few minutes, my boss and good friend looked me straight in the eye and said the most freeing thing I've ever heard: "*Tammy, you are not as important as you think you are.*"

To some that might seem harsh, but it was exactly what I needed to hear. I tend to have an over-inflated sense of personal responsibility that serves me well at times but can cause me to think more highly of myself than I should (like I should be able to fix or control everything). My friend's words were an encouraging and truthful reminder that while God wants to include us in advancing His Kingdom, He does not need us to accomplish His purposes.

Several years after this foundational conversation, God again made this truth very real to me through my 2 year old nephew.[21] I had been laboring in Kochevnikstan for 5 years, and I was back in the U.S. for a U.S. Work Assignment. During this time, I lived with my brother's family including his 2-year-old son, Rhett (yes, as in Rhett Butler from *Gone With the Wind* – we are a southern culture family!) I am a morning coffee drinker: it's my ritual and at the time I was very into French press coffee. Rhett quickly learned that Aunt Tammy made coffee every morning, and he decided that he wanted to "help" me. He'd pull up a chair to the counter as I was putting in the coffee and pouring the hot water. Then his job was to push down the plunger. It was a real job, an authentic contribution to my morning coffee routine. When he did his job, I praised him generously. And like every 2-year-old (maybe not just 2-year-olds), he loved being made much of. Did I really need Rhett to help me push down that plunger? No. I was perfectly capable of doing the job on my own, and honestly, doing it better than Rhett. So why did I invite Rhett to help me if I didn't really need his help? Because I was delighted to simply have Rhett with me, doing some-

---

21   I love that God used a 2-year-old little boy to teach me one of the most foundational lessons of my life. God can use anything in any place at anytime to teach us. The question is whether or not we are prepared to learn.

thing that I cared about. For his sake, I wanted him to make a authentic contribution to the process.

The reality is that none of us are as important as we think, and God is far more interested in developing our character than He is in our contribution to His cause.

Like Rhett I desperately want to help my Heavenly Father with what He is doing in the world. I want to contribute, to make a real difference, and if I'm honest, I want to be made much of. But God used Rhett to teach me something very foundational: I am not as important as I think AND I am far more dearly loved than I can possibly imagine. This simple but profound truth helps me stay grounded and reminds me that God is God and I am not. I can rest in the reality that He will ultimately accomplish his plans!

Recently, I heard a veteran missionary who has spent 20+ years in Africa say, "*I think that I needed Africa more than Africa needed me.*" That is the way God works. In our youth we are zealous and long to change the world, to advance the Kingdom, to make our mark. These "contributions" are cast in front of us in our campus ministries, churches, and missions organizations. These things are noble, biblical goals. God does call his children to invest in eternal things. He delights in our authentic contribution. But the reality is that none of us are as important as we think, and God is far more interested in developing our character than He is in our contribution to His cause.

📖 FOR FURTHER STUDY

Read the following verses: Ezekiel 36:22-30 (how many times does God say, "*I will*"?), Job 42:1-6, Isaiah 46:8-13, Acts 4:27-28, 2 Timothy 1:8-9

What do they teach us about God's purposes and our contribution?

Persevering in the Pressure Cooker

6-9 months

PLAYGROUND VS. BATTLEGROUND

Imagine that you are a child on a playground with all of your friends. While playing a game, you trip and fall, skinning your knee and hitting your head. You start to cry both because it hurts and also because all your friends saw you fall, and you feel embarrassed.

Now imagine that you are on a battleground with your fellow soldiers. While running to take cover from enemy fire you fall, skinning your knee and hitting your head. What do you do? Do you start to cry? Do you feel embarrassed that your fellow soldiers saw you fall? I don't think so. You get up and keep running because your life – and the lives of your buddies around you – depend on getting to cover.

How do YOU view your life and your labor in the Kingdom of God? Are you on a playground or a battleground? Do you get your feelings hurt at the slightest slip up? Do you worry more about what people think of you than you do about the realities of the war being waged around you? How we view ourselves – as children on a playground or soldiers on a battleground – has everything to do with how we respond to things that happen to us and around us

A.W. Tozer was a pastor in the mid-20th century who wrote many practical essays concerning the Christian life. Below is an excerpt from his essay on the concept of Playground or Battleground:

> "Things are to us not only what they are; they are what we hold them to be. Which is to say that our attitude toward things is likely in the long run to be more important than the things themselves…One such fact is the world in which we live…The world is for all of us not only what it is; it is what we believe it to be…In the early days, when Christianity exercised a dominant influence over American thinking, men conceived the world to be a battleground…Men looked forward to…a return from the wars, a laying down of the sword to enjoy in peace the home prepared for them… Sermons and songs in those days often had a martial quality about them, or perhaps a trace of homesickness…That

view of things is unquestionably the scriptural one. Allowing for the figures and metaphors with which the Scriptures abound, it still is a solid Bible doctrine that tremendous spiritual forces are present in the world, and man, because of his spiritual nature, is caught in the middle...How different today...Men think of the world, not as a battleground but as a playground. We are not here to fight we are here to frolic. We are not in a foreign land. We are at home. We are not getting ready to live, we are already living, and the best we can do is to rid ourselves of our inhibitions and our frustrations and live this life to the full. This, we believe, is a fair summary of the religious philosophy of modern man, openly professed by millions and tacitly held by more multiplied millions who live out that philosophy without having given verbal expression to it...A right view of God and the world to come requires that we have also a right view of the world in which we live and our relation to it. So much depends upon this that we cannot afford to be careless about it.[1]

✎ ON YOUR OWN

What is your view of the world? Playground or battleground? Think about situations in your life. How would you respond differently if you viewed your world as a battleground?

How often does Scripture use wartime analogies, illustrations, or metaphors? Make a list. How does Scripture describe the battle we are a part of?

---

1   From *The Best of A.W. Tozer* p. 84-86

HOW DO I FEEL?

The following is a section out of my journal written during a day of prayer around my 6-month mark. Keep in mind that these are honest feelings and not necessarily the right perspective.

I don't know how I feel - *has probably been my most common feeling. Numb might be another way to say it. I just read through my journal and this phrase is repeated several times. It's not that I'm depressed, or overly happy. Most of the time I just am.*

Numb - *I don't feel excited or fearful, eager or unmotivated. I don't feel much of anything. I can't conjure the passion and vision that pulled me here (the same passion and conviction that I shared will all my support team). I KNOW I am where I need to be and yet I don't feel anything. I have only cried once since I've been here (which is not the norm for me). I find myself lifting up the words of a song "don't let my vision die; don't let my love grow cold; you know my heart my deeds, I need your discipline; Father light the fire again."*

Bored - *This was another common emotion in my journal. It's not that life is not busy. Sometimes I feel like I have nothing to do but no time to do it in. I know it's crazy but it's true. Recently I haven't felt very bored because life is beginning to fill up. But I'm not sure I want it to "fill up." I'm not sure I'm ready. It's like I think my capacity is greater than it is and then I do something and it completely wipes me out. I'm not sure what I need to do or to change. One of my most common - almost daily - thoughts lately has been from Ps. 139 - YOU have searched and YOU know me, YOU know what I need and I don't! Please give me what I need!!!*

I miss the way my life was - *It's not that I miss home, because the truth is what I loved about my "home" doesn't exist there for me anymore. Lives have changed and people have moved on. And that's the way it ought to be. But I miss being in the middle of a movement - lots of momentum that pulled me with it. I miss being a part of the major changes (marriage and new babies) taking place in my close friends' lives. E-mail is great but it's not the same as being there. I don't want to go back because it wouldn't be the way it was and yet I miss it all the same. It's that bitter sweetness of finishing a book that you loved - you are glad that you finished it and are ready to read a new book but you sort of wish it weren't over because it was so good.*

I don't belong anywhere *- which is of course NOT true. I do belong - I have a wonderful team which is more than many people who arrive on the field for the first time have. But it's hard to leave behind such a huge network of relationships. This is one thing I had been forewarned about and knew in my head would be a struggle, but it's just a reality that I live now instead of something I know. I'm still "investigating" fellowships so while I have some friends at different places I rarely go to the same place twice in a week. I have friends but the network is limited. But then I feel guilt sometimes when I think this way because I think of [my friend in East Asia] who has doesn't even have a team or an ex-pat community.*

I'm never going to... *- learn language, culture, feel adjusted, change, etc., etc., etc. The list goes on. I know that I am learning and getting more settled every day, but I don't always "feel" that way. I keep reminding myself that I've only been here for a few months.*

I feel defeated *- not just by outward things (like language) but inwardly too. All my sin is spewing out like a geyser and it's ugly and gross. I feel like I don't even know how to say a kind word (even though I want to). What I say comes out defensive and oversensitive. I give myself a hard time rather than accept the grace that is freely given to me. My eyes are so much fixed on "me" and not on "him". It's like looking at mirror - the longer you look at yourself in a mirror the more* *you see what is wrong with you. You see every wrinkle, every blemish, every imperfection. I read a great A.W. Tozer quote today "While we are looking at Him we do not see ourselves - blessed riddance (amen). The man who struggled to purify himself and has had nothing but repeated failures (that's me!) will experience real relief when he stops tinkering with his soul and looks away to the perfect One. While he looks at Jesus Christ, the very things he has so long been trying to do will be getting done within him. It will be HIM working in him to will and to do." So simple yet so hard. My spirit is willing, but my flesh is weak.*

__I feel tired__ - physically tired and emotionally tired. I've never slept so much in my life. 9 hours is nothing for me now. I average 7-8 hours and less than that exhausts me. I'd like to blame it on the climate or the culture but Jenny didn't sleep that much when she was here. I wonder sometimes if I'm just escaping into sleep or if I really am more tired. My capacity is shrunk - which I knew it would but again it's one of those things where what I've heard to be true is a now a reality in my life. And I'm not just physically tired - I'm tired emotionally too. Life just takes more out of me. Language can be draining - more than I usually realize - and so the simplest tasks become emotionally draining. This is one of those things that I usually blow off as "it's not a big deal" and push myself until some small things causes me to crash. Like most people I guess being emotionally tired puts me in this terrible cycle - I don't have emotional energy so I pull away from people and become unsocial (my response to being drained); that makes me feel "un-fun" which is a major insecurity in my life; the more un-fun I feel the more uninviting I become and so begins the awful circle. I'm in the middle of a "unsocial, un-fun, un-inviting" cycle.

__I feel melancholy__ - this has been just recently and it's funny because one of the "dangers" I wrote down before I ever came was my tendency to become melancholy. It's too easy for me to take myself, and life and others too seriously. I need fun *"play partners" and people who just make me laugh. Jenny was that for a while when she was here (we really miss her). But there really isn't anyone here like that now. I think too that the Sept. 11 tragedy[2] really put our team in a different place than we expected to be the first few months. It brought up some hard issues about leadership and how we relate to one another. It revealed differences in perspectives that had to be worked through. It's extremely stressful for me to watch people I respect disagree with one another - even if it's a good thing and necessary for making a relationship stronger. Jenny's leaving - while a good thing in many ways - left gaps for us all (like I said she was my "play partner"). And there was the stress of knowing that we really might have to pack up and leave - that left us in limbo for several weeks. We couldn't really "get settled into a routine" because at any moment we might have to leave. Anyway - I don't think any of that is why I've been feeling melancholy lately. I feel melancholy because I am not choosing to rejoice. I've been so wrapped up in what is "wrong" or "hard" that I haven't thought about all that is good and right.*

I read through what I just wrote and I sound depressed - which really isn't true. Intermingled with all of those feelings have been joy, peace, eagerness to learn, stability, humility, excitement, happiness, awe, and thankfulness.

✐ ON YOUR OWN

Do your own self-evaluation. How do you feel? Don't worry about what is the right or wrong perspective, just be honest with yourself and with the Lord. He can handle all of your emotions!

---

2   I had been in Kochevnikstan 5 months when 9/11 happened. I watched the twin towers fall in real time from my Kochevnik neighbor's living room.

SQUEEZED AND SHAKEN

What happens when you squeeze a tube of toothpaste? What happens when you squeeze it harder? Toothpaste oozes out, and the harder you squeeze the more it oozes!

When you shake up a glass of lemonade, why does lemonade spill out? Think about it a minute. The most common answer people give is *"because you shook it up."* Or another favorite: *"Because you didn't put a lid on it."* Both are legitimate answers but not the real reason. The real reason that lemonade spills out of a glass when you shake it up is because lemonade is what's inside!

There's a deep spiritual and emotional truth in these simple analogies. When you move to a new country and an unfamiliar environment where culture stress is your constant companion, you get shaken up like the glass of lemonade or squeezed like a tube of toothpaste. When that happens, what's inside of you (sin, insecurities, old habits, etc.) is what spills out. You can blame your circumstances for what is spilling out of you like the person who says, *"Quit shaking the glass of lemonade."* Or you might muster up all the self-generated willpower in your reserves and force yourself to *"put a lid on it."* But neither response will sustain you for very long. You can't control your circumstances – life will happen to you and it will squeeze you and your own strength won't sustain you indefinitely.

Let me pause for a minute and clarify. When you get shaken up, sometimes godliness comes spilling out. If you are a mature believer and you've learned to recognize lies in your life and have chosen to believe the truth instead, then sometimes when you get shaken up, you choose a godly response in spite of your natural fleshly response. That is sanctification at work in us. We ARE becoming more and more like Jesus. As we walk with Jesus, we grow in Christ-likeness, our minds are transformed, and our actions and choices are also transformed. Our capacity to recognize lies and our capacity to war against our flesh increases with each situation; we grow in godliness.

When you make a cross-cultural move, your world gets turned upside down – not just outwardly but inwardly as well. You are squeezed and shaken in new ways and in new places you didn't even know about. Old sins and struggles you thought you'd conquered resurface. You revert to old habits and sinful styles of relating as a means of coping with the stress. Insecurities and weaknesses you thought were behind you begin to ooze out once again. Your capacity to war against your flesh diminishes, the same way your capacity to do simple tasks diminishes under the stress of adjusting to a new culture. In the same way you have to rebuild outward capacity, you also have to rebuild capacity inwardly.

My first year in Kochevnikstan, what spilled out of me as I got squeezed and shaken was anger, insensitive words, control, self-protective sin, demandingness,[3] and independence (not the healthy kind but the kind that says, "*I can do it myself!*").

So take joy in being squeezed and shaken; it is God at work bringing freedom to your life and glory to His name.

My anger wasn't so much outward. I wasn't hitting things or yelling at people (at least not verbally). Although, I do remember wishing I could get my hands on one of those blow-up Bozo the Clown punching bags so I could hit it anytime I wanted! I couldn't find Bozo, so I actually bought a real punching bag – for exercise purposes of course!

Journal entry at three months:

What have been my biggest struggles?

Anger - *The hardest thing for me the last month or so has been struggling with anger. It's all in my mind - I get frustrated because things aren't going the way I want (that's my control issues) and I have these angry conversations in my mind. This is something that I've done for a long time but*

---

3   One of the most influential books in my life is *Inside Out* by Larry Crabb. In it he unpacks what sin in our heart (vs. sin in our behavior) looks like including self-protective sin and demandingness.

it has been really bad recently. This summer a friend made this off-handed comment one day about anger being addictive and how we can get a high from it. That statement has come back to me often, and I've thought "maybe I get a high off of feeling angry the way some people get a high from pornography (a gross comparison maybe, but I think it's true). Having these angry conversations in my head makes me feel in control (I always win the arguments in my mind). It's like an addiction. Strange thing is that I don't really think I'm an angry person in real life - only in my mind (but that's where it all starts). For the most part it's not hard for me to submit to actual decisions. The real life discussions are almost never as heated as the ones in my mind. In fact the topics in my "made up" conversations are usually based on my own assumptions rather than on truth (isn't all this a terribly scary thought - I'm being really honest here!). It's all in my head - a struggle to take my thoughts captive. I think part of the reason it's so prevalent right now is that I have so much free mental time. Before I was always thinking of something, doing something, thinking for someone or running somewhere. But I have more free time now and I'm having to really discipline myself to think on true and right things. Since I've recognized this, I've been trying to take steps to really take my thoughts captive. One specific thing is that I try to listen to worship music in the morning when I'm getting ready - morning seems to be a particularly vulnerable time for me. The music gives me something to focus on and I'm less tempted to let my thoughts just wander on their own. It's still a struggle, but God has been faithful in the last few weeks to begin to change me in this and I'm so thankful.

Critical Spirit *- along with the whole anger thing and something that feeds it - is my own critical nature. I look at something (or someone) and see everything that is wrong with it. It makes me angry that it (or he or she or me) isn't perfect. This has been especially true of how I look at our team. I love our team, and because I love us I have high expectations on us - unrealistically high expectations. My tendency is to look* *and see what needs to change. And that's not all bad. I'm discerning (you know the whole strength misused thing). I've been reminded lately of one of my favorite quotes "discernment is for intercession not for fault finding." That has become my battle weapon for dealing with my own critical spirit. As a result, praying has become a major theme in my life, to really bring big things - character things - to Him and trust HIM to change it. Not just in others, but in me as well.*

With the benefit of hindsight, I can look back at this honest journal entry and have some insight I didn't have at the time. I thought that one contributor to anger pouring out of me was that I had more mental free time than usual – and that was probably true. But as I look back now, I see that my anger was the result of blocked goals. You want to do something, but your goal is blocked. You get angry because you can't do what you want. Blocked goals were my whole life that first year…

I had goals to be proficient in language. Blocked.
I had goals to get multiple things done in one day. Blocked.
I had goals to disciple women. Blocked.
Goal. Blocked. Goal. Blocked.

Squeezed and shaken – what spilled out was anger. I wanted to control my surroundings, my own life, but so much was out of control (hence the conversations in my own head that I was always able to control!). In His goodness, the Lord squeezed, forcing me to grow through my own control issues and trust him in new ways – to trust Him to be in control even when I wasn't and to be accomplishing His goals even when I couldn't accomplish mine.

Anger that results from blocked goals and being out of control might not be what spills out of you when you get shaken. Perhaps it's insecurities in what people think about you – are you doing the right thing? Do people like you? Maybe you feel incompetent or unloved or misunderstood. The point is that living cross-culturally, especially in your first year, is like riding a roller coaster. You know one of those old rickety ones that jerks you around and shakes your insides out. It's not a matter of IF you get squeezed and shaken, but how you will respond

WHEN it does happen. What will you do with what spills out?

1 Peter 1:6-7 says, "*...though now for a little while you may have had to suffer grief in all kinds of trials. These have come so that your faith of greater worth than gold, which perishes even though refined by fire – may be proved genuine and may result in praise, glory and honor when Jesus Chris is revealed.*"

God himself is the one who squeezes and shakes. He may use circumstances to do the actual shaking, but He is the one controlling it. He is Sovereign. He shakes and squeezes, because He desires our faith to be proved genuine. A refiner's fire. In His goodness and commitment to making us holy, He turns up the heat bringing to the surface the dross, or sin, so that He can remove it from us and purify us. Just when we think, "*I can do this,*" God squeezes a little more and shakes a little harder, because He is committed to our holiness and keeping us dependent on Him. Truth sets us free – not keeping our sin hidden deep inside the bottom of the lemonade glass by avoiding anything that shakes us or by tightly keeping a lid on anything that might try to spill out. "*You will know the truth and the truth will set you free*" (Rom. 8:32). So take joy in being squeezed and shaken; it is God at work bringing freedom to your life and glory to His name.

✒ ON YOUR OWN

In what ways are you getting squeezed and shaken as you adjust to your new culture? What emotion, insecurity, or sin is spilling out? Be honest with yourself and use the "4 Why" method to go deeper into the root issue. See "Language Learning I: It's just hard" for the "4 Why" method.

What can you practically do to grow through this refining process? Remember, the goal is not to control the squeezing or keep what's inside from spilling out but to know what to do with what spills out. (See "Notes to Self" for practical suggestions)

5 Ds OF CHARACTER DEVELOPMENT

How does God develop character? Romans 5:3-5 says *"...we also rejoice in our sufferings because we know that suffering produces perseverance; perseverance, character; and character, hope. And hope does not disappoint us, because God has poured out his love into our hearts by the Holy Spirit, whom he has given us."*

Character is revealed by trials and developed through perseverance in the midst of those trials. Remember the lemonade illustration in "Squeezed and Shaken"? What spills out when you get shaken up? Whatever is inside! There are 5 tools God uses to shake us up and reveal and develop character as we cross cultures (I'm sure there's more than these, but these 5 are nicely alliterated "D" words).

DELAY
Patience and flexibility is the missionary mantra. There's a reason for that. Living internationally is full of delays and changes in plans. EVERYTHING takes longer than we think it should. Out of 10 things on your to-do list, expect to get 2 done. If you are running to the store, expect it to take 3 times as long as you think it should.

When you think about waiting (what we are supposed to do in response to delays), what comes to mind? An angelic face quietly and calmly lingering until the desired result comes to pass? That is so not me! Patience – calmly waiting – is not my strength. Years ago, in an attempt to cultivate greater patience in my life, I was studying "waiting." God gave me hope when I came across Psalm 34:7: *"Be still and wait patiently for him."* The word "wait" in this verse is translated only one time in Scripture as "wait." The rest of the time, it's used in association with childbirth – to writhe and dance in pain. A woman in labor is "waiting" for the joy of her child to be born (John 16:21), and the waiting is anything but quiet and calm.

DISAPPOINTMENT
When plans and hopes are not fulfilled in the way we had envisioned, we feel disappointed. We desperately want to see someone come to know the Lord, and yet the ground remains hard. The new believer

we are meeting with simply disappears to who-knows-where, and we can't get in touch with him or her (this happened in Kochevnikstan multiple times). While editing this chapter today, I got an e-mail from my friend who still labors in Kochevnikstan. A girl we love and have both helped grow has decided after 4 years that she doesn't want to be a believer anymore. What do you do with that kind of disappointment – disappointment in her, in yourself, in God? Elisabeth Elliot talks about "material for sacrifice,"[4] bringing the disappointments of life to a loving Father and offering them up to Him. A good heart check question for me is, "*Where is my hope?*" Is it in the Lord or in His provision of the thing I so long for? As we persevere through the difficulties of life, God develops our character. Consider Joseph who must have been devastated when his brothers sold him. God was doing something bigger than Joseph's immediate circumstance – both in Joseph as well as in the world around him.

DARKNESS[5]

Fears of the unknown, the unfamiliar, the uncertain are dark places of life that we don't understand. Depression and discouragement press in and threaten to destroy us. We ask, "*Why Lord?*" but He is silent. He doesn't explain or give understanding. His answer is not an answer at all, but only "*Trust me.*" "*God is light; in him is no darkness at all,*" but the reality of our world is that it IS a dark place and many of the places you serve are behind enemy lines where Satan rules for the present time (1 John 1:5). God's promise to us as we persevere through the dark places (and we must persevere through them and not give in to them) is "*I am the light of the world. Whoever follows me will never walk in darkness, but will have the light of life*" (John 8:12). Perseverance builds character and character builds hope.

DISTURBANCE

Our comfortable routines get shaken up, revealing what is underneath. Contribution is about the external but character is about what is INTERNAL. What's inside is what spills out when the disturbances of life

---

4   From *Passion and Purity* by Elisabeth Elliot
5   There are whole books written on spiritual darkness and depression. If this is something you struggle with, talk with your team leader or your organizational staff care team.

shake us up. What things "disturb" your life and reveal what's inside? Internet problems? Culture clashes? Relational conflict? How do you respond when your life is disturbed? How you respond has everything to do with the character God is revealing and developing in you.

DEFEAT

We can feel defeated about a lot of different things in life – relationships, ministry, family, etc. Language is a place that every missionary feels defeated at some point. Whether it comes easy or it seems impossible, it is so tempting to trust too much in my own ability rather than leaning on the promises of Scripture and the leading of the Holy Spirit. The longer we walk with God, the more we learn to re-define success by His standards rather than the standards of the world (or the standards we set for ourselves). Winston Churchill wisely observed, "*Success is never final and failure is never fatal.*" In fact, when we evaluate and learn from our mistakes, failure is far more valuable in developing character than success!

Character is revealed by trials and developed through perseverance in the midst of those trials.

PRACTICAL PRINCIPLES FOR DEVELOPING GODLY CHARACTER

Hebrews 5:14 is a definition of maturity: "*Solid food is for the mature who by constant use, have trained themselves, to discern good from evil.*" Developing godly character is a lot about what God stirs up in our lives (the 5 Ds), but it's also about how we take personal responsibility to habitually respond to those situations. A few practical principles to help you begin "training yourself":

1. Remind yourself often that you are not as important as you think you are, but you are more fully loved than you can possibly imagine! (1 John 3:1, 2 Corinth 1:9-10)

2. Make time to reflect on what God is teaching you. Developing character is not about what you know but what you apply!

Experience is not a great teacher; evaluated experience is a great teacher.

3. Train yourself to ask "what" and not "why." Instead of "*Why are you doing this, God?*" ask, "*What do you want me to learn about you or myself in this situation?*"

4. Choose to be honest. Even if no one asks, choose to share your struggle. There is something powerful about speaking things out loud. "*Godliness is not the absence of sin but the absence of hiddenness.*"

5. Seek out people who:
- Will ask you the hard questions
- Speak truth to you (even when it hurts)
- Help you laugh at yourself
- Help you interpret what you are learning

✎ ON YOUR OWN

Which of these 5 Ds is God using now in your life to reveal your character? How will you respond to the Lord when (not if) these 5 Ds surround you?

Read 2 Corinthians chapters 1, 4 and 12. What should our perspective be on trials, hardship, and difficulties?

What sustains us in our struggles?

What practical steps can you take to allow God to more deeply develop character in your life?

NOTES TO SELF

I love one liners – it's the sentences that impact my life more than the chapters or books. And one of my favorite "one-liners" is something a trusted pastor told me about taking our thoughts captive. He said that we should "*talk to ourselves more than listen to ourselves.*"

Have you ever been talking to someone, sharing with them or giving them biblical counsel, and you hear what you are saying and think, "*That is exactly what I need to hear*"? When we talk to ourselves, we are more likely to speak what we know to be true – what our head believes. But when we listen to ourselves, we can get lost in emotions, uncertainties, and doubts. Listening to ourselves is important. It is essential in understanding what is really going on inside of us – where our heart is. Otherwise, we end up lying to ourselves and not being honest with our emotions. But when it comes time to take action, we need to cultivate the habit of talking to ourselves more than listening to ourselves.

As I was being squeezed and shaken in new (and old) ways my first year, I began to put into practice something I learned early on in my walk with God. I began to identify the lies I was believing, and replace them with truth directly from Scripture. What developed out of that exercise was what I called "Notes to Self" – a way to tangibly talk to myself more than listen to myself. It was a one-page list of truths directly countering the lies I tended to believe. These were truths that I wanted to focus on, choose to believe, and pray into my life. I wrote down the truths and the Scripture that went with them, and I kept this one page "Notes to Self" in my Bible. For months, I read and prayed through these "Notes to Self" every day, or at least several times a week, asking God to make these truths a reality in my life.

In writing this chapter, I've gone back and looked over these "Notes to Self." While God has grown and changed me over the years, I find that I still struggle with the same basic weaknesses, and the same truths need to be applied to my life. I still need to be reminded to "let people be where and how they are" and to "delight in the differences." I still need to "choose to rejoice" and to give Him time to do His work.

The core lies we believe, the basic weaknesses of our personality, don't change. We just learn – over time and in the power of the Holy Spirit – how to bring those things under the Lordship of Christ, to be transformed more and more into His likeness and with His attitude (Rom. 12:2-3, Phil. 2:5).

While God has grown and changed me over the years, I find that I still struggle with the same basic weaknesses, and the same truths need to be applied to my life.

You may or may not be the kind of person who makes a list of truths (I love lists and sometimes even make them for fun). And certainly your "Notes to Self" will not be the same truths as ones I listed to counter my personal weaknesses and struggles. But regardless of the form your "Notes to Self" take or the exact promises you choose to remind yourself of, we all need to learn ways to talk to ourselves more than listen to ourselves. We all need to remind ourselves of God's promises and truths and pray them into our lives in a consistent way.

✔ LET'S GET PRACTICAL

Read through the sample "Notes to Self" and then make your own list. Commit to pray through your list daily for at least 2 weeks.

SAMPLE NOTES TO SELF

"Your attitude should be the same as that of Christ Jesus…" (Phil. 2:5)

"Be joyful always, pray continually; give thanks in all circumstances, for this IS the will of God for you…" (1 Thess. 5:16-18)

"Do not let any unwholesome talk come out of your mouths, but ONLY what is helpful for building others up according to their needs, that it may benefit those who listen." (Eph. 5:29)

Choose to rejoice because God is always good.

I'm not responsible to "fix" everyone's problem. Discernment is for intercession NOT for fault finding.

If no one else changes, I can change – I am not responsible before God for their lives, but I AM accountable to the Lord for my own. Even if they don't change, I can choose to change.

Choose NOT to try to solve everyone else's challenges – in reality OR in my head OR in conversations with other teammates

Let people be where they are – don't try to "fix" them.

Accept people where they are and HOW they are.

"A man's wisdom gives him patience, it is to his glory to overlook an offense." (Prov. 19:11)

"It is not good to have zeal without knowledge, nor to be hasty and miss the way." (Prov. 19:2)

"He who guards his lips, guards his life, but he who speaks rashly will come to ruin." (Prov. 13:3)

"A fool finds no pleasure in understanding but delights in his own opinions." (Prov. 18:2)

JOY IN THE JOURNEY

In Kochevnikstan, there was a waterfall outside Orchard City where we often took summer teams camping and hiking. The trail crossed back and forth over a small stream before reaching the waterfall, and if you were really adventurous, you could scale the rock wall that ran alongside the waterfall to a beautiful meadow at the top. I loved the views – both from the base of the waterfall and from the meadow at the top. But I found that once I got to the waterfall and soaked in a little of the beauty, I was ready to get moving again. I think that is often the case in our lives. We are so in a hurry to get to where we are going, but once we get there and rest a while, we are ready to get going again. Why? Because the real joy is in the journey, not in the destination (heaven might an exception to this – that is one destination that WILL BE better than the journey!).

Journal entries after 7 months:

> *Time is a challenge. I see all the things that need to be done (i.e. setting up house, learning language, familiarizing myself with the culture, building relationships, etc.) and in my impatience, I want them to be finished and settled "right now." I sometimes want to be as experienced at my new life as I was at my old life. But I know that all things take time and I MUST pace myself. I must concentrate on doing a little at a time rather than trying to do everything all at once. There's joy in JOURNEY!*

> *I was reminded of this just this week when a co-laborer in the States wrote and asked my advice about some campus work she is doing. I KNEW what to tell her (I had lots of ideas, opinions, and experiences), because I did her exact job for 10 years before I came to Kochevnikstan. I had something to offer, because I have been where she is now. I didn't always know these things about U.S. campus work. I learned them as I lived and worked in that environment. And my memories of those ten years are so sweet – not memories of knowing everything, but memories of the journey. That's*

how it will be here. Right now, I feel like I know nothing well – not language, not culture, not even the rhythms of my own life – the same way I knew nothing when I started on campus ten years ago. But ten years from now, I WILL have something to offer those who come behind me – experiences, philosophies, ideas – because I will have lived it.[6] Not only do I want to endure the challenge of learning for what I will know, but to enjoy the journey to get there.

"Life is a journey" – [this lesson] keeps coming round to be front and center in my life. I can't escape it. Every book I read, every character I study, every lesson I learn somehow has this truth stuck in there. I get in a hurry and impatient and want things to be "there" (fluent language, full fledge movement in place, a particular character trait firmly rooted in my life). I start thinking...why don't I have it all together. And then I read a biography about Martin Luther who was older than me when his greatest works were done. Or I think about Moses who was still learning Egyptian ways when he was my age (and he had 40 additional years to go in the desert before he started his "real" work). Daniel spent 3 years learning language and culture in Babylon; Paul spent 15 years in solitude before he began his public work; Amy Carmichael was in China and Japan before she ever landed in India. And the list goes on - I can't get away from this truth and yet I can't seem to really grasp it either. I still get impatient and in a hurry. I think, "I've been here 7 months, why don't I have this down." But I've ONLY been here 7 months.

✐ ON YOUR OWN

Do you wish you could be as experienced at your new life as you were at your old? Why or why not? What does it practically look like in your life for you to take joy in the journey?

---

6   This book is living proof that 10 years later I DO have a few thoughts and ideas to share!

SPEAKING THINGS OUT LOUD

Sally was driving me crazy. She talked all the time – seriously I don't know how she could breathe in, because there were always words coming out of her mouth. We were only a few days into our pre-field training and I was already wondering how in the world I was going to last a full year listening to this incessant chatter. To make it worse, in my own sin and selfishness, I started to simply tune Sally out. She would talk, but I quit listening. Initially, she didn't even notice my half-hearted listening, but then she started asking me to respond – demanding my attention. Sally and I were going to be roommates for a full year, not just apartment mates but actually sharing the same room. I could not survive this kind of relationship for a few weeks, let alone a full year. It wasn't that Sally was in sin because she talked so much or that my need for quiet was sinful. But our personalities clashed and we needed to come to some kind of compromise if we were going to live and work together.

Talking to Sally was on my mind all the time. How do I talk to her, explaining I need more quiet without making her feel like she was wrong for talking all the time? And how do I make sure that in my heart of hearts, I really do NOT believe that she is wrong for talking all the time? Finally, I did the only thing I knew to do – be honest and tell Sally how I felt.

I'd learned the hard way that words are powerful. When bringing up a charged topic, I needed to not only be aware of what I said (is it true?) but how I said it (my tone of voice) and when I chose to bring it up (my timing). After thinking and praying about this for several days, God opened a door for me to honestly tell Sally how I felt. With uncharacteristic gentleness, diplomacy, and tact – definitely supernatural from the Lord – Sally and I were able to bring our frustrations with one another into the light. It was GREAT. Sally knew she talked a lot, had been told that by many other people. She was trying to work on it but didn't know how. She recognized that I needed my quiet and space. We both wanted to respect one another. Finally, we came to a mutual agreement. Sally could talk all she wanted and I was allowed to tune her out (seriously, it was her idea). If she really needed me to listen to something, she would ask me for my full attention for a few minutes, and I would stop what I was doing to give it to her. It may sound crazy, but it's absolutely true. And it worked for us for a year. Sally and I were great friends that year and have stayed in touch casually since then. We learned the value of speaking things out loud. That year we committed to be honest with one another when we felt hurt or confused. If something bothered us, we committed to ask about it. In that way, we eliminated a lot of misunderstanding.

One night after the lights were out and we were going to sleep, Sally said she needed to ask me something. Was I frustrated with her about her talking at night before we went to bed? I told her that I was perfectly content with our agreement that she could talk all she wants as long as I don't have to always listen intently. *"Then why do you sigh every night before you go to sleep?"* she asked. I had no idea what she was talking about. She went on to inform me that I sigh quite loudly before falling asleep. Sally thought it was directed at her personally. It hurt her feelings until she brought her hurt into the light and asked me about it. As it turned out, my sighing had nothing to do with her – just a reflexive response to winding down before falling asleep. But she wouldn't have known that had she not been committed to speaking things out loud!

Over the years, my conviction about the importance of speaking things out loud has continued to grow. My experience is that there is something powerful about saying things out loud – not just thinking it but speaking it and speaking it to another person. It can be confessing sin, verbalizing an insecurity, sharing a weakness, declaring your dependency and neediness, or bringing out into the open something that bothers you about another person or about a particular situation. Usually with the "big" things – obvious sin or sin against another person – we know that we need to confess, confront, and reconcile. James 5:16 says, *"Confess your sins to one another so that you may be healed."* But it's not the big things I'm thinking about here, it's the little things. Those little passing thoughts, a moment of jealousy, being bothered by some random comment someone else makes, or even those little insignificant private thoughts that we'd feel foolish telling someone about. It's easy to blow off the little things and convince yourself that *"it's not really important"* or *"it's not that big of a deal."* Yet little things can easily become big things if allowed to take root. When something is held in (in secret, in the dark), it grows like a balloon being filled with air. Speaking things out loud is like deflating that balloon – it takes all the oomph out of it so that this empty thing (whatever we say out loud) loses all it's power over us and keeps the enemy from gaining a foothold in our lives and in our relationships (Eph. 4:27).

We already said that confessing our sins to one another is clearly scriptural (James 5:16). But what about this idea of speaking little things out loud? I believe that is.

1 John 1:5-7 says *"...God is light, in him there is no darkness at all. If we claim to have fellowship with him yet walk in the darkness, we lie and do not live by the truth. But if we walk in the light, as he is in the light, we have fellowship with one another and the blood of Jesus purifies us from all sin."*

Have you ever noticed how shameful things often happen in "darkness." Bars, strip clubs, porn shops all have darkened windows (keeping the darkness in and the light out). The majority of their activity takes place at night. And when we sin, our natural, fleshly response is to keep it hidden – to keep it in the dark.

Throughout Scripture we see that light represents everything that is good. God himself is light according to 1 John 1:5. When we read of darkness in Scripture it is always associated with Satan, evil deeds, and separation from God. *"Satan masquerades as an angel of light"* implies that his natural state is one of darkness (2 Corinth. 11:14). *"Men loved darkness instead of light because their deeds were evil"* (John 3:19). *"I am sending you to them to open their eyes and turn them from darkness to light, and from the power of Satan to God..."* (Acts 26:18). *"For he has rescued us from the dominion of darkness..."* (Col. 1:13).

Speaking things out loud is a way of bringing it into the light. It's seeking truth in the inmost parts (Ps. 51:6). It's exposing this seemingly insignificant thought for what it really is – a ploy of the prince of darkness to keep us in bondage and/or to plant seeds of division and dissension in the body of believers. Secrets and hidden things are associated with darkness. The secrets we see in Scripture are people hiding their sin, shortcomings, or weaknesses. For example, David kept his affair with Bathsheba a secret and Achan hid his sin – literally (2 Samuel 11, Joshua 7).

Just a word of clarification here – I am not saying that we should always speak out loud everything we think or feel. Scripture is clear that there is a time to be silent, and certainly Scripture has much to say about the virtue of holding our tongues (Eccl. 3:7). There is an element of wisdom in choosing what we say and do not say. *"The heart of the righteous weighs its answers, but the mouth of the wicked gushes evil"* (Prov. 15:28). It's not wise to speak something out loud simply because I want to vent my anger (Prov. 29:11), or make sure everyone knows my opinion (Prov. 18:2), to speak out of a reckless lack of self discipline (Prov. 12:18), or to say something for the evil purpose of hurting someone with my words (Eph. 4:29). When I talk about speaking things out loud, I am referring to an attitude of humility that speaks for the purpose of exposing dark thoughts – those foolish or insignificant things that "feel" more comfortable left unsaid (Eph. 5:11).

Speaking things out loud is a way of bringing it into the light.

Ultimately, we must each listen to the Holy Spirit in us and His prompting. We will each answer to the Father for what we do or do not say out loud. *"But I tell you men will have to give account on the day of judgment for every careless word they have spoken. For by your words you will be acquitted and by your words you will be condemned"* (Matt. 12:26). Our words will acquit us: speaking things out loud can and will bring freedom. But our words, ones rashly and recklessly spoken, can and will condemn us. Only you can know your heart and it's motivation for speaking something out loud or keeping silent. But beware of the danger of keeping silent as a sign of *"…never [being] able to acknowledge the truth…"* (2 Tim. 3:7).

Let's look again at 1 John 1:5-7: *"God is light, in him there is no darkness at all. If we claim to have fellowship with him yet walk in the darkness, we lie and do not live by the truth. But if we walk in the light, as he is in the light, we have fellowship with one another and the blood of Jesus purifies us from all sin."*

One of the benefits of walking in the light, exposing and speaking out loud to others our "hidden" thoughts, is that genuine fellowship will result. It's a promise from the Word. As we confess our sin, there is healing (James 5:16). As we speak truthfully to our neighbor, we protect our relationships from giving the devil a foothold (Eph. 4:25-27). As we share our insecurities, weaknesses, and dependency, we allow others the opportunity to meet our needs and help us in our burdens (Gal. 6:2). Speaking things out loud provides opportunities to pray for one another and breeds an attitude and environment of encouragement and support rather than comparison and competition.

"But what fellowship can light have with darkness?" (1 Corinth. 6:14). While the primary context of this verse is that believers and non-believer cannot have true fellowship, I believe that it can also be applied to relationships between believers. If one person is walking in the light, honestly confessing sin and exposing his dark, hidden thoughts to the light, and a second person is not, there cannot be any depth of fellowship. Even if that second person is a believer and he is IN the light because he is IN Jesus, if he is consistently keeping parts of his life in darkness, if he is keeping secrets and afraid to expose his inmost thoughts, this will hinder genuine fellowship. Some fellowship may occur since both people are believers and are in the light, but the fellowship will be shallow and lacking real depth.

Finally, we consistently see in Scripture that where there is real fellowship, there is great growth in the Kingdom of the Father of Light. *"Many of those who believed now came and openly confessed their evil deeds...in this way the word of the Lord spread widely and grew in power* (Acts 19:18,20). As real fellowship occurred in Acts 2:32-47, the result was that *"the Lord added to their number daily those who were being saved."* And Jesus himself said to his followers, *"Love one another. As I have loved you, so you must love one another. By this all men will know that you are my disciples, if you love one another"* (Jn. 13:34-35). The ultimate goal of speaking things out loud is love. And by this love, those outside the light will know that we are different, that our relationships are different, and they will want to join us in the light.

✎ ON YOUR OWN

Ephesians 4-5 has much to say about living as children of light. Read Ephesians 4:17-5:21. What can you learn about "living in the light" from these verses?

What very practical counsel do these verses give about how we are to relate to others?

Is there something in your life that you are holding in? That you feel uncomfortable sharing with your roommate/team-mate? If so, what makes you hesitant?

Do you have a Sally on your team – someone whose personality is different than yours and gets on your nerves? If so, how can you bring this into the light in a way that both respects your "Sally" and helps you both move forward in how you relate?

SUBMISSIVE REBELLION

I was mad. I was having an angry conversation with my boss, the kind where I presented irrefutable logic as to why he needed to listen to me. This was the kind of argument I always won – at least in my head where the argument was happening!

My boss would not give me permission to go on vacation. Who was he to tell me when or where I could go on vacation?[7] I thought about quitting – not really of course, because I knew God had called me to Kochevnikstan – but telling myself that I could always quit if I wanted to made me feel like I had control over my life. After all, it was MY life, and I could do whatever I wanted – or so the argument went in my head.

I had been in Kochevnikstan for almost a year. It was the end of a long winter – snowy, cold, dreary – my first real winter anywhere. I grew up in south Mississippi. Cold was the temperature dropping to 40 degrees Fahrenheit, and if it snowed, everything closed down and the whole city had a play day. Even if it did by chance get a little cold, the sun still showed itself. That first winter in Kochevnikstan, I think the sun came out only 4-5 days in the WHOLE month of January. Locals said that it was the coldest winter on record in 20 years. I was tired of winter. I was tired of language study. I was tired of feeling bored with nothing "productive" to do. I was tired of the 7+ people I knew in the entire city. I was tired of the same monotonous routine. I had cabin fever and I wanted OUT! My solution was to take a vacation. I wasn't asking to go to America, just someplace away from here! But my boss said "no" – actually he didn't come right out and say no. He did that frustrating thing that my parents used to do by putting the decision back on me: *"Do you really think that's a good idea? What would be the best thing for your consistency in language study and cultural adjustment?"* He might not have said "no," but he wasn't going to say "yes" either.

---

7 Although it sounds ultra-controlling, most supervisors in international contexts (even in secular companies) DO have the right to tell their team where as well as when they can go on vacation. It's a legal security issue, a responsibility that international supervisors have that most U.S. bosses don't.

I'm a pretty logical person and usually insightful. I knew there was something going on inside of me that was about more than going on vacation. I knew that ultimately I wasn't mad at my boss, but I was mad at God for keeping me "stuck in this place." I believe that God is good and "*no good thing does He withhold from those whose hearts are his*" (Ps. 84:11). I really believe that's true. And yet in this situation, I was rebellious like I have rarely been rebellious in my life. It wasn't outward rebellion: I'm far too much of a do-gooder for that. It was a heart level submissive-rebellion like the little girl who says defiantly to her parents, "*I may be sitting down on the outside but on the inside I'm standing up.*" I prayed and confessed my sin in not trusting God to give me what was good for me. Usually "talking to myself" about what is true is enough to bring my heart around. But as much as I confessed my lack of trust in God, I could tell my heart wasn't really broken over my sin. I wanted what I wanted, and that was it. I may not get it, but I was not going to let go of wanting what I wanted. It was demandingness in its finest form.

It's only when we open our hand – releasing what we are holding on to so tightly – that God can pour His goodness and grace into it.

Finally, I think God had enough of my childish tantrum – not unlike Job when God says, "*Brace yourself like a man and I will question you*" (Job 38:3). God, a loving but firm Father, sat me down for a heart to heart: "*Malishka (an endearment in my host language meaning "little one"), I love you, and I want you to have what is good. But I won't negotiate with you. You can't have what you want, so you have a choice to make. You either submit to me, trusting my goodness, or you continue to fight against me, which will only make you more tired and frustrated. You choose.*" I'm so thankful for God's patience and for the fact that he never gives into our temper tantrums or whimsical wants. God's love for me and my knowledge of his past goodness in my life finally won out and in genuine brokenness; I repented of my desire to control my own life rather than trusting my Father to make better decisions for me than I could make for myself. I felt free for the first time in weeks. So what if I didn't go on vacation – that wasn't the point anyway. God would provide what I really needed, and if that wasn't a vacation then so be it. I would trust Him.

My heart to heart with the Lord that resulted in genuine brokenness was on a Sunday night. I remember precisely, because on Monday morning my boss came over to my apartment. He'd gotten a call on Sunday night from a mutual friend of ours – our old boss – with a special request concerning me. My boss had thought about coming to talk to me about it on Sunday night (he lived in my building), but decided it could wait until morning. There was a situation with a U.S. staff woman that prevented her from participating in the international summer training project she was supposed to help lead. They were considering me to fill her position for the upcoming summer. The project was in New Zealand. The staff and students were people I knew. And my boss thought it was a great idea. I sat dumbfounded and unable to speak (that doesn't happen very often!). At the VERY time that God was humbling me and asking me to trust him, He was arranging for me an opportunity that was far better than any vacation I could have planned for myself.

It wasn't a coincidence that my boss waited to come talk to me on Monday morning instead of Sunday night. God had work to do in my heart – to remind me that HE is God and I am not; to remind me that I gave Him control of my life years before (Gal. 2:20); to remind me that while He will never negotiate terms with me, that He will always choose do what is good for me. God's choice to "give me a break" from the mundane existence of my current life (that's how I felt about it) was so much better than what I was stubbornly convinced I wanted. He not only sent me to an interesting place,[8] but he gave me a job there doing something I loved, something refreshing that I missed about my old life – investing in maturing women – something that simply wasn't yet in place in our pioneering work in Kochevnikstan.

Had I gotten what I so desperately wanted, to go on vacation, I would

---

8   One of my life goals is to visit and share the Gospel on 6 continents (no interest in going to Antarctica where the only thing indigenous is penguins!). Australia/New Zealand was my last continent. In addition to spending 2 months in New Zealand – north and south islands – the trip allowed me to spend a few days with some good friends laboring in Australia.

have settled for so much less than what God was preparing for me. A simple picture reminds me of this truth. Close your hand tight making a fist. This is you holding on to whatever it is you think you want. But when our hand is closed we are unable to receive from God what He wants to bless us with. It's only when we open our hand – releasing what we are holding on to so tightly – that God can pour His goodness and grace into it.

✎ ON YOUR OWN

Have you ever felt "submissively rebellious" – like the little girl sitting on the outside but standing on the inside? What were the circumstances? What did it take for God to break through to you?

Read Psalm 84:11 and Psalm 34:10. Do you believe that God is good in everything? Do you really believe it in a way that affects your actions? How would your life look different if you completely embraced this truth?

CHOOSING CONTENTMENT

"Contentment is not getting what you want, but wanting what you have."

Often we associate discontentment with being single. But discontentment comes in many forms. Discontentment says I'd be really happy…

If my life were just more exciting
If my job were just more challenging
If I could just speak the language better
If I just weren't so tired
If I just had a child
If I just had a little more money
If someone would just listen to me

It's a vicious cycle that doesn't end with getting what you want. The self-made millionaire, J.D. Rockefeller, understood this. Someone once asked him, *"How much money is enough?"* to which Rockefeller replied, *"One dollar more."* Discontentment is a condition of our hearts and ultimately, as believers, it's a statement of our belief (or lack of it) in the goodness of God.

As I write this chapter, I have been in Kochevnikstan for 10 years. I'm in a time of transition and change – in some ways similar to my first year of adjusting to a new culture. The past few months have been ones in which discontentment has knocked on my door more often than at any other time I can remember. Even as a single woman, I have never struggled with feeling discontent as much as I have recently.

I've been struggling to make a decision about whether or not to leave the field. I've loved my time in Kochevnikstan, my friends here, my team. But a few months ago, I found myself everyday in my quiet time coming back to the same thought: *"It's just not enough."* Not enough to do, not enough teamship, not enough leadership, not enough stimulus, not enough breadth, not enough relationships, not enough, not enough, not enough…

I remembered a friend once telling me that in our lives, when we are struggling, there are usually real circumstances – practical things – that need to change. But in our sinful nature, we often respond wrongly to those circumstances and tell ourselves, *"If this could only change then..."* But changing our circumstances alone is not enough – that's a superficial band-aid that isn't addressing the deeper issue. We have to first deal with our perspective (our sin), and then look realistically at the practical changes (circumstances) that need to be made. This was certainly the case in my situation.

I knew that seeds of discontentment were taking root in my life. I could see it in my response to my circumstances, but I felt powerless to change it. I didn't want to be discontent. I didn't want to be frustrated, and I was tired of my own thoughts constantly cycling downward in a discouraging, discontent thought pattern. There were realities I needed to face – realities about my job, my life, and my current circumstances – but before I could objectively address those realities, I needed to get my heart right with God. I needed to choose contentment.

We have to first deal with our perspective (our sin) and then look realistically at the practical changes (circumstances) that need to be made.

I confessed the seeds of discontent I saw taking hold of me, and I began to ask the Lord to root out my sin. I prayed this way for at least a month, still wrestling regularly with my own wrong thoughts, unable to consistently maintain a right way of thinking. I prayed from Philippians 2:13 that God would work in me *"to will and to act according to his good purposes."*

After more than a month of praying that God would root out this sin and help me move forward, I heard a talk on contentment. One of the main references was from Psalms 16. I was convicted. God answered my prayer. In my journal I wrote:

> *Lord, you are at work in my life. I confess not only have I been discontent with that work, but that I've said in my*

heart – without even realizing it – that what YOU are do-ing ISN'T ENOUGH…[my thoughts of] 'I want/need more' have ultimately been against you – that you are not enough or what you are doing in my life is not enough. Lord, I know there are some real circumstances to be addressed. I do not want to settle for just OK – I do want more – I want every-thing that YOU want to give me, whether that is boredom or excitement, joy, or hurt. YOU ARE ENOUGH! You know me. You know what I want and need. You see what I don't [see] and know what's ultimately good for me. Teach me to be content in any and all circumstances [Phil 4:11]. The things I think I want -- I want to trust YOU, not people or even myself, to provide these things… to provide them (or not) in whatever way YOU know is good.

YOU have assigned me my cup and my portion
YOU have made my lot secure
YOU have set my boundary lines in pleasant places
YOU have given me a delightful inheritance
YOU fill me with joy in your presence
YOU counsel and instruct me
YOU have made me secure
YOU make known the path of life
YOU fill me with eternal pleasures
Lord YOU ARE ENOUGH! [From Psalms 16]

God had answered my prayer to "*will and to act according to His good purpose.*" He dealt with my discontentment – my heart issue – and only then was my heart in a right place to be brutally honest with myself about the specifics of my circumstances. Changing our circumstances won't necessarily change our hearts. In my case, I did end up leaving Kochevnikstan, making changes in my circumstances to pursue an-other path the Lord had laid out for me. But I didn't leave because I was discontent; I didn't leave because anything was "not enough." I came to the same conclusion, that it was time to leave, but with a totally differ-ent heart motivation.

✏ ON YOUR OWN

Finish these statements (what is the very first thing that comes to mind?)

"If only I could........ then I'd be content."

"If only I had........... then I'd be content."

"If only .... then I'd be content."

How do you behave, think, interact if you are feeling discontent? What are the yellow flags in your life when you are discontent that you can learn to recognize?

Are there other areas in your life where you need to deal first with a wrong perspective before dealing with practical changes in your circumstances?

GOD IS ALWAYS GOOD

"God is always good…always God is good." This phrase is one of the favorite mantras of my teammate and close friend Dan. He and his family have lived in Kochevnikstan for more than 17 years and there have been plenty of times that their confidence in this truth has been challenged. Yet this truth that God is good has sustained them through the painful places in life.

Do you really believe that God is good? Before you answer with a quick automated response, stop and think. Do you really believe that God is always good? Is God good even if I'm in an accident and paralyzed because of it (think of Joni Eareckson Tada)? Is God good if my parents divorce, leaving me with all kinds of emotional baggage? Is God good if one of my children is molested? Is God good if teammates I hoped and prayed for turn out to be unbearable to labor with? Is God good when I see so much suffering around me in the country where I labor to make a difference but never see a change?

It is easy to say that God is good – as a Christian that is the "right" answer. I would never say that God is bad, and I doubt you would either. But is He always good? Where the rubber meets the road and my life hits the bumps, what do I really believe in my heart?

What is your perspective on suffering? Hardship? Difficulties? Where do you see God in those things? What is your view of Him when life goes sour and either you or the people you love are wounded and beat down?

These are important questions to ask yourself. Your perspective on suffering in this world, on hardship in our lives, will be put to the test living in another culture. It's not that life is easy when you live in America or that suffering is avoided. But living in another culture brings out these things in a new way, and your view of God will be tested, refined, and purified.

Years ago, one of the girls I discipled was sharing with me what God was teaching her. She quoted Psalm 34:10, *"those who seek him lack no good thing.*" How did she apply this? With conviction, she said "*...if that's true Tammy, then anything I don't have right now I don't have because it's not good for me.*" This insight has stuck with me and become a foundational truth in my life – the thing I come back to whenever I doubt that the circumstances of my life are "good." God does not withhold good things from his children. If I am seeking Him, then I can be confident that what I have – welcomed or hard – is ultimately good for me.

What you think about God is the most important thing about you.

We often quote from Romans 8:28 when we talk about things being "good": "*And we know that in all things God works for the good of those who love Him, who have been called according to his purpose.*" The problem is that often – without even realizing it – we define "good" as being something that makes our life better or easier or more comfortable. But "good" is defined in verse 29 as being "*conformed to the likeness of his Son...*" Being like Jesus is anything but comfortable or easy. Jesus humbled himself for the sake of people not at all righteous (Phil. 2:5-7); he was "*despised and rejected by men, a man of sorrows, and familiar with suffering*" (Isaiah 53:3); he was falsely accused and ultimately murdered (Matt. 27:11-56). If we want to truly be like Jesus, then it will likely mean that we experience many of these same things – rejection, sorrow, suffering.

The promise of Scripture is that all things ultimately work out for the good of those who love the Lord. But we need to re-think our definition of what is "good". Good as defined by what standards? The world's? Our own? Does good mean easy? Comfortable?

Take some time to mediate on these questions and the verses in FOR FURTHER STUDY. A.W. Tozer says that what you think about God is the most important thing about you. Whether you believe that He is always good or sometimes good will have far reaching consequences on your daily responses to situations in your life.

📖 FOR FURTHER STUDY

Read Exodus 13:17- 14:31 – The Crossing of the Red Sea. Where does God tell the Israelites to go (14:2)? What happens there (14:9)? How do the Israelites respond? How do they feel about their circumstances?

What does God do in the place He has intentionally led his children?

Is God "good" in this situation? How or how not? What can you learn about God's character from His actions? What can you learn/apply from this story about how God works in your life?

Read through the passages below meditating on these three questions:
    How does God's goodness play out in your life?

    What promises can I claim for my life?

    Write out your own definition of "good".

Genesis 50:19-20   John 16:21-22
Psalms 23:1   John 16:33
Psalms 34:9-10   John 15:18-22
Jeremiah 29:11   1 Peter 4:12-16
Jeremiah 32:30, 38-41

Prayer: *God, I trust you to be good in all you are doing in my life. Choose for me better than I would choose for myself.*

THANKFULNESS

Journal entry from 7 months:

> *...the biggest application to my life in the last few weeks is thankfulness - that is the remedy to being me-centered, angry, melancholy, and critical. In* Words that Hurt, Words that Heal *Carole Mayhall says that, "Self pity cannot coexist with thankfulness." And it's so true. The other night during our team worship we took a few minutes - in honor of Thanksgiving - to say something about a teammate for which we were thankful. It was amazing how the atmosphere changed. Not that it had been bad before, but it just lightened. I could physically feel it. And I see the power of thankfulness in my own life - in the little things. Instead of looking at all that is wrong, why am I not looking at all that is right? The list is long. When I'm thankful for my team and the specific things each member brings to the team, I'm not as likely to be angry that they are ["something" I think they should be]. When I'm thankful for what God has done in my life I don't feel melancholy or sad. It's all about perspective.*

There are only a few places in Scripture that expressly say, "*It is God's will...*"[9] One of those places is in 1 Thessalonians 5:16: "*Be joyful always; pray continually; give thanks in all circumstances, for this is God's will for you in Christ Jesus.*" Absolute words are always a good place in Scripture to meditate – God loves absolute words. He doesn't say to give thanks in easy circumstances or to give thanks in some circumstances. He uses the absolute word – give thanks in ALL circumstances.

Thankfulness is God's penicillin: it will cure just about whatever ails you in mind and spirit. In the face of a thankful spirit:

Worries disappear
Complaints vanish

---

9   According to my own study there are 4 – but don't take my word for it. It's an interesting study to find out what things are clearly stated "it is God's will" in the Scriptures.

Joy is restored
Courage increases
Decisions become clearer
Sacrifice becomes satisfying
Peace is experienced
God is glorified

I love movies, and one of my favorite classics is the 1960s version of *Pollyanna* starring Haley Mills. In the movie, Pollyanna is the daughter of a missionary pastor to Africa who returns to the U.S. after the death of her father. She goes to live with her aunt – a wealthy, but controlling and unhappy, spinster. Pollyanna turns the whole town upside down with her indomitable joy and thankfulness. In one scene, she is sitting with the maids in her aunt's house on Sunday afternoon. Everyone is complaining, so Pollyanna teaches them a game that she and her father used to play – the "glad" game. When things are hard and you feel sad, think of something about which you can be glad. The maids don't think there is anything to be glad about on Sunday (the hardest work day of the week for them), until finally Pollyanna says, "*Well I guess we can be glad that Sunday only comes around once a week.*"

"*Give thanks in all circumstances….for this is God's will for you…*" No matter the situation, giving thanks is the key to adjusting our attitude and reminding us of the goodness of God.

✔ LET'S GET PRACTICAL

Take a few minutes and play the "glad" game. Think about the hardest things in your life to date. Think about both current and past difficult circumstances.

What can you be "glad" about in these situations? Give thanks to God for these things.

Take a few more minutes and make a list (either written or in your mind) of all the good things you have to be thankful for in your life. Be specific and don't take for granted anything!

Use the list below to get you started:
Body

    Brain (thinking)
    Blood
    Bones & muscles
    Nose (smell)
    Tongue & Teeth (taste)
    Skin & nerves (feel)
    Eyes (see), Ears (hear)
    Arms & Legs, Hands & Feet
    Thumbs (imagine how hard life would be without
    thumbs or big toes)

Abilities

    Learn & Think
    Read & Write
    Remember
    Speaking English
    Walk (not everyone can)
    Sit & Stand
    Sleep, Eat, Breathe
    Your specific abilities

Spiritual

    Forgiveness
    Word of God
    Men of Faith (David, Peter,etc.)
    Holy Spirit
    Body of Believers
    Spiritual Gifts
    Christian Heritage (personal and/or as an American)
    Purpose

Nature

    Mountains, Clouds
    Rivers, Seas, Oceans
    Sunsets, Colors

Grass, Flowers, Trees
Snow, rain, fire
Sun & Moon
Water (think of all the things water does)

Possessions
Coffee Maker
Bed
Toilet Paper & toilet
Books
U.S. Citizenship

Technology
Electricity
Telescopes & microscopes
Internet
The micro-chip
Washing machines (and dryers!)

Family & Friends
Give thanks by name and contribution to your life. For
example, "thank you Lord for my parents who taught
me generosity and hospitality.

Mentors & Teachers
Give thanks by name and contribution to your life

THE HEART OF THE MATTER

"We are not sinful because we sin, we sin because we are sinful." St. Augustine

In his *Confessions*, St. Augustine writes about the sin in his life that he most regretted. Before becoming a Christian, Augustine was an anti-God, womanizing, alcoholic, partying heathen. But none of these actions were what weighed on his heart or caused him to feel ashamed of his life before Christ. Rather, it was an incident as a young boy that Augustine remembers and regrets. He and some boyhood friends jumped a fence into a neighbor's yard and stole fruit from the neighbor's tree. They didn't steal the fruit to eat it but vindictively destroyed it out of sheer malice. Although the incident was seemingly innocent compared to his other sins, Augustine remembered it later in his life and it reinforced his belief that we are not sinful because we sin (all the sinful actions we do), but we sin because we are sinful (the malicious nature of our sinful hearts).

When I became a believer at 17, there wasn't much outwardly that changed about my life. I knew I was sinful, but my sin was "small" compared to others – or so I thought. During my 1-year stint in Kochevnikstan[10] I began to see just how deeply rooted my sin was, that it wasn't about how I behaved but about what was in my heart. God began teaching me what Augustine had learned centuries earlier.

The most penetrating truth that year came from the book *Inside Out*. In it, Larry Crabb talks about "self-protective sin" which he defines as:

> *"...when our legitimate thirst for receiving love creates a demand to not be hurt that overrides a commitment to lovingly involve our self with others. When that demand for self protection interferes with our willingness to move toward others with their well being in view then the law of love is violated.*

---

10   This was the very first time I went to Kochevnikstan in 1991. I moved there long-term in 2001.

> *The violation is often subtle. It feels natural to protect your-self, just as a desire to make money is natural for someone whose family and friends are poor. He can count on no one else to pay the bills. If he can't trust someone else to take care of what deeply matters to him, then he'd better look out for himself. Self protective relational styles are hard to identify not only because they seem so normal, but also because they are easily disguised in conventional, attractive Christian clothing."*[11]

As I reflected on my life, and as God allowed challenging situations and relationships to cross my path during that year, I began to see just how deeply rooted this self-protective sin was in my life. God opened my eyes to see how much more of my energy I spent protecting myself from being hurt, looking foolish, or making sure I was "right", than I spent loving other people.

That year in Kochevnikstan, I was on a team of six people. Just six of us. There was nowhere to run. Nowhere to hide. When I had relational conflict with one of these six people, I couldn't just avoid them. I couldn't just hang out with a different group of people or go away for the weekend. I was stuck with them and I had a choice. Either I listened to the things God was teaching me and faced my sin of self-protection head on – calling sin "sin", confessing it and begging that HE would change me – or I chose to become hard and calloused, ultimately alienating the only six like-minded Americans I had to relate to for that whole year. I wish I could say I always chose the former, but that's not true. However, by his grace, I did choose more often than not to confront my sin head on and beg God to change my life from the inside out.

In our modern day of counseling and psychological "issues," it's easy to blame others for our sin. We feel justified in our response to others who have hurt us – especially when it was deep hurt or hurt over a prolonged period of time. Our desire to protect our self from hurt overwhelms and snuffs out our desire to love others unconditionally (as Jesus commanded), and we end up "blaming" others and rational-

---

11   *Inside Out* by Larry Crabb p. 117

izing our violation of God's commandment to love. In her book *Lies Women Believe* Nancy Leigh DeMoss says:

> *"When we are angry, depressed, bitter, annoyed, impatient, or fearful, our natural response is to shift at least some of the responsibility onto the people or circumstances that "made" us that way...The enemy tells us that if we accept full responsibility for our own choices, we will be plagued with unnecessary guilt. The truth is that only by accepting full responsibility for our actions and attitudes can we ever be fully free from guilt."*[12]

A friend of mine told me about a dream she had once. She was shut up in a dark room and there were all these frogs – thousands of them everywhere. She hated the frogs, and she wanted to be rid of them. She was ashamed to let anyone know that her room was full of frogs, so she kept all the doors and windows closed. That way no one could see the frogs. But it also meant that the room could never be free of frogs. Finally, in her dream, she got so tired of the frogs filling her room that she swung open the doors and windows. Light streamed into the room and the frogs fled. Sin is like these frogs. We want to keep it shut up so that no one sees it, and yet by shutting it up we prohibit the light from getting in and keep ourselves in bondage.

Scripture tells us to confess our SIN (not our wrongs or weaknesses or badness), and he will forgive us and cleanse us from all unrighteousness.

The crux of the matter is learning to call sin "sin" and to not rationalize it away (the deeper the sin, the harder it is confront it head on). We tend to say that we are weak or wrong or bad. We say we have deep psychological issues because of our upbringing, or that we are the way we are because of what someone else has done to us. But none of these things have any remedy. What can I do if I am "bad"? Can I change to become good? Many people try just this and end up exhausted. If I am

---

12   *Lies Women Believe* by Nancy Leigh DeMoss pp. 104-105

just "wrong" how can I make things "right"? The truth is that I can't. When I say that I am bad or wrong or weak, there is no remedy for these things – only harder work on my part that results not in change but in exhaustion, defeat, and discouragement. BUT when I call sin "sin", when I acknowledge that what is wrong with me is deep within me and beyond my control, then I have a remedy. His name is Jesus. Scripture tells us to confess our SIN (not our wrongs or weaknesses or badness), and he will forgive us and cleanse us from all unrighteousness (1 Jn. 1:9). Nancy Leigh DeMoss quotes:

> "Sin is the best news there is, the best news there could be on our predicament. Because with sin there's a way out. There's the possibility of repentance. You can't repent of confusion or psychological flaws inflicted by your parents – you're stuck with them. But you can repent of sin. Sin and repentance are the only grounds for hope and joy."[13]

I'm so thankful to God that, in his graciousness to me that year in Kochevnikstan (and subsequent years), He has revealed to me this sin of self-protection. Over the years, He has continued to use people and circumstances to root out this subtle and ugly sin in my life that pops up in unexpected places at unexpected times. By his grace, I have developed a habit of taking personal responsibility for MY sin – no matter what the "other person" has done to me. The result has been great freedom to love others better and receive love from them.

📖 FOR FURTHER STUDY

Read Ephesians 4:26-5:2. What happens when we don't deal with sin (4:27)? How are we to love others according to 5:1? Ask yourself, "Do I love others this way?"

When you read my story of self-protective sin – sin in my heart – what is your response? How do you feel?

---

13 *Lies Women Believe* by Nancy Leigh DeMoss p. 105 quoted from John Alexander "And that's that: Sin, Salvation and Woody Allen," *The Other Side*

Meditate on Psalms 51:6 and Psalms 19:12-13 as a prayer. Ask the Lord to open your eyes to your own sin in your heart (versus sin in your behavior).

What is your view of sin? Be honest – is it more about what you do or what is in you?

Meditate on Mark 12:30-3. What does it mean to love the Lord with all our heart? Soul? Mind? Strength? What would it look like in my life, in practical application, if I did this?

What does it mean to love my neighbor as myself (think about my story of self-protective sin)? What would it look like in practical application in your life if you loved your friends and family as you loved yourself?

For even further study, see "B.R.I.D.E." or "H.U.S.B.A.N.D." in the Practical Resources section.

FORGIVENESS FAQs

Forgiving one another is *"the act of setting someone free from an obligation to you that is a result of a wrong done against you"* (Charles Stanley).

PRINCIPLES

Jesus set the example of forgiveness at the cross (Lk. 23:34).

We are to forgive as God forgave us (Eph. 4:32).

Forgiveness is never referred to as a feeling, but it is given as a command to be obeyed (Lk. 6:37).

Harboring unforgiveness hinders my fellowship with God (Lk. 6:37).

It is by faith I forgive – not of myself, but of God's grace on me (Lk. 17:3-4).

"We are never expected to forgive the sins of others but we are expected to forgive others" (Zodhiates commentary).

FREQUENTLY ASKED QUESTIONS - ON FORGIVENESS FROM MAN TO MAN

Are forgiveness and reconciliation the same thing? If not, how are they different?

They are not the same.

Reconcile = to re-establish a close relationship between; to settle or resolve; to make compatible or consistent (American Dictionary). Reconciliation appears only one time in Scripture in reference to a man being reconciled with his brother (Mt. 5:24 1259). Another reference in 1 Corinthians 7:11 refers to a wife being reconciled to her husband. The other times, reconciliation is used to refer to God reconciling man to himself through Jesus.

Forgive = to excuse a fault or offense, pardon; to stop feeling anger or resentment; to absolve from payment (American Dictionary). Forgiveness is used in Scripture to refer to both God forgiving man and man forgiving man. The relationship between two people does not necessarily have to be restored in order for forgiveness (me forgiving another) to take place. Reconciliation is a desired, but not necessary, result of forgiveness.

Is reconciliation by mutual consent between two people? What if only one side wants to reconcile?

In biblical reconciliation, God does all the initiating, but we must accept his overtures in order to be reconciled to Him. We must accept his forgiveness of our wrong doing. (Although Scripture only refers to reconciliation once between brothers, we can – by the example of God's forgiveness – say that reconciliation must be mutual. Even though it is initiated by one person, it must be received by the other.)

Is forgiveness a feeling? Do I have to feel forgiving to forgive?

Scripture never refers to forgiveness as a feeling. It is most often a command to be obeyed. By faith, we trust that the Lord will give us the "feeling" of joy and confidence that comes with obeying his commands.

What are the results of forgiveness? Unforgiveness?

If forgiveness is a command to be obeyed (Lk. 6:37), then like all obedience, forgiveness brings fellowship with God and thus manifestations of the fruit of the Spirit (Gal. 5:22). Likewise, unforgiveness, like any sin, hinders my relationship with God. I cannot approach God to fellowship with him with unforgiveness harbored in my heart (Mk. 11:25; Matt. 6:14).

Is confession/repentance necessary for forgiveness? Does a person have to ask for forgiveness for me to forgive them?

Scripture does associate repentance and confession with forgiveness man to man (Lk. 17:3-4), but it does not seem to be a prerequisite for my forgiving an offense committed against me (Mk. 11:25), since forgiveness is an act of obedience to God. However, my forgiving an offense done to me IS necessary to God's forgiving me (Lk. 6:37).

How often is forgiveness (our forgiving others) associated with faith?

At least twice. First, in Luke 17:1-6 when the Lord says that we should forgive as many times as someone asks for forgiveness. The disciples' response is, *"Increase our faith."* Also in Mark 11:25, Jesus teaches that we will receive whatever we ask for in prayer if we believe it. The next verse commands us to forgive anything we hold against anyone so that God will forgive US our sins (so that our prayers will be heard).

SUMMARY

Forgiveness is supernatural; on our own we cannot forgive hurts against us. Our fallen, sinful nature won't allow it – at least not time and time again. The basis for our forgiveness is faith in God, that HE will give us what is needed to forgive others. Philippians 2:13 says, *"God is at work in us helping us to want to obey him and then helping us do what he wants"* (TLV). Let us say with the disciples, *"Lord, increase our faith!"*

✏ ON YOUR OWN

Is there anyone in your life you need to forgive? Anyone you need to ask forgiveness from?

Do your own study on forgiveness starting with the key verses mentioned in this chapter. What does the Lord want to stay to you about forgiveness (His forgiveness of you or your forgiveness toward others)?

Deepening Your Understanding

9-12 months

SEEK TO UNDERSTAND
Seek to understand before being understood

The deeper we get into a culture, the more we uncover the good, the bad, and the ugly. It's easy to be judgmental and critical of things that are different. Remember, *"different isn't wrong it's just different."* But what if things aren't just different? What if they ARE wrong? What if we see in the culture (our own or our host culture) things that are clearly a violation of Kingdom Culture values? Take lying, adultery, corruption, and injustice for example; those things aren't just different, they are wrong according to Scripture. Right?

One of my good friends loves to remind me that life is messy. It is simply not as black and white as we wish it was. Abraham, the father of Christianity, lied about Sarah being his wife (and asked her to lie for him) in order to protect himself. Jacob, the patriarch of the 12 tribes of Israel, cheated his brother out of his birthright and lied to his father about it. Judah slept with a prostitute, who was really his daughter-in-law deceiving him, which resulted in twin sons who are ancestors of Jesus. David, a man after God's own heart, committed adultery and tried to cover it up with murder. Peter, an intimate disciple of Jesus, lied about his relationship to Jesus in order to protect himself and save face. These were great men of faith – our spiritual ancestors – but their lives were messy!

As you begin to uncover differences and messy situations in your new culture, it's important that you seek to understand before being understood. What is the value that drives this behavior? What's the result of this choice in the culture? Where does this belief come from? I'm not saying that we in any way compromise the truth. But if we want to have any lasting impact, it's essential that we seek to understand the underlying motivations and traditions that drive our cross-cultural friends.

Jesus was brilliant at understanding what motivated people – of course he is God, so He knows everything – but we can learn a lot from how Jesus related to people and asked questions. I love the way Jesus was able to put the Pharisees in their place with one question and the way he lovingly cut through the traditions and excuses of an adulterous woman with a series of probing questions and statements (Mark 12:13-17, John 4:1-26).[1] Jesus didn't make snap judgments based solely on outward appearances; he sought to understand the deeper things going on in a person, a situation, or a culture.

As you begin to uncover differences and messy situations in your new culture, it's important that you seek to understand before being understood.

Following Jesus' example, we need to grow in our understanding of people and the things that drive them. *"Wisdom is supreme; therefore get wisdom. Though it cost all you have get understanding"* (Prov. 4:7). The next two chapters, "Lying" and "Cheating," are based on my own real struggles with "wrong" things in Kochevnik culture. As I pushed through the "wrongness" and sought to understand, I found that this understanding helped me move from judgment and criticism to grace and compassion for my new culture.

📖 FOR FURTHER STUDY

Do a study on the questions Jesus asked as he interacted with people. You can use Mark 12:13-17 and John 4:1-26 as a starting point.

Do the "Understanding Bible Study" in the Practical Resources section.

---

1   In his book *Desiring God* pp. 73-76, John Piper calls Jesus a Soul Hunter and unpacks Jesus' conversation with the Woman at the Well in light of this.

LYING

It was already 7:00pm, and I had invited two girls from my English class to come to dinner at 6:00pm. After an hour of waiting, I decided that something had happened. Not only were they not coming, they were not going to call and let me know they weren't coming. In that moment, I understood why locals never cooked the hot dish until after the guests arrived; they were never sure the guests were really coming!

The next day at the university, I saw these two girls and naturally asked them what had happened. They looked a little uncomfortable, and one of the girls shared that her dad had a heart attack. How awful! I felt so bad that I had been frustrated with the girls for not showing up, and something had happened that was far worse than missing a dinner invitation. I asked a few questions, gave my condolences, and we went our separate ways. About a week later, wanting to show my genuine concern for her and family, I asked again about the girl's father. She looked a little sheepish and said that yes, her dad was fine. He was out of the hospital and back at work. Back at work a week after a massive heart attack? In Kochevnikstan, people spend a week in the hospital for a bump on the head. The more questions I asked in attempts to understand, the more the girl got uncomfortable until she and her friend finally hurried off, eager to escape my inquisitiveness. I stood there trying to comprehend what had just happened, and then somehow, God opened my eyes – I understood. The girl's dad had not really had a heart attack. It was an excuse for not coming to my house for dinner.

I come from a family where lying is the ultimate sin. No matter what you did, it could never be as bad as LYING about what you did! For me, lying about something as serious as your father having a heart attack was incomprehensible. If the girls didn't want to come to dinner at my house, all they had to do was say so. I did not understand, but I wanted to seek to understand why someone would lie about something so big over something so small.

As I thought about it and talked with other ex-pats about this phenomenon, I began to gain some insight. In Kochevnikstani culture, as in most Asian cultures, saving face is one the greatest values. People do whatever they have to in order to avoid being shamed or shaming others. If lying saves face, then lying is justified. These girls either couldn't come to my house for dinner or didn't want to, but either way, they didn't want to tell me that directly. They didn't want to shame me by saying no, and they didn't want to feel ashamed for not "honoring" me since I was their elder and teacher. So they did what their culture teaches them, and lied to me - lied to my face! When the lie is so big and unbelievable, I'm supposed to know somehow that it's a lie and to not be offended that they lied. If I know it's not the truth, then it's really not a lie – at least that's how the local logic goes.

Scripture is pretty clear that *"lying lips are an abomination to the Lord"* (Prov. 12:22). One of my local friends who had just become a believer called me one day, asking me what "abomination" meant. She had read this verse in her English Bible and didn't understand. It became one of her favorite words, and from that day on, she was very convicted about lying. She swam against the culture in her attempt to never lie.

Lying is a messy thing. Didn't Rahab lie to protect the spies in her house (Joshua 2)? While lying might be messy, it is certainly NOT a Kingdom Culture value that we want to promote. Personally, I still hate it. Lying is NOT a way I want to become culturally relevant. Telling the truth is ingrained in me from childhood and reinforced by my understanding of Scripture. BUT this pursuit of understanding helped me become less judgmental of the cultural lying I encountered every day. I have a better understanding of why it happens, and that cultivates patience and compassion in me instead of frustration and criticism.

✏ ON YOUR OWN

What cultural values in your host culture seem outright "wrong" to you? Begin to seek to understand why that "wrong" thing happens.

Think about your own family values (like honesty was for me). How do these come into play in how you view your new culture?

CHEATING

Cheating is rampant in Kochevnikstan. It is accepted and expected. Students share homework, test answers, and term papers. You can buy test answers on the street – often because the teacher has sold them to a student who passes them on for a profit. Students are incredibly creative in coming up with new ways to cheat, and as a teacher it's almost impossible to control it.

I taught English at a prestigious university. These were not poor, uneducated students but the cream of the crop: intelligent, self- motivated, ambitious, future leaders. And yet, they cheated all the time. It was against school policy to cheat and punishable by expulsion. And yet they cheated. My North American mind could NOT comprehend the reason behind this behavior. Why would these students not WANT to learn? And for those who did want to learn, why would they allow their friends to cheat off them. Ultimately you aren't helping anyone learn if you let them cheat off of you, right?

One day in my classroom, I had enough of the cheating. I stopped class, ditched my lesson plan, and we had an open debate. I was determined to understand what motivated these bright and gifted students to cheat. I set the stage by telling my students that they could be completely open and honest with me. I was not judging them, but I really wanted to understand WHY they cheat. Did they really think cheating helped them? Helped their friends? Could they "cheat" when they were in the workplace? How did cheating help them get a better job or be prepared to do a good job? The students opened up, were honest, and really engaged with me and each other over the topic. What emerged from that discussion was a deeper understanding – not just for me, but for them too – of WHY they cheat. The bottom line was that relationships are more valuable than learning and more valuable than the fear of breaking the rules (i.e., cheating).

My students tried to explain it to me: *"If my friend asks me to let him cheat off my homework paper – I HAVE TO help him. I have to let him cheat because he's my friend."* Logically a North American might say (and believe me, I did in our classroom discussion) that you aren't really helping your friend in the long run. But in an Asian culture, the here and now relationship is more important than the future one. Even if they don't really want to cheat, they can't say no because the friend is more valuable than not breaking the rules. For those who take a stand against helping their friends cheat, there's often a social exile that isolates them from the rest of their groupmates. America is an individualistic culture, but Asian cultures are collective and the person who refuses to abide by the collective value is ostracized. Given the choice between helping a friend cheat or saying no to helping him – my students all agreed they would help their friend.

If relationship is the real value – a Kingdom Culture value – then how can I help my local friends embrace this value and apply it in more productive ways than cheating?!

I still hate cheating and don't think it's a good thing – for anyone. But I DID gain insight and understanding. From their point of view, their action made sense. And while cheating may not be a Kingdom Culture value, a relationship certainly is. We are to love one another, serve one another, consider one another, submit to one another, etc.

Seeking to understand the value (relationship) driving the action (cheating) not only helped lessen my frustration at my students for cheating, but it also gave me a place to begin to champion in them a Kingdom value they already held dear. If relationship is the real value – a Kingdom Culture value – then how can I help my local friends embrace this value and apply it in more productive ways than cheating?!

✔ LET'S GET PRACTICAL

What can you do to create an open discussion – like I did in my classroom – that will give you and some local friends an opportunity to discuss issues in the culture (or the differences between your two cultures)? What are the issues you think the group needs to discuss?

MARTHA'S STORY: CONFLICTING VALUES

*A first-hand account of how conflicting values
can play out on the field[2]*

"If it's not illegal, immoral, or life-threatening, then use your own good judgment." That's what my parents used to say when I asked them for advice. I still think that's wise. But there's a small problem: "good judgment" is based on some set of values. And when you're living cross-culturally, you get caught between two sets of values.

HOW VALUES PLAY OUT AT WORK

So there I was, in an office with 4 or 5 girls, facing a daunting pile of exams that needed to be graded. They were multiple-choice exams on fill-in-the-bubble pages that look like Scantron sheets, only we don't have that technology in Durvistan yet, so we were supposed to grade them by hand with a red pen. Fun, fun.

As the other girls were slowly plugging away at that, some of them were muttering to themselves *"B...C...B..."* – not exactly helping my concentration. So I filled in a clean answer sheet with the correct answers from the key and taped it to the window. I could hold an exam up to my key, see where all the wrong answers were immediately, and have it graded in like 10 seconds. Work smarter, not harder, right?

Wrong. The other girls were aghast. *"Don't do it that way! Mr. Ali will catch you!"* I didn't get it. Can't I just explain to Mr. Ali [the man in charge of this exam-grading operation] that this is a better method, and won't he appreciate my time-saving ingenuity?

Apparently not. The other girls were convinced that Mr. Ali would feel really disrespected to find someone who wasn't following his instructions. Plus they were skeptical about the accuracy of my method (just for the record, I was skeptical about theirs as well).

One girl, Jen, finally saw the light and came over to the window to start

---

2   This story was written by a friend who works in a Muslim background country of "Durvistan" - a made up name. All names are aliases to protect her local friends. "Mama Pearl" is my friend's host mother.

grading tests like I was. The work was really picking up speed then. But she kept glancing towards the door saying, *"If Mr. Ali comes, someone shout, and I'm going to hide what I'm doing!"*

Was I doing something wrong? Not at all, if you judge by American values of efficiency and pragmatism. But it was outside the lines if you judge by the Duvari values of respect, doing exactly as you're told, and working in such a way that no one can criticize you later. They don't feel like they have the right to think independently much of the time. So much depends on values.

HOW VALUES PLAY OUT WITH GUESTS AT HOME

It's been a month since Mama Pearl's surgery, and we've had guests over almost every single evening to support her in her recovery. Last night, there were guests in the house when I got home from work, like always. They had shown up unannounced, like always.

When guests show up around mealtime, we have the option to have them eat with us or to just serve tea. This time there didn't happen to be enough food ready to feed the 10 people who were in the house… so those of us who lived there had to wait until after 9 when they left before we could eat our dinner. Which, by the way, we didn't manage to finish before the next round of guests arrived.

That's kind of a worst-case scenario, but you can see why it's a bit exhausting psychologically to have as many guests as we have this month; you never know when someone is going to show up, and you're going to have to drop everything and sit with them (but don't interpret this as complaining – they are, after all, people I like).

Could I just run off to my own room and be alone in the evenings? As an American who "needs" space, absolutely. But as an honorable Duvari daughter of a respected family, not without some explanation.

Is there something wrong with the way this culture is set up? Yes, if you judge with American values like comfort, respect for others' time and space, and the idea that people should control their own schedules. But not if you judge with Duvari values of supporting each other,

195

spending time together as a priority over other plans, hospitality, and earning respect in the community.

HOW VALUES PLAY OUT IN HOUSEWORK

Mama Pearl is feeling pretty well now, but still can't do much housework. We finally went out and bought a washing machine for laundry! I feel like we just fast-forwarded a few decades in our house!

But not when it comes to vacuuming. Their method of vacuuming involves crawling around on the floor with a brush in one hand to brush the dirt up from the carpet, and the open vacuum cleaner hose in the other hand sucking it up – no attachments, long handles or fancy nozzles involved. Mama Pearl is definitely not up to that yet.

Vacuuming has to be done every other day, because... well... I guess because that's the standard (never mind American values of convenience, efficiency or having enough privacy in your own home to be immune to other people's judgments of it...Here it's all about cleanliness, aesthetics, doing things the "right" way, and respectability!).

The three village relatives who had been staying with us for the month just left. So now the vacuuming duties probably fall to yours truly. Mama Pearl really hates asking me to do it, but who else can help vacuum? (Nope, not a boy job here. That would insult their value of masculinity.) Her values of hospitality and respectability trump the idea of leaving the house dirty or hiring some stranger to come clean.

Could I refuse to do it? Could I say, "*this is why I pay rent money, so I don't have to do things like this?*" Yeah, I could. But that would be saying, "*I care about myself more than about you,*" and would drive a wedge into the mutual understanding that our family has built. Could I go out and buy a nice modern vacuum? Probably, but she wouldn't trust it to do the job as well as a brush and hose.

So there we are. If it so happens that I'm laughing to myself, crawling around on the carpet every other day before work for the next few weeks, you can pray that I won't feel enslaved by American values OR by Duvari values, but that I will rejoice in the relationships that have been built here and that my mind will be fixed on what takes first priority in God's book (Heb. 12:2)!

✏ ON YOUR OWN

What parts of Martha's story resonate with you? What conflicting values have you encountered as you assimilate into your host culture?

If you were in Martha's shoes what would your response be in each of the situations she mentions? (I wish I could honestly say that I would respond the way Martha does, but I'm not sure. I so respect Martha's love of people and willingness to do whatever it takes to build bridges.)

GOD'S WORD IS NOT CHAINED

Journal Entry at 9 months:

*In addition to TIME and PERSEVERANCE being key ele-
ments in language learning, I realize – not for the first time –
learning language is HUMBLING. Of course it's humbling,
because you walk around sounding like a child (but looking
like an adult). But for me personally, it's more than that.
I take pride (yes, there is that ugly word) in my ability to
communicate. You might even say it's one place I frequently
put significance. I LIKE being able to say EXACTLY what I
mean in EXACTLY the way I mean it (of course some might
argue that I'm not good at doing that!). Last night before I
started studying I was talking with my local roommate who
had a small "crisis of faith" in her life. Without understanding every word of what she was telling me, I understood
that it was simply a matter of being afraid to "step out in
faith." I KNOW how to counsel, encourage, and exhort her
in English – but in this new language? I was humbled at
MY inability to "speak words of wisdom" (I know it sounds
arrogant that I would even think that?). I couldn't communicate adequately. I said what I could – but even that kept
being interrupted by my need to use an example to explain
a word that I was trying to use so that my "normally logical counsel" rabbit trailed until it was unrecognizable! It's
amazing that she understood anything! And in reality it IS
amazing – it's amazing because it is HIM who gives understanding – NOT MY WORDS whether they are in English
or in my second language. I keep thinking of the verse from
Paul's Second letter to Timothy – 'though I am in chains,
the word of God is NOT in chains.' It is HIS words – not
my clear communication in English or my childlike words of
this new language – that changes lives!*

*"Remember Jesus Christ, raised from the dead, descended
from David. This is my gospel, for which I am suffering
even to the point of being chained like a criminal. But*

God's word is not chained. Therefore I endure everything
for the sake of the elect, that they too may obtain the salva-
tion that is in Christ Jesus, with eternal glory."

2 Timothy 2:8-10

I love the second chapter of Second Timothy, but to be honest I had never thought about these verses until I started learning language. I feel like I identify with Paul; I'm not physically in jail, but in a very real way I felt like my tongue was chained in those early years of learning language. No matter how hard I tried, I simply could not make myself understood – at least not in a way that I thought was effective. I realize that not everyone is as much of a words person as I am, but for me this place of "inability to communicate" was a major shake up point in my life. God squeezed, and what came out was a deeply rooted sense of self-sufficiency in my own ability to clearly communicate the Gospel. It's not that I would have ever said that my words changed people's lives. But when I was unable to say what I wanted to say, I realized how I put more confidence in my words than I thought.

Instead of me giving advice, and people unintentionally becoming dependent on my words, I turned people directly toward THE Word.

God is good and uses everything in our lives for good. Through this experience of not being able to say what I wanted to say in the way I wanted to say it, I learned to rely on God's Word more and more. Not just for what His Word could teach me, but for how HIS word was the most powerful way to speak into the lives of others. Instead of me giving advice, and people unintentionally becoming dependent on my words, I turned people directly toward THE Word.[3] I would write down a list of verses that spoke to whatever subject we were talking about and either my local friend would read on her own or we would read the verses together (she read, I followed along); direct interaction with the Word of God, not second translation (through my words). It

---

3   I realize that some readers might be in a culture that does not have the written word of God. In that case, I honestly don't know what to tell you except to pray the Word of God into people's lives.

also forced me to pray more that the "living and active" word of God (Heb. 4:12) would penetrate deeply into my friend's life and that the Holy Spirit would convict her of sin and righteousness.

As my language abilities increased, I became better able to communicate what I wanted to say. But this lesson that God's Word is not chained has stuck with me. Even in English when I can pretty much say everything I want to say with the appropriate nuance of meaning, I realize that my words will not change someone's heart or mind. I can challenge and promote and point out, but ultimately ONLY God's Word is living and active, sharper than a double edged sword that is able to pierce a heart. John writes that *"He must become greater, we must become lesser"* and language learning is one very effective means to that ultimate end (John 3:30).

✏ ON YOUR OWN

Does it bother you if you can't say what you want to communicate? If so, why? Use the "4 Why" method to go deeper into this reflection.

How might it be possible to engage a non-believing local friend in a "conversation" about some topic using only the Word of God? For example, I had a friend who was very existential in her thinking. I asked her to read Ecclesiastes so we could talk about her thoughts on it.

CONFESSIONS OF A MONOLINGUAL

What do you call a person who speaks three languages?
What do you call a person who speaks two languages?
What do you call a person who speaks one language?[4]

If you've never heard this joke, chances are you will abroad. It's a common international perception – and a true one most of the time – that Americans are monolingual people. We grow up speaking English and nothing else.[5] Perhaps we have some friends who speak another language or we have adopted a few words of another language into our vocabulary (English is full of adopted words),[6] but we are by and large comfortable in speaking and hearing one language.

My point here is not to be disrespectful to my own culture but to be realistic. Much of the world grows up in a multi-lingual environment. South Africa has 11 official languages. Educated Europeans who grew up on the continent (and not in England) usually speak their native language, English, and one of the other common European languages (e.g., French, German or Spanish). It makes sense; if you drive a few hours in Europe you're not just in another State, you are in another country! As North Americans with limited opportunities to actually speak a second or third language in real life situations, we are used to being part of and listening to monolingual dialogues.

I remember the first time I realized – not just in my head but through experience – that I was not living in a monolingual country (Kochevnikstan is trilingual – three primary languages with a few other ethnic languages mixed in). I was walking through the bazaar, taking in all the sights and listening to the sellers sing-song voices trying to convince shoppers that they had the best bargains. I was listening

---

4   Trilingual, Bilingual, American
5   There are a few areas of America where this might not be true. Perhaps your region is Spanish or Chinese speaking or heavily saturated with a particular immigrant culture. But by and large, America is monolingual when compared to other nations. South American Spanish speakers might be the one exception.
6   The museum on Ellis Island in New York City has this amazing display of hundreds of words that have been adopted into English from other languages – the great American melting pot.

for new vocabulary in the language I was learning. I'd hear a string of words I recognized and then a word or two that was completely foreign – words from one of the other primary languages. The sing-song voice never paused, just integrated the two languages into one sentence. So what does this have to do with language learning?

God is not limited to working through just one language, and HE is comfortable in a multi-lingual environment.

After being in Kochevnikstan for about 2 years, I started to feel frustrated with my language development. It wasn't progressing. I could communicate basic things, but once I got to a certain point, it seemed I couldn't go any farther. On top of that, I felt like my English was digressing. I would forget simple English words. I spoke in choppy, grammatically incorrect sentences (because that is what I was hearing from my English-as-a-second-language friends on a daily basis). I picked up ways of saying things that were not the way we say things in English (like "*I feel myself...*"). Of course, my English was still much better than my new language, but it felt like I could speak neither language well. The worst part was that Satan, in his deceitfulness, latched onto my frustration and fed me lie after lie.

"*You'll never be able to speak well enough to clearly share the Gospel.*"

"*If you can't say everything you want in this new language, then you should say nothing at all.*"

"*You can't speak truth part in Kochevnik and part in English – that is unacceptable.*"

I remember sharing my frustrations and feelings of defeat with an American friend who had been in country longer than me. She listened to me vent and then gently but directly said, "*Tammy, those are lies from the pit of hell. If you can't say all of what you want to in the local language then say what you can and then switch to English. It doesn't have to be either or; use BOTH languages. God is not limited to working through just one language, and HE is comfortable in a multi-lingual environment."*

Such freeing words for me – simple but true. I began to realize that my monolingual upbringing made me feel like I needed to be operating fluently in one language or the other. But the reality of my life was that I was living in a multi-lingual culture where people were used to switching back and forth from one language to another. It's the way they grew up. While it felt unnatural to me, it did not seem unnatural to my local friends. My own limiting mentality was a stumbling block for me being confident sharing the Gospel. It was another reminder that God's Word – and His words through my limited bilingual language – is not chained.

✎ ON YOUR OWN

Is your new culture monolingual? Bilingual? Or perhaps speaking multiple languages at one time? How do your local friends think about this? Have a discussion with a trusted local friend about growing up in a world that naturally incorporates 2-3 or more languages.

Do you experience any of the same frustrations I did at living in a multi-lingual world? What are the lies you have a tendency to buy into? What is the truth that counteracts those lies?

WARTIME LIFESTYLE

My first major purchase in Kochevnikstan – and my biggest purchase in life besides my car and house – was a custom made green suede-like sectional and sofa bed. It was beautiful and comfy (not hard like the majority of couches in Kochevnikstan). I wrestled for months trying to decide if it was really worth the cost. After all, I could have just "made due" with some second hand local piece of furniture (although second hand furniture was rare – Kochevnikstanis don't get rid of stuff like Americans, and when they do finally get rid of something it's because it isn't usable anymore!). But the question that nagged at me was "*is this really a worthwhile investment*"? Yes, I needed (or at least wanted) a couch to sit on, and if I'm honest, I wanted it to be beautiful and comfy. I wanted my home to be inviting and a "safe" place. But at the end of the day, what were the cost benefits of investing in such an expensive piece of furniture?

Different people have different values on how things should look and how much money is an "acceptable" cost. At the time I was wrestling with whether or not to purchase this couch, I had two single guy teammates who grew up on a farm and were very frugal. I don't think I ever knew them to buy a piece of clothing in the 3 years they lived in Orchard City, and they certainly did not buy any furniture (not even a mattress). For the longest time, they only ate white food (bread, rice, boiled chicken, pasta) because it was easy as well as cheap. How things looked was simply not important to them and it never seemed to bother the stream of college guys they always had at their house.

My goal is not to draw conclusions about how one should or should not spend his money; that is an individual decision and in my experience every person is different in the decisions they make about money.[7] My goal here is to introduce a perspective that has given me a grid of thinking about spending money in a way that evaluates more than just how much something costs (i.e., if it costs a lot, it's not worth it; if it costs a little, it's a good deal).

---

7   I DO encourage each person to give intentional thought to his or her own values and principles about how to spend, save, and invest money.

I first heard of this revolutionary (but simple) perspective in a biography I read about Dr. Ralph Winter who was, at the time, the Director for the U.S. Center for World Missions (USCWM). The Winters lived what they called a "wartime lifestyle." A wartime lifestyle differs from a simple lifestyle. To live simply is really about how much something does or does not cost with an emphasis on needing as little as possible. But according to Ralph, "*If a man is out in a trench and he's eating K rations [military issued food packs], he's not using up much money, but a guy who's flying a fighter plane may be using up $40,000 a month of technology. In other words, during wartime one doesn't judge according to the same model of lifestyle. What's important is getting the job done.*"[8]

The Winters practice what they preach and live out a wartime lifestyle. At the time this biography was written, Ralph drove a car that was in its third 100,000 mile cycle. He was "*often seen wearing the same blue sports coat that he picked out of the missionary barrel.*" But the offices at the USCWM made use of the latest computerized technology and expensive express mail services.[9] Whatever it takes to win the war!

Consider a lesson from World War II. The U.S.A. was fighting a war on two fronts, and the federal government halted the production of many consumer items. For example, car manufacturers were told to stop regular production and instead assemble armored vehicles for use on the battlefield. The Federal government also implemented the use of "ration stamps," encouraging the American people to conserve, conserve, conserve. "Normal" household items like gas, oil, butter, and meat required ration stamps and were only allowed to be purchased in limited quantities. The American people were making more money but had fewer items to spend their earnings on, so they saved for the future,[10] which is a major contributing factor to the end of the Great Depression.

At the same time that the Federal government was asking the general population to conserve, conserve, conserve, they were spending more money on defense than ever before. In 1941, 47% of all federal

---

8   From *Jerusalem to Irian Jaya* by Ruth Tucker p. 481
9   From *Jerusalem to Irian Jaya* by Ruth Tucker p. 481
10   From http://www.shmoop.com/wwii-home-front/economy.html

spending went to defense. By 1945 that number had almost doubled – 89.49% of all federal spending was directed toward the war effort, the defense of the nation.[11] While the American people sacrificed everyday necessities, the federal government spent generously. Both made decisions and choices committed to the same goal – whatever it took to win the war!

A wartime lifestyle is about evaluating every purchase and decision through the matrix of "what will it take to win the war?"

After much wrestling and asking God for wisdom, I bought my comfy couch which eventually became known as "green couch." It was the most expensive piece of furniture I ever bought. For the sake of comparison, when I moved back to the U.S. ten years later, I purchased my whole house full of furniture second hand for about a quarter of what green couch cost! But it was an investment in eternity. That beautiful and comfy couch was the site of many significant conversations about the Kingdom of God. It moved with me 4 times and came to represent "Tammy's house" – a place of safety and refuge where students I invested in and teammates I labored with could relax and feel at home. Eventually green couch was passed on to one of my teammates where it continued to be used to advance the Kingdom. It became so much a part of our team and family that when these friends moved to a new house, their teenage son made one request: green couch had to move with them!

You can laugh at the silliness of naming a couch or talking about it like a person (really, I laugh at it myself!). The financial cost of that couch was nothing compared to the eternal value of it. When we think about our standard of living, what we really need, the place to look is not around us but to look to the Lord and ask Him, *"Will this advance the war effort? Is this purchase an investment in eternity?"*

A wartime lifestyle is about much more than living "simply." It's about

---

11   1941-1945 GDP figures calculated using Bureau of Labor Statistics "CPI Inflation Calculator"

more than not spending money. A wartime lifestyle is about evaluating every purchase and decision through the matrix of *"what will it take to win the war?"* What are the things that I can sacrifice now (and store up treasure in heaven) that will help move the war effort forward? And what are the things I need to "splurge" on to contribute to the end goal of moving the war effort forward? At the end of the day only YOU can answer those questions for yourself, and you alone will stand before God answering how you have stewarded the resources He's provided you.

📖 FOR FURTHER STUDY

Read the parable of the talents (Matt. 25:14-30). Which of the three servants lived with a wartime mentality? Which did not? What does the master say to the servant(s) who invested wisely? To the servant who did not?

Read 2 Corinthians 4:16-18. In a culture that sells us "buy now, pay later" how can you intentionally cultivate an eternal perspective, fixing your eyes on what is unseen?

Honestly evaluate your own life. In what ways do you live a wartime lifestyle? In what ways can you "sacrifice" what does not contribute to the war effort and "splurge" on what does?

POOR TALK AND OTHER FOUR LETTER WORDS

Years ago I heard a series of talks about our perspective while raising support. The thing that stuck out to me the most was the speaker talking about how those of us in ministry often fall prey to "poor talk." Poor talk is when we make subtle comments about how much money we don't have. Things like *"I'm so poor I can't afford..."* or *"Us poor missionaries..."* Maybe the comments are made in jest with a quick laugh, but often comments made in jest reveal a deeper attitude we don't even realize we have.

"Poor talk" comments reveal one of two things. First, there might be something deeper going on – a lie that's taken root that I don't have what I "need" or that I don't have "enough." We would never consciously say that God has not provided for us, and yet with our "poor talk" we are saying just that.

The second thing that might be happening when we make a "poor talk" comment is that we are simply saying something out of habit. In my opinion, this is even worse than comments made because of a lie we believe. Careless words are dangerous. Even if at a heart level we don't believe the "poor talk," just by saying it we are either planting the seed of untruth in our own life as a self-fulfilling prophecy or in someone else's life.

"Poor talk" is specific to comments about money, but the same idea applies to other "four-letter" words. If someone asks how you are doing, what is your most common answer? Is it good, fine, busy, or tired (I realize "tired" is a 5 letter word)? Good and fine are so non-descriptive that they don't tell anyone anything; they are "habit" words. And are you really busy? Do you even want your life to be "busy"? And if you are so tired, why is that? What are you doing in your life that makes you so "busy" or so "tired"?

I remember getting to a place in my life where I was tired of saying that I was tired all the time, so I chose to eliminate the word "tired" from my vocabulary. While there were things in my life that caused me to be emotionally more tired than usual, I realized that my habitual, default answer was only reinforcing in my own mind the feelings of being tired. Through this exercise, I became more aware of what was really going on in me. Every time I started to say, "*I'm tired*," I caught myself and in my mind I thought, "*Is that really true?*" If it IS true, why is that? Jesus says in Matthew 11, "*Come to me all who are weary and burdened and I will give you rest.*" Does God really want me to live a tired life? Choosing to eliminate the word served to heighten my awareness of just how often I defaulted to it.

Careless words are dangerous.

Beware of common habit words especially "shoulda woulda coulda" syndrome. For example, when I look back at a situation I realize that I "*should have done this differently*" or "*I could have changed that*" or "*if only I would have known this sooner.*" I can learn from my past choices so that I make different ones in the future. Honest evaluation is healthy. But what is not healthy is wallowing in the shoulda woulda couldas and not being able to move forward. God is just as sovereign over my mistakes as he is over my victories.

Words carry weight and we have a responsibility to be wise with how we use them.

✎ ON YOUR OWN

What are "habit" words you find yourself saying all the time? How often do you use them? Ask yourself why you say this all the time. What's going on in my perspective/attitude when I say this word?

Make a list of your "habit words," then find a Scripture verse that speaks truth to that word.

For example: I am poor (Phil. 4:19), I am tired (Matt. 11:28), I am busy (John 17:4), I should have (Eph. 1:11).

LEADING FROM YOUR KNEES

One of the most challenging stories I've heard about prayer is about an itinerant minister in China. This minister had four different village pastors that he traveled to visit several times a year, encouraging and strengthening them in their faith. During a particularly rainy season, there was a mudslide that cut off the itinerant pastor from visiting one of the four village pastors. He decided that he would commit to pray for the village pastor and for his flock every day until the rainy season passed and he was able to visit him in person. He continued to visit the other three village pastors as usual, and he faithfully prayed daily for the fourth pastor. Eventually the way was clear enough to visit the fourth village pastor.

When he arrived in the village, the itinerant pastor was amazed. Not only was his friend and disciple flourishing in his own spiritual growth, but the village church had grown exponentially in the short time the way had been closed for the itinerant pastor to visit. Indeed the fourth village pastor and his church was spiritually healthier than the other 3 pastors the itinerant minister had been faithfully visiting. His prayers had a greater effect than his visits. (I can't confirm 100% that the story is true, but even if it's not, I believe the principle behind it is – and it challenges me).

Praying is not only a way to eternally influence the lives of the men and women God entrusts to us, it's also a way we consciously depend on God.

When I heard this story I was convicted, to say the least. It's not that I don't pray, but if I'm honest, it's not always my "first" response. I take a lot of pride (the wrongful kind) in my ability to communicate, to encourage, speak truth, or offer wisdom. I DO believe that God uses me in these ways to sharpen and strengthen the body. But only God causes growth in people's lives (1 Corinth. 3:6-7). I'm sure you've heard the old proverb: spend more time talking to God about people than talking to people about God.

When I got to Kochevnikstan, learning to pray for people took on new meaning; more often than not it was the ONLY way I could really influence their lives. My language was limited, which really hinders your ability to speak words of truth, wisdom, or encouragement.

A friend once told me, *"It's the hardest thing in the world to trust God to do in someone else's life what He's done in your life."* And I believe it. Praying is not only a way to eternally influence the lives of the men and women God entrusts to us, it's also a way we consciously depend on God. Prayer is a reminder to us that only God causes the growth and that the best leaders lead from their knees.

📖 FOR FURTHER STUDY

In Luke 11:1-4, Jesus teaches his men to pray. HOW did he pray? WHAT was on His Heart? WHAT did He pray?

In John 17, Jesus prays for his disciples. HOW did He pray? WHAT did He pray for them?

Read through the Gospels ND take note of other examples of what, when, and how Jesus prayed.

EXPANDING YOUR COMMUNITY

Thanksgiving was one of my favorite holidays in Kochevnikstan. I know that's strange since Thanksgiving is not a Kochevnik holiday and is very American. But Thanksgiving in Kochevnikstan came to represent for me a picture of the international body of Christ and how I belonged to it.

My very first Thanksgiving in Orchard City, I celebrated with over 60 people from 7 different countries. The day was a "normal" work day for Kochevnikstani's: people went to work, nothing was closed, no painted turkeys in shop windows. Even the international school had class for half the day. But at my teammate's house an international community gathered for a day of celebration. We ate traditional American Thanksgiving food alongside Australian cookies, Dutch dessert, and Kochevnikstani bread. We spent time in worship and thanksgiving – the voices of the nations raised in praise. There were skits by all the kids (and even a few adults). My favorite activity that day was a sing-along of all kinds of 60s, 70s, and 80s oldies with my Japanese friend leading the way – her knowledge of American music amazed me! We even introduced an international flavor to our sing-along with "Waltzing Matilda;" over the 11 years that I lived in Kochevnikstan this became a Thanksgiving tradition. There was a tremendous sense of unity among foreigners working in Orchard City.[12] It was a beautiful experience of the body of believers – people from different nations, tongues and organizations – coming together to celebrate the abundance and bounty of the Lord over the past year. Thanksgiving took on a whole new meaning for me.

Living in another culture is full of challenges, many of which we've talked about in this book. One of the more subtle, but often most difficult, challenges is living in community with other believers. Hopefully you will have good, healthy, and sharpening relationships with your teammates. But even the best teams cannot meet all your needs.

---

12   I'm very thankful for the sense of international community I experienced in Orchard City. I realize that isn't always the case. And yet I find that in many places, organizational lines fade away as the larger body of believers labor side by side in the hard places.

During my time in Kochevnikstan, I found it really helpful to have a few friends who were not part of my sending organization or team. One of my best friends that first year, who is still a dear friend, was another single woman with a different organization. Her name was Angel and after my first 6 months, she moved into the apartment across the hall from me. Angel, my roommate, and I spent many evenings laughing together, or crying depending on the events of the day. Angel was so refreshing not only because she had been in country longer than I had, but because she had a fresh perspective on issues going on within our team. She was a place of refuge, an outsider, who I could safely "vent" to not only about frustrations in learning my new culture but also frustrations with my team. (Note: Someone who is an ex-pat does not always make them a safe person to "vent" to. Be wise in what you say and to whom. The ex-pat community is usually small and information spreads quickly within it.)

The guys on my team found outlets with other ex-pats through playing sports (a Thursday night basketball pick up game or Sunday afternoon ultimate Frisbee). The families on our team connected with parents from other organizations through their children's school. We took intentional steps to expand our community beyond our own team.

As you adjust and settle into your new culture, it will be natural to develop new networks of relationships with locals as well as other ex-pats. Depending on your location and your personality, you will probably lean more heavily toward one or the other.

One of my American friends is the most incarnational person I know and lives with locals (non-believers) who have become her second family. On the reverse side, there is danger in being so caught up in the ex-pat world that you find yourself wondering, "*Why am I living in* _____ *if I spend all my time with Americans/foreigners?*" For parents with kids in an international school, this is a real temptation because so much of your time is invested (rightfully so) with your kids in their environment. It's easy to find yourself gravitating toward other people who are "like" you and provide a measure of security and familiarity, especially when you are experiencing "*I hate this culture*" days.

In your early months and years it's important that you seek to expand your relationships in BOTH of these groups. Locals are the reason you've uprooted your life and moved to this new country. Invest in these relationships! On the other hand, ex-pats understand your challenges and struggles in the culture in a way that local friends cannot. It's not a matter of either/or but of both/and.

Expanding your community from your immediate family and team to include local friends and international ex-pats is one the greatest joys – in my opinion – of living overseas. We are ONE body, and we belong to each other. Like my first Thanksgiving, it is a beautiful picture here on earth of what will be in heaven: people from every tribe, language, nation, and race worshipping together before the throne of God.

🖉 ON YOUR OWN

Take some time to do a self-evaluation: Who are the people you spend the most time with? How do those people encourage you? Drain you? How do you encourage them?

In your life, do you have healthy relationships with your teammates? Other ex-pats? Locals? How can you take intentional steps to expand your community and network of relationships?

What we want and what we need are not always the same. Sometimes we want something so badly (like a local friend) that we work hard to get it but forget to ask God for it. Or sometimes God withholds something we want (like an ex-pat friend), because He is busy doing something else in our lives.

Take a few minutes to listen to the Lord. What is HE saying to you about your relationships with others? What do you want to ASK Him for in terms of your relationships?

SINGLE PERSPECTIVE

Let me start by making a distinction. Being single in your 20s is different than being single in your 30s, which is different from being single in your 40s and 50s, which is different from being single in your retirement years. "Single" gets put in a life stage category in the way that newlyweds, parents with young children, or empty nesters is a life stage category. But unlike these other stages, "single" covers the whole age range from birth to death. It is true that sometimes "single" gets divided up into single never married, single divorced, or single widowed (which gives you a hint as to the age of the "single"), but for the most part single just means "not married." And while there are similarities to singles in different age groups, it's my opinion that the differences are very significant.

Going into an exposition on all the nuances of singleness is not the point of this chapter. I only mention it briefly here to state that I am assuming that the majority of my readers are singles in their 20s, and therefore their singleness takes on a specific feel and look that is different from older singles. I also assume that the majority of my readers will likely be married within the next 5-10 years.

ON FINDING A MATE

Immediately after I graduated from college, I spent a summer in Bangkok, Thailand on a short-term trip. There was a 30-something single woman there named Lucy – a blonde, white woman who stuck out in a crowd of brown-haired and brown-faced Thais. But her language was so good that Thais would say that if their back was to her they couldn't tell from her language that she wasn't Thai. She loved the Thai people, was readily accepted by them, and as a result had an incredibly fruitful ministry. One night a group from my team sat with Lucy, and as often happens with young women, the conversation turned to marriage and singleness. Someone asked Lucy, "*So are you afraid that if you stay in Thailand you won't get married?*" I will never forget Lucy's answer. In a very matter-of-fact and confident way, she said, "*If I have a heart and love for Thailand, then the very best place for me to meet a man with the same heart for Thailand is in Thailand.*" After that summer, I never saw or heard from Lucy again. I don't know if she ever did meet that man in Thailand, but what I do know is that her wise words influenced and forever changed the way I viewed my own singleness.

Just recently I was talking with a young man, still in university, who has a growing heart for Muslims. He was feeling more and more called to labor in the hard places of the world, outside the camp (Heb. 13:13). After we had talked for a while, he asked me about being single and my view on it. He wants to be married and, like most men and women his age, he's thinking about the when and how and where he might meet a woman with the same heart as him. I told him what Lucy told me so many years ago – the best place to find a woman or man with a heart to labor among Muslims is IN the Muslim world. And then I told him these two stories...

The woman who discipled me in college lived and labored in Thailand as a single woman for many years. She desired to be married and to be a mom (she was an elementary school teacher by profession and loved children). But she also knew that God had called her Thailand to labor with college students there. So in obedience (and joy) she went where she was called.

One day she was walking in downtown Bangkok (a city of 11 million people), and literally bumped into a handsome American man. Not only was this guy an American, but he was a believer. Not only was he a believer, but he was on staff with a Christian organization. He was working on a project that brought him to Thailand several times a year. They became friends and eventually married. They now live in Florida, have 4 children (the youngest of whom is adopted from China), and are still on staff with the husband's organization that keeps him traveling throughout Southeast Asia and North Africa.

Maybe Bangkok is a cross-roads for many Christian workers, and even though it's a city of 11 million people, you can psych yourself up to believe that you could meet a potential mate there. But what about Jinja, Uganda? My "niece" (my teammate's daughter) had long felt a call to love the unlovely of the world. During college she did a short-term trip to Uganda working with AIDS orphans, and after she graduated she wanted to go back for an extended period of time to continue a photography project she'd started, using pictures to be a voice for the voiceless.

My niece and a few friends who went with her to Uganda had just come to the "big city" of Jinja after spending several weeks in a small village. They treated themselves to a trip to a small western style coffee shop. When they walked into the shop, they saw a white faced young guy who chivalrously gave up his chair so they could sit at his table. My niece noticed he was reading a Bible, and they struck up a conversation about spiritual things (the guy just happened to be in that coffee shop that day, wrestling with the Lord over whether or not to stay in Uganda or return to the States in hopes of meeting a like-minded woman to co-labor with in the unreached places of the world). To make a long story short, my niece spent the next few months working at the same AIDS orphanage as the coffee shop guy, they fell in love, married, and at the time of this writing are now co-laboring in Uganda.

"If I have a heart and love for Thailand, then the very best place for me to meet a man with the same heart for Thailand is in Thailand."

If these friends had not been obedient to what God was calling them to do and to where He asked them to go, they might not have met their mates – mates who have the same heart and calling that they do.

My counsel to young single men and women considering long-term cross-cultural labor (or laboring in the U.S. for that matter) is to walk with the Lord where He leads you. Trust Him to do just what he's done since the very beginning as told in Genesis 2:22, "*God brought the woman to the man.*"

ON BEING AN AUNT (OR UNCLE)

I mentioned my "niece." One of the greatest joys of my single life has been choosing to be an aunt – not only to my own brother's two kids – but also to the children of my closest teammates (and later on to their friends by association). My blood niece (my brother's oldest child) was born the year I moved to Kochevnikstan, and when I arrived in Kochevnikstan, there were two families on my team with young children. I was 30-something at the time, and I remember thinking, "*I don't know if I will have my own children or not. But I DO know that these kids are right in front of me. I want to choose to be an aunt to them.*"

I decided to intentionally initiate to my nieces and nephews. At birthdays, I would try to do something special with them (rather than just giving a gift): ice skating, shopping, bowling, or a movie night at my house. I went to basketball games when I could as well as other school events. I'd ask the boys about girls they were interested in and give friendly advice on how to be a gentleman. We played games. I would offer to babysit when they were younger, and sometimes I even helped with homework (although never math – they all know how bad Aunt Tammy is at math). I became the hairstyle specialist and would not only do my nieces' hair for banquets and formals in Kochevnikstan but also their friends' hair (recently one of my nieces even asked me to do her hair for her wedding – what a joy!). I developed a whole "identity" as "Aunt Tammy" since all my nieces' and nephews' friends in Kochevnikstan – not knowing what else to call me – called me Aunt Tammy, too.

I also initiated spiritual conversations, especially with my nieces. I met with my nieces and their friend(s) to do Bible study, help them learn how to reach out to their friends, plan their time, and talk about purity and singleness. As they got older, I was also a safe place for them to vent about their relationship with their parents – normal challenges every teenager and parents of a teenagers walk through.

The single guys on my team were great uncles as well. They played sports with the boys, teaching them great lessons about sportsmanship, teamship, and humility. They were also wonderful role models for the girls, setting a standard of the kind of godly men the girls' parents would want them to marry.

In the U.S., being an aunt or uncle is a joy. I love my brother's kids and work to build memories with them. I'm the crazy aunt who travels all over the world and sends them weird gifts and food from weird places. However in another culture, where my interaction with families and friends was limited to a small network of people, being an aunt took on all new meaning. It became a way that I "unplugged," a way that I became something else besides just the foreign worker. While I made a choice to be an aunt in order to serve my teammates and engage in a meaningful way with their kids, it also was a decision for me. Being an aunt brought a new dimension to my life that made me more well-rounded. I wasn't just the "single woman" on the team – I was a part of the family.[13]

ON DEVELOPING WHO YOU ARE AS A PERSON

Develop who you are as a person. Be a learner of yourself: your temperament, you values, your likes and dislikes. You may not always be single, but you will always be you. Part of learning who you are, especially in your 20s, is trying a whole lot of new things. Try out different hobbies, serve in different ways, explore your new culture. I mentioned in an earlier section that when I first arrived in my new culture, I took one day a month to explore my city by taking pictures. Later I started writing essays of my experiences. Both photography and writing are hobbies I enjoy, and I incorporated them into my new culture. Read books, take a local folk dance class, join a local sports team. And as much as you are allowed (based on the security of your location) or are financially able, travel both within your country and to the neighboring region. You'll never again in your life have the freedom to travel and explore such a variety of different places and activities.

IN CONCLUSION

Make good use of your time as a single person. The likelihood, statistically speaking, that you will be married at some point in the not so distant future is high. Don't worry so much about getting married that you miss out on the joys of being single. Don't miss out on God's plan for your life because you are too afraid that following Him will take

---

13   Not all families are as inviting aunts and uncles as my teammates were. And I know that for some singles (I labored with a few in Kochevnikstan), it's hard to engage in "family" activities because it only makes you want a family of your own. But I encourage you to get beyond that and choose to be an aunt or uncle. Ask the Lord to give you a family (whether its on your team or not) that you can become a part of by choosing to serve and encourage them. But beware that you don't look to this family to meet YOUR needs. The joy and love you feel as you engage as an aunt/uncle is a blessing not an expectation. ONLY God can fully satisfy you – no husband, wife, children, nieces or nephews can fill a need that only God was intended to fill.

you down a path that doesn't lead to marriage. God is GOOD, and he delights in giving good things to his children. Enjoy the gifts he gives you today (including the gift of being single at the current time). Trust that as you delight yourself in Him that He will give you the desires of your heart (Ps. 37:4).

✔ **LET'S GET PRACTICAL!**

What are some things that you really like to do or would like to learn? Is it possible for you to do that in your host culture? Is there a family you would like to get to know? How can you initiate to serve and encourage them?

Meditate on Psalms 34:10. What does it practically mean in your life (in terms of singleness) that "*those who seek the Lord lack no good thing?*"

Challenging Your Paradigms

12 months and beyond

PLANTED IN THE LAND

I remember sitting in a taxi with one of my good friends of many years. We were discussing our first few months living in our new city. I'm not sure which of us made the comment first, but one of us said, "*I don't want to just exist here, I want to live here.*"

When moving to a new culture, it's easier than you might think to just "exist" rather than choosing to be fully present and "live" there. It's sort of like going on a long vacation or to summer camp. You learn the routines, you do what you need to do, but in the back of your mind there is always this knowledge that this isn't "real life," that you don't really "live" here and you never completely settle in or put down roots.

One of my goals my first full year overseas came out of Jeremiah 29:3-7. Most of us know verse 11: "*For I know the plans I have for you, plans to prosper you and not to harm you; plans to give you a hope and a future.*" But what we often don't know is the full context of that promise. That verse is in the middle of a letter that Jeremiah writes to the exiles in Babylon. God tells the Israelites that He will bring them back to the land He had promised them. During the 70 years they live in this foreign land God says:

> "*Build houses and settle down; plant gardens and eat what they produce...increase in number there, do not decrease. Also seek the peace and prosperity of this city to which I have carried you into exile. Pray to the Lord for it, because if it prospers, you too will prosper.*"

The context of the good God promises in Jeremiah 29:11 is the exhortation for the Israelites to "plant in the land" where God had sent them.

Journal entry from my first year:

> *I feel a need to really "plant myself" in this land. I think I've realized that for my first several months here I - in a way - mourned my old life. Not necessarily "living" in the States because the truth is that the life I lived there even a year ago*

doesn't exist anymore. Most of my friends are married or moved on. It's not the actual place or even my house (which I do love and miss) that I am mourning - it's the way my life was. I had deep, old and intimate friendships for the last 8 years. Now I have only a few. My breadth of relationships has been diminished to almost nothing and it takes time to build it back up. I'm realizing that so much of life here up to this time has been in English language and American culture. One of the things I've been thinking of and asking God for is to incorporate Kochevnikstani culture into my "comfort zone". For example my apartment is a "safe place, a comfort zone" for me. But most of time spent in my apt is in English. I've just set a goal to watch TV only in Kochevnik (including movies) and to try to read in Kochevnik several days a week. That brings the culture into my home.

I remember the first time I felt like I lived in my new city. You know how you feel when you are in a random place (like Wal-Mart) and you bump into an old classmate you haven't seen in years? It reminds you that "you live here," that there are relationships you have that you don't always see on a regular basis. When I saw someone I knew out and about in the city for the first time, I felt like I could fly. It wasn't even someone I knew personally; it was the sales lady from the souvenir counter at the city department store. I "knew" her, because the summer I had arrived, I helped a short-term visiting team buy souvenirs often. I was on a bus when I saw her, and I knew she recognized me. I smiled and she smiled back. It was faint, but I'm sure it was a smile! She recognized me! I actually saw someone in the city who was NOT one of the 7 adults I saw on regularly. It made me feel like I lived there!

When I moved to Kochevnikstan, I didn't travel back to the States for two full years. I wanted Kochevnikstan to become my home, and all the "experts" say that moving back and forth between your home culture and your new host culture never allows you to really live in either place. In fact, many organizations have stipulations about how often you can travel back to America. By the time I'd lived in Kochevnikstan for two years, it felt like home. God answered my prayer to plant me in the land.

Journal entry from 3 years later:

> *It's fun to look back and see that 3 years ago I started ask-*
> *ing God to plant me in this land, to make this place feel like*
> *"home". And now three years later, I see that the Father has*
> *and continues to do this. I DO feel like this is my home.*
> *When I was in the States I was eager to get "home" to my*
> *"normal" life. When I talk with people, I usually refer to*
> *Orchard City or places here as "our" – our city, our roads,*
> *our bazaars. I know I'm not "local" in the sense of being*
> *Kochevnikstani, but I AM a local in Orchard City. I know*
> *the city better than first year students from other regions.*
> *I have places I like to shop, a network of local and ex-pat*
> *friends – too many to get enough time with. There are still*
> *some things not in place but those things are in process. I*
> *love my job. I'm known at my university and sought out. I*
> *still do most of the initiating in my relationships, but I have*
> *several old relationships that are very comfortable. I see that*
> *Kochevnikstani culture is more incorporated into my life.*
> *I'm still looking for my "niche" of being a foreigner in this*
> *culture, but I think the girls [I disciple] like that I'm not "lo-*
> *cal" and do some things in my American way.*

✏ ON YOUR OWN

Do a self check. Are you "living" in your new culture or are you just existing? Talk about this with your teammates.

Read Jeremiah 29:3-11. What does it look like in your life to "build houses," "settle down," or "plant gardens"? Set a time to "pray for the peace and prosperity of this city."

Do you believe God when He promises that he has *"plans to prosper you and not to harm you"*? If you truly took hold of this promise, how might your current attitude change? How might you pray differently?

SIMPLICITY

After my first year in Kochevnikstan, I had the opportunity to spend a summer in New Zealand with a group of U.S. students doing a summer training project. We planned a one-week exposure trip to the south. As we started preparing and packing I was a little overwhelmed with how much "stuff" everyone was taking.

One of the things I learned living in Kochevnikstan is that Americans accumulate stuff like no one else. We have this need to always have it all with us. For just an overnight trip, an American needs a backpack full of pajamas, a change of clothes, toiletries, a book to read and/or Bible, slippers or extra shoes, and a pillow. A Kochevnikstani needs a toothbrush and even that can be forgone. An American's motto is "*be prepared*"; a Kochevnikstani's motto is "*be resourceful.*"

Just for fun, and to make a point, I gave the team in New Zealand a challenge. I offered to give anyone $20 if they could pack less than me for the one-week trip. If I were truly a Kochevnikstani, no one could have beaten me! But only 1 year of uncluttering my life was not enough to completely eliminate all the stuff I felt I had to take with me. I ended up with a medium-sized backpack full of my must have items. Out of 20 people on the team only 2 – both guys – packed less than me. They got their $20 each, and everyone got a chance to evaluate how they could simplify their lives.

Simplicity is not an easy concept to define. My Cambridge International Dictionary lists 6 different definitions for "simple:" plain, easy, one part, no more than, natural and foolish. Trying to do a Bible study on "simplicity" gets confusing because the word "simple" almost always refers to something insignificant or foolish (as in a "simple-minded" person or fool). So what is simplicity? What does it mean to live a "simple" life? Is simplicity nothing more than eliminating stuff (like taking less clothes on a trip or having less stuff in your house)? Or is it something more? Think about it. How would YOU define simplicity? In *Knowing God*,[1] J.I. Packer defines divine simplicity as "*the fact that*

---

1 *Knowing God* by J.I. Packer p. 99

there are in him [God] no elements that can conflict, so that, unlike us, he cannot be torn in different directions by divergent thoughts and desires." Godly attributes that cannot be possessed by humans are called incommunicable. And theologians define "simplicity" as an incommunicable attribute of God.[2]

One way I work to "simplify" my life is by eliminating the clutter of self-imposed guilt born from comparing myself to others.

So if simplicity is an incommunicable attribute of God, something we can never fully possess, how do we cultivate simplicity in our lives? In our human nature, we can never be completely free from contradictions and divergent thoughts. Until we get to heaven, our flesh and the Spirit in us will war against each other. However, we can pursue greater integrity[3] in our lives. In other words, we strive to bring our internal thoughts, values, and perspectives into greater continuity with our external actions, behaviors, and possessions. Here are a few personal examples of how I work toward greater simplicity. I'm not always successful, but I work at cultivating simplicity into my lifestyle habits.

ELIMINATING PHYSICAL CLUTTER
In Kochevnikstan, I moved 10 times in 11 years. Nothing helps to eliminate clutter better than moving! What do I really need? What things, memories or heirlooms are valuable enough to me that I am willing to carry them around the world and move them up and down 5 or more flights of stairs? In general, if I haven't used it in a year, I don't need it. I do allow myself one trunk full of old journals and childhood memories – mementos for future generations. Eliminating clutter is not just about getting rid of "stuff" – it's about deciding what things are most valuable to me.

CLARIFYING DECISION MAKING VALUES
One of my favorite re-entry exercises was spending a half day in Wal-

---

2   *Knowing God* by J.I. Packer p. 99
3   I'm referring here to a "structural integrity." In engineering, a building is considered structurally sound when the inside frame can support the outside building.

Mart "re-learning" what products I liked and didn't. I get easily overwhelmed trying to decide what is the "best" product, because there are so many contradictory values to consider. What is the cheapest? The most healthy? The most effective? The most environmentally safe? Which of these values are most important to me? An initial time investment (a few hours in Wal-Mart reading labels and discovering new products since my last trip to the States), helped me clarify my decision-making values. In the end, it made my life much simpler. Now, I can spend 1 minute choosing shampoo and peanut butter rather than 10 minutes on each item every time I go shopping. The decision has already been made (outside behavior), because I've already thought about what I want (inside value). Clarifying decision-making values helps to simplify our lives. (Note: This same principle applies to other decisions that are far more important and have greater consequences than peanut butter: e.g. dating, work, commitments, standards, etc.).

BEING COMFORTABLE WITH WHO I AM AND WHERE I AM IN LIFE

Internal conflict and contradiction can drain emotional energy and make life feel more complicated than it has to be. When I give in to comparing myself to others (or to the standard of the world), I am complicating rather than simplifying my life. As I move through different stages of life, I have to choose to be comfortable with who I am, even the ways I'm different from other people. For example, I don't wash my hair everyday (silly as it sounds this used to cause me stress because other women wash their hair every day so maybe that is the "right" thing to do); I live alone (none of my teammates live alone so is it "wrong"); I love to watch TV (not very "spiritual"!). Even seemingly petty things like these examples can cause internal turmoil that saps energy. One way I work to "simplify" my life is by eliminating the clutter of self-imposed guilt born from comparing myself to others.

A book I've found helpful in thinking about simplicity is called *Intimacy with the Almighty* by Chuck Swindoll. This small book is a powerhouse of "simple" truths that focus on 4 areas to foster greater intimacy with the Lord:

1. Surrender – submitting to the Goodness of the Lord and obeying him in everything

2. Simplicity – eliminating the clutter of our lives (physical, emotional, spiritual, mental, etc.)
3. Silence – practicing times of silence (a "test" Swindoll suggests is to turn off the radio in your car; most people are uncomfortable with silence and surround themselves with noise)
4. Solitude – extended times of being alone

Like many "good" things, simplicity can become an idol in our lives. If simplicity means getting rid of stuff more than eliminating contradiction, we can begin to focus too much on asceticism, eliminating all worldly things in our lives. This is the way of Buddhist monks and many Christian monks of past centuries. In doing so, we become prideful in our ascetic lifestyle choices and often judgmental of those who make different choices. As I was studying simplicity, I saw this begin to happen in my life. I noticed that I more frequently asked myself *"how can I simplify my life?"* than I asked *"how can I be like Jesus?"* The two questions can sound similar since Jesus was – by J.I. Packer's definition – perfectly simple. Even good things can become idols when we focus more on the goal than on the person who exemplifies the goal.

🖊 ON YOUR OWN

How would you define simplicity? Using that definition, is your life "simple"?

What are specific areas where you can begin to eliminate clutter and contradiction in your life (physically, emotionally, mentally, spiritually)?

Is simplicity primarily about behavior or perspective? Why?

Think about the following process. In what ways does this apply to your life?
    Simplicity to Complexity to Perplexity to Humility to Simplicity

TIME

Microwaves. Frozen foods. Instant potatoes. Online shopping delivered to your door. Home banking with same day bill pay. Immediate answers to almost any question accessed right from your mobile phone. Flights that will take you the ends of the earth in under 24 hours. Skype, Google hang out, and FaceTime that allow real time communication with anyone almost anywhere in the world. No more waiting weeks to receive a single letter from home or weeks more for them to get a return letter. We live in a world of instant gratification; waiting is a thing of the past. Or is it?

I am in awe of time, the fourth dimension: how it flows, how it's spent, how it can seem to stop. Time can be seized. It can be used or invested or wasted. But it cannot be stopped. It cannot be controlled. There is never more or less time to be had – it is constant. Isaiah 55:8 says, "'For my thoughts are not your thoughts and neither are your ways my ways,' declares the Lord." I think there are few places in the 21st century where that verse is more true than in the differences between how God views time and how we view time.

God is not slow (2 Peter 3:9) nor is He in a hurry. He allowed the Israelites to remain in bondage for 430 years before rescuing them (Ex. 12:40). Time is a tool in the hands of the Lord to accomplish HIS purposes in our lives and in the world. It is a means of training, firmly rooting, healing, and preparing.

Think about Moses. Exodus 2 covers 80 years of Moses life. He spends 40 years growing up in Pharaoh's household learning the language, culture, and ways of the Egyptians. Then, he spends another 40 years in the desert humbled by his own failure to rescue his people, which resulted in him killing an Egyptian, being despised by his people, building a family, and learning patience (as a shepherd). Finally, at the end of Exodus 2 when God has firmly prepared Moses according to HIS plan, He calls Moses to do the very work Moses wanted to do in the first place. God had a plan for Moses' life, but the timing was not what Moses expected. When we read the story of these 80 years of Moses life, it takes us 3-4 minutes to know what Moses will end up doing and being. But Moses lived every day of those 80 years not knowing the end of the story.

Abraham is another example of how God's use of time is not what we would expect. Abraham was chosen by God and promised that he would be the father of many nations. But Abraham had no son. Abraham (at Sarah's impatient urging) tries to "help" God out, resulting in the birth of the Islamic nation. God tells Abraham that while Ishmael will become a great nation, he will not be the son with whom God makes his covenant (Gen. 17). God will give him another son with Sarah, even though they are impossibly old. Abraham waits a total of 25 years for the fulfillment of that promise. Can you imagine waiting 25 years for God to keep a promise? I think I would give up hope or think that maybe God got it wrong (actually Abraham had a similar moment of weakness in Genesis 17 when he asks God to make Ishmael the son of the promise).

We can read a story spanning 25 years from start to finish in a matter of minutes. With that immediate perspective, it's easy to be judgmental and wonder why Abraham wasn't stronger. But "in the middle" of my life (as Abraham and Moses were), I know I wouldn't be any stronger or more patient. I like instant results, instant gratification, and instant confirmation that what God has promised will indeed come true. However, instant gratification does not seem to be God's chosen training method!

Time is a tool in the hands of the Lord to accomplish HIS purposes in our lives and in the world. It is a means of training, firmly rooting, healing, and preparing.

I like to read biographies. One of the things I've learned about reading biographies is that I have to keep in mind that although I'm reading the whole story from start to finish, the person I'm reading about actually "lived" in the moment with all the turmoil of waiting and not knowing how the story would end.

I was reading a biography summary of David Livingstone, and there was one sentence that captured my attention. *"David spent 12 years in the mill."* This short sentence encompasses 12 YEARS of Livingstone's life. It may have taken me only seconds to read these 7 words, but David Livingstone LIVED each day of these 12 years working in the mill. This is NOT what we think of when we think of David Livingstone but as an explorer and missionary pioneer of the Dark Continent. Those 12 years must have felt "mundane." The details weren't interesting enough to record in the biography of his life; imagine how boring it would be to read a book about 12 years of working in the mill. That information isn't what we want to know about David Livingstone. We want to know the "exciting" stuff, but those 12 years were very influential in his preparation; he read constantly during his years working at the mill.

TV programs are similar. Crime dramas solve the mystery in under an hour. Stake outs last only minutes (instead of days or weeks). Have you ever noticed that on TV people rarely go to the bathroom or sit for hours in traffic? The mundane parts are cut out, because they are not exciting. Time is not actually stopped or sped up in the movies, but it IS manipulated to make us "feel" like it is.

What is the point in these musings over time? The flow of life is not always as it seems in the movies, in books, or even in the Scriptures. The "fourth dimension" influences how we view life. And in your new culture, time will probably "feel" different. It will either feel sped up with so many new things happening every day that one day feels like a years worth of experience. Or time will "feel" slow: mundane and boring like you will never get to where you want to be (the exciting parts!). However time feels to you, remember that it never stops. It is never actually faster or slower. Time is never outside of God's control. He is never racing a clock. And He is never slow in accomplishing His purposes. By the grace of God learn to live *"In His place...at His pace."*

✎ ON YOUR OWN

Time yourself reading Exodus 2 out loud. How long did it take you to read an 80-year account of Moses's life? Take a few minutes to think about how Moses experienced those same 80 years you just read about. How would you have felt if you were Moses – not knowing the end of the story – during your 40 years in the desert? (Think about "slow" times in your life – what is your natural response?)

How do you think God views time? Uses time? What Scripture can you think of to support your thoughts? What does this tell us about the character of God? How does this view of God influence my life?

What are practical ways that you can cultivate an eternal (vs. microwave) perspective in your life? The line and the dot illustration has helped me have perspective. Think of a clothesline stretched out over the entire length of your yard. Then, picture a black marker dot on that clothesline. Our life is like that dot and the clothesline represents eternity. Will you live for the dot? Or for the line?

BRONZE SNAKES

"...he broke into pieces the bronze snake Moses had made, for up to that time the Israelites had been burning incense to it."

2 Kings 18:4

In Numbers 21:4-9 we are told a story about the disgruntled Israelites wandering in the desert.[4] They get impatient, and they start to speak out against the Lord and against Moses. Why have you talked us into leaving our home? We are going to die in this place! There's nothing good to eat; we hate all the food here! The Lord responds by sending venomous snakes among the people. The snakes did what snakes do: they bit the people and many died. Motivated to rethink their complaints, the Israelites come to Moses and say, *"We have sinned when we spoke against the Lord and against you. Pray that the Lord will take the snakes away from us. So Moses prayed for the people"* (Num. 21:7). The Lord then asks Moses to do something that seems unusual – one of the many unusual things the Lord does in history. He tells Moses to make a bronze snake, put it on a pole, and raise the pole. When the people look at the bronze snake they will be healed and live.

In John 3:14-15, Jesus refers back to the bronze snake and reveals it as prophetic picture of the Son of Man being lifted up on a cross, so everyone who looks to him may have eternal life. I love how God paints pictures in the Old Testament that reflect the realities of Jesus in the New Testament. The bronze snake is one of many such pictures. But that picture is not the point of this particular story.

In 2 Kings 18, we are introduced to King Hezekiah who *"did what was right in the eyes of the Lord"* (v. 3). He removed the high places, smashed the sacred stones, and tore down Asherah poles. He destroyed all the things that represented the Israelites' worship of idols. He also *"broke into pieces the bronze snake Moses had made, for up to that time the Israelites had been burning incense to it"* (v. 4). Unlike the Asherah poles,

---

4   The Israelites always seemed disgruntled and ungrateful, complaining about one thing or another. We give them a bad rap, but I often wonder if I am any different in my "wanderings" through this life!

the bronze snake was not a foreign idol. In Moses' time it was a means of salvation for the people of God. It was a God-given means to bring healing and hope, a picture of what was to come. But in Hezekiah's day the people had taken something that was created by God for a specific time and place and began worshiping the method of salvation rather than the Savior.

God may choose to use a "bronze snake" to save me or to point me to Jesus, but HE is the one who empowers it. The snake has no power in and of itself...

The concept of "bronze snakes" hit home with me after several years of living cross-culturally. I began to ask myself what methods of ministry, philosophies, even theologies had become "bronze snakes" in my life. What things are more rooted in their productivity in a specific time and place than they are rooted in principles that span time and space?

The clearest (though not only) example of God revealing bronze snakes in my life is in the area of "church." Church is a loaded word, meaning different things to different people. It is NOT my intent in this short space to promote or discourage various forms or functions of church.[5] However, if you live overseas church planting will be a hot topic of discussion. Even if you are not specifically part of a church planting team, there will be those around you who are, and you will be forced to evaluate what you think church is and what church should look like in your host culture.

My exhortation to anyone in a new culture – or even to those who have never left their home culture – is to be willing to look closely at the things we hold dear in our lives, the things we've known to be effective and productive in the past. In an attitude of prayer and invitation to the Spirit to give insight, we need to evaluate our traditions, our patterns

---

5   There are whole libraries of books written about church planting and growth. If this is an area of interest, talk to your team leader or organization about their particular philosophy of church and ask them to recommend a few books that embrace their viewpoint.

of spiritual disciplines, our philosophies and methods of ministry, our theologies of church, suffering, spiritual warfare, etc.

God may choose to use a "bronze snake" to save me or to point me to Jesus, but HE is the one who empowers it. The snake has no power in and of itself, and when it ceases to become useful to God it should cease to become important to me. We are wise if we closely evaluate the places in our lives where "bronze snakes" have become idols that replace the power of the living God.

When I was 20-something, I had a long list of non-negotiables, or things that I was convinced were absolutely true no matter what. But as I've gotten older, I find that my long list gets shorter and shorter. I'm not denying absolute truth, and I'm definitely not embracing or encouraging relativism. I'm simply admitting that there are things I don't understand. God works in mysterious ways, and the best I can do is to obey what he tells me at the time he tells me. The teacher sums up this truth in Ecclesiastes 12:11: *"Fear God and keep his commandments, for this is the whole duty of man."*

✎ ON YOUR OWN

Ask the Lord to open your eyes to any "bronze snakes" in your life.

Think about your belief system. What is your theology about church? Suffering? Spiritual warfare? Can you articulate it? What Scriptural basis supports your belief system? Are there things in your theology that are rooted more in tradition and your American culture than in Scripture?

A MOVEMENT OF THE GOSPEL

One of the bronze snakes God revealed in my life after several years of laboring cross-culturally was that there is a big difference between developing a movement on the campus and a movement of the Gospel. My U.S. ministry experience is almost exclusively on a college campus. I was involved in campus ministry as a student. When I graduated, I had a full-time job, but my main ministry focus was still on the campus. I was a member of a local church, but I was primarily involved in the collegiate ministry. Then I came on staff with a Christian organization, and college ministry became my full time job.

I was one of two staff who pioneered a new campus work, and it was exciting to see this new work grow into a full-blown generational ministry. We went from having a few key students involved to having multiplying ministries in many of the sororities and fraternities as well as with independents and athletes. We were training student leaders who were influencing the strategy and direction of the overall campus ministry. We were sending over a 100 students every summer to either a U.S. based or international summer training program. In 5 years time, there was a growing movement on the campus.

U.S. based campus ministry has a prevailing philosophy: you train and develop students during the 4-5 years they are in college in the context of the campus movement, then you mobilize them into a local church or community ministry. You maintain personal relationships with graduated disciples, but the focus of your ministry stays on the campus. That is the bread and butter of maintaining a campus movement, and some part of your staff team starts over every two years with investing in the incoming freshmen. You don't "follow your fruit" off the campus.

For 10 years I invested in women, training them in the context of a campus movement and mobilizing them into various opportunities after graduation. At the risk of sounding prideful, I was very good at it. Then I moved cross-culturally and started laboring in an eastern education system. Everything I thought I knew about developing a campus movement was challenged. To start with, it took 2-3 years for someone to come into the Kingdom rather than 2-3 months. That left little time to train them before "mobilizing them into the community." Mobilizing them into the community took on an entirely new meaning, too – what community? In the U.S. there are many well-established, Gospel-teaching churches. There are multiple ministries that focus on helping the poor, planting new churches, and ministering to people of various life stages. The possibilities for "mobilizing" from the campus movement to another movement is almost limitless in the U.S. But in Kochevnikstan there were very few, if any, possibilities to mobilize people into, even if they were ready to be mobilized after 4 years of college.

I love campus ministry. I love students and their influenceable place in the life since they are in college. I loved my time in campus ministry in the U.S.: I saw lots of fruit, and I loved the opportunity to "start over" every few years. The "campus movement" philosophy worked in the U.S., but my frustration grew as I tried to implement that same campus movement method in my new host culture.[6] It took 3 years of sharing my faith before someone became a believer, then another 6 weeks for my first discipleship group of 2 girls to meet together at the same time. My well laid out discipleship "plan" was constantly re-adjusted, because the girls I was meeting with had no Bible background. If I made a passing statement about David dealing with sin, I had to spend 30 minutes explaining who David was and how he had sinned. I was starting from scratch, not building on any previously laid spiritual foundation (at least not a biblical one).

I was frustrated and felt like a failure. I questioned everything I thought I knew about campus ministry and discipling women. I knew discipleship was God's means to develop his people, but my methods were not working. It was a time of great character development as I begged the Lord to show me what I was doing wrong and what needed to change.

---

6   Campus movements such as we are familiar with in the U.S. can still be effective models in cross-cultural settings. But it depends on the background of the host culture and the time available to bring a new believer to maturity. Non Judeo-Christian background cultures – such as Muslim cultures – take longer to see people come into the Kingdom, lengthening the time of investment to bring a new believer to maturity. Cultures that are traditional and collective - where students live with their families while in college making them less available - can slow down the maturing process.

After several years of struggling unsuccessfully to create a movement on the campus, I had a paradigm shift. The ultimate goal was NOT creating a movement on the campus; that was only a means to an end. The real end-game was creating a movement of the Gospel into a culture.[7]

There's nothing wrong with building a movement on the campus. It was an effective method for me for many years and continues to be an effective method in many collegiate ministries. But it had become a bronze snake in my life. The method had become more important than the real goal – a movement of the Gospel into the nations. My context – a Muslim background, collective, Asian culture – meant learning to work through natural networks of relationships versus working through shallow university friendships. A movement of the Gospel meant that I needed to "follow the fruit" past college instead of "starting over" ever few years. It meant establishing and equipping people as they moved into their professional and new family lives, because there was a lack of community ministries into which to mobilize them.

We all have bronze snakes in our lives, paradigms that seem so right we can't even imagine that there could be another way to view things. One of the greatest joys of living cross-culturally is that God uses the experience to turn us upside down and inside out to show us that He will NOT be put in a box. No matter what we think we know, the reality is that there is so much more that we don't know.

✒ ON YOUR OWN

What are the ways you've seen the Gospel advance in your *home* culture, on your campus, or in your community?

Are there any paradigm shifts or bronze snakes God is revealing to you? Ask the Lord to give you insight into what it will take to advance the Gospel into your *host* culture. Talk about this with your team.

---

7 Prepositions are important words for creating nuances of meaning. It's one thing to advance the Gospel *to* a nation but quite another to advance the Gospel *into* a nation.

THEODIDACTIC
Meaning "God taught"

[A letter written to a friend 4 years after arriving in Kochevnikstan]

One of the things God has been doing in my life recently is reminding me just how much someone's growth is NOT dependent on me. I KNOW that God wants to use me – I'm an instrument in his hand. I don't have a problem believing that. But I often get caught up in an over-inflated sense of responsibility – that someone's growth is directly related to me. How often I spend time with them, my ability to communicate with them, what wisdom I impart to them. I can start to believe that if I (emphasis on the I) am not in someone's life on a regular basis that they won't grow. How very ME-centered, ME-sufficient, ME-focused is that? My mind knows, of course, that this isn't true – I know 1 Corinth. 3:7 that "...only God makes things grow...". I KNOW this and yet my actions don't always line up with the truth I say I know.

Let me give you a few examples of what I mean.

> *This last week was Reading Week – a week long fall break. During this week (actually more like 12 days) my group of girls didn't meet, and I saw each of them at best 1 time, some of them not at all. I feel guilty for not taking advantage of all this "free" time to invest in my relationship with them. If their growth depends on me, then not seeing or talking to them for almost 2 weeks is like not feeding a baby for two weeks – the baby will starve to death.*

> *This same group of girls meets on Friday mornings at 8am – and even though we all agreed on this time they come sporadically, because it's so early (8am IS early here, especially for students). I know that our group time is not the point. But how can I teach them anything if I don't see them during our planned meeting times? If their growth depends on me then I'm frustrated with them when they don't show up for our "meetings."*

> *I know that the "right answer" to these things is that I should*

> *"spend more time talking to God about people than talking to people about God." And I do intercede for these girls – but the truth is that I don't pray for them nearly as much as I think I should. If their growth depends solely on how much I pray for them, then they aren't growing much.*

These are just a few examples of how I see this familiar truth (that a person's growth is not dependent on me) rattling my cage in a new and deeper way. The other day I was listening to a John Piper sermon, and in his opening prayer (that had nothing to do with his theme) he asked that the people would be "as the Thessalonians who were God taught and not John Piper taught." That caught my attention. I searched through Thessalonians and found what I think is the passage he was referring to.

> *"May our Lord Jesus himself and God our Father, who loved us and by his grace gave us eternal encouragement and good hope, encourage your hearts and strengthen you in every good deed and word...the Lord is faithful, and he will strengthen and protect you from the evil one. We have confidence in the Lord that you are doing and will continue to do the things we command. May the Lord direct your hearts into God's love and Christ's perseverance." (2 Thess. 2:16-17; 3:3-5)*

It's a verse I want to memorize and begin asking for all the people my life touches. I know that The Father wants to use me and yet in the process of using me I never want for others or for myself to become dependent on ME for their growth. I long for people to be God taught, not Tammy taught. Tammy taught is so limited – they can only become what I am if I am their source. I would never say that I believe myself to be the "source" of someone's growth, and yet my life reflects that truth so much more often than I realize. Simple truth – not new, not something I've not learned before and yet revolutionary when applied to every level of my heart and life.

God IS going to grow his children. This is truth. The more important thing that the Lord is doing in MY LIFE is revealing just how deep is MY pride and ME-centeredness. It's humbling for someone's growth to NOT come from my input in their lives. There is a part of me that wants them to grow based on me – I find significance in this. I feel better about myself when I'm doing the things I think I should to invest in someone's life. But the truth is that I am helpless, inadequate, and ill-equipped. If not for the Lord's working through me, I would have no impact whatsoever. As the Lord reminds me that HE causes the growth, he is also reminding me of just how desperate I am for HIM and in need of HIS presence in MY LIFE. I'll close with another verse I've been meditating on from Exodus 33:12-14:

> *Moses said to the Lord, "You have been telling me, `Lead these people', but you have not let me know whom you will send with me. You have said `I know you by name and you have found favor with me.' If you are pleased with me, teach me your ways, so I may know you and continue to find favor with you. Remember that this nation is your people. The Lord replied, "My Presence will go with you, and I will give you rest."*

✐ ON YOUR OWN

What – if anything – about my confession resonates with you? Do you have an over inflated sense of responsibility for someone's growth and spiritual maturity? Do you inadvertently create a dependence on yourself (or allow others to become dependent on you) because you find significance in helping people grow?

What will it look like in your ministry for your Bible study or discipleship group or non-believing relationships to be "God taught"? How can you cultivate this in the lives of people you influence?

MENTORING VS. DISCIPLESHIP

My freshmen year in college was a crucial turning point in my life. I had just become a believer (started a real relationship with Jesus as opposed to doing religious activities) and wanted to grow, but I didn't really know where to start. I had pledged a sorority and several of my sorority sisters were strong believers. One in particular (J.D.) initiated with me and helped me get into the Word. J.D. strongly recruited me to my first ever summer training program. It was there that I first remember being challenged with The Great Commission. That God had given me a purpose in life, to know Him and make Him known, was life-changing. My sophomore year another sorority sister (C.C.) challenged me to meet with her and a third sorority sister in a discipleship group. I wasn't the easiest disciple; I questioned and challenged everything, but C.C. was faithful to initiate with and invest in me. My senior year, the staff woman on my campus (D.R.) invited me to be part of a senior leaders accountability and study group. In this last year of college of D.R.'s investment, a lot of things about discipleship, multiplication, the nations, and God's glory really began to "click" for me.

For four years I had women who challenged me to a discipleship relationship: they intentionally initiated with me and invested in my life. My discipleship groups in college were leader-initiated and my primary (not only, but primary) source of spiritual input. I was eager to grow, but looking back, I did much less initiating to my own spiritual growth than I do now as a mature laborer.

Allen Hadidian in *Discipleship: Helping Other Christians Grow* defines discipleship as (parenthesis addition is my own):

> ...*the process by which a Christian with a life worth emulating* (character of the discipleship leader)
> *commits himself* (commitment)
> *for an extended period of time* (time-frame)
> *to a few individuals* (selection)
> *who have been won to Christ, the purpose being* (evangelism)
> *to aid and guide their growth to maturity* (establishing)

and equip them (equipping)
to reproduce themselves in a third spiritual generation.[8]
(end goal = generations)

The Gospels give us one of the clearest examples in Scripture of a discipling relationship. Jesus discipled his men for three years, intentionally developing in them a framework for their future spiritual growth. Jesus did not do everything needed in these men's lives, but he laid a foundation that would aid them in their journey towards maturity.

When we mature spiritually we need a variety of mentors who are helping us to grow and develop in all aspects of our life.

I hope you have experienced, as I did in college, a leader-driven discipleship relationship focused on laying a foundation for future spiritual maturity. Even if you haven't experienced discipleship in this way, it's likely that you are no longer an infant in the faith.[9] As we grow and develop, we need less and less of a discipleship type relationship (and in reality have less and less availability for it). An infant needs a parent to care for him providing all of his needs until he is able to care for himself. But an adolescent, young professional, or newlywed needs a variety of adults (not just parents) speaking into his or her life (coaches, teachers, friends, co-workers, supervisor, etc.). In the same way, when we mature spiritually we need a variety of mentors who are helping us to grow and develop in all aspects of our life.

Those who have had a positive discipleship experience (especially recent college graduates) commonly make the mistake of wanting and looking for a discipleship leader who will think for them, initiate with them, and tell what to study. But part of the maturing process is taking on more and more responsibility for our own spiritual growth. Hebrews 5:14 defines maturity as someone who "...*by constant use has*

---

8 Page 29
9 Since you're reading this book, I'm assuming that you are a cross-cultural laborer and possess some spiritual maturity as deemed appropriate by your organization.

trained themselves to discern good from evil." Discipleship and mentoring are both essential parts of our spiritual growth. Though similar in form, they are different.

WHAT IS MENTORING?

A mentor is a person who shares his or her knowledge, experience, and life with someone less knowledgeable in the desired are of growth. Mentoring is an essential way that we intentionally grow, learn, and develop even after we are mature adults (physically and spiritually).

How is mentoring different from discipleship?

Initiative. Discipleship is leader-initiated; the discipleship leader thinks for the needs of the disciple and prepares a study plan to help meet those needs.

Mentoring is initiated by the mentoree. The mentoree evaluates his or her own development needs, seeks out a mentor (who models the desired growth area), and initiates both the relationship and the "plan" for meeting together.

Focus. Discipleship focuses on a broad base of primarily spiritual development issues and is done life-on-life with the disciple.

Mentoring focuses on a particular skill, character development area, or general exposure. The mentor is a resource the mentoree meets occasionally (less frequently than with a discipleship leader).

Part of the maturing process is taking on more and more responsibility for our own spiritual growth.

How are mentoring and discipleship alike?

Relationship. Both are relational in nature. Long-term friendships often develop out of discipling or mentoring relationships.

Time frame. Both have a clear starting and ending point. Both discipling and mentoring relationships make a commitment to meet together on a regular basis for an agreed upon time (not indefinitely).

KINDS OF MENTORS

Skill focus. These mentors are "experts" in a particular skill area that the mentoree would like to grow in. The specific skill area can be spiritual (prayer, evangelism, Bible study, etc.) or general (budgeting/ finances, time management, cooking, auto repair, etc.). Depending on the skill, it's possible to do this kind of mentoring using modern technology (e-mail, Skype, etc.) or even from a book.

Exposure/Apprentice Focus. These mentors are those who do a certain job or have a ministry focus that you would like to learn more about. The goal is to get practical exposure and hands on experience by being around people who do something you would like to learn to do better. This can have a ministry or non-ministry focus (e.g., landscaping, working with orphans, business practices, campus ministry, working with Muslims, etc.). This kind of mentoring is *more caught than taught*" and therefore requires close life-on-life proximity.

Character Focus. These mentors are those who demonstrate or model a particular character quality the mentoree would like to grow in (e.g., patience, graciousness, loving people, freedom, faith, etc.). The idea here is that you become like people you spend time with. This kind of mentoring ideally happens in "real time" (not via the internet), although it can also happen through biographies or books that model the desired characteristic.

Lifelong. A lifelong mentor is usually someone who has played a significant role in the mentoree's life (parent, discipleship leader, boss, coach), someone with whom you've spent quantity time at some point. The mentoree comes to trust and respect this more mature person and seeks him or her out for counsel and advice in a variety of situations over the course of his whole life. Lifelong mentors often do not live in close proximity to the mentoree. They are wise counselors occasionally sought out for insight to specific life issues or struggles.

📖 FOR FURTHER STUDY

Read through the Gospels paying close attention to what Jesus did with his disciples. How did he spend time with them? What did he teach them? What was the clear start and end point of their discipling relationship?

Look at the lives of these men and women of faith: Moses, David, Joshua, Peter, Abraham, Ruth, Esther. Who were mentors to these people? Who did they mentor? What was the focus of their mentoring? Who initiated the mentoring relationship? In your life how have you seen a difference between discipleship and mentoring (or maybe both)?

Consider doing the "Mentoring Challenge" in the Practical Resources section.

WHY DID JESUS COME?

It is a thought provoking question if you really stop and think about it. Of course those of us who grew up in "Christian culture" know the right answer: Jesus came to save the world, for forgiveness of sins. That is the right answer, but what does it really mean? I was challenged by this thought through a non-believing friend.

I was a part of a student theater group on a university campus. My main objective in getting involved in this group was using it as a means of building new relationships with college students. When you work in full time ministry, it can be challenging to get natural time around non-believers. That sounds crazy since the whole point of my job is reaching out to the lost world, but it's true. So much of my time is spent with believers – counseling, encouraging, training.

I DID have contact with unbelievers, but it's usually in a very "contrived" setting. I was intentionally talking to a person in order to bring up spiritual topics or the person has come to talk to me specifically about a spiritual topic (I wish that happened more often!). Being part of this theater group was different because it gave me real context with people. We worked side by side for three months learning lines, gathering props, rehearsing, and doing it all over again. In fact, we worked so hard on the play that I had to often remind myself why I got involved in the play in the first place – for the sake of being among the lost world.

Although most of the cast were college students, a few were older community folks. One woman in particular (we'll call her Julie) was the catalyst for re-thinking this thought provoking question: why did Jesus come? Julie was in her late 30s, and she lived cross-culturally for half of her life. The very first time I met Julie she told me, "*People where I'm from (Northwest Canada) hate people from where you are from (the Bible belt south).*" She would never call herself a Christian, and by her own admission doesn't really like Christians. She's a teacher and social activist. She cares about people and is a professionally trained counselor. It's true that she is abrupt and sometimes abrasive in her manner, but she is genuinely motivated to make the world a better place. In short, she is a "good" person who has done many "good" things in her life.

One day I was talking to Julie about her experiences. She shared about working with street prostitutes in Thailand, fighting for rights of native peoples, and her heart to see poor and underprivileged kids free from the baggage of emotional and physical abuse. I was challenged by her love for people. She had done more in her lifetime to care for the poor and down trodden than I had even thought about doing. Here I am, a self-proclaimed follower of Jesus, and yet this woman (who hates traditional religious beliefs) was spending her life on behalf of the poor and needy.

Julie and I had some conflict during the course of the play – conflict that was almost entirely caused by me. I was clearly in the wrong and humbled myself, confessing my wrong to Julie. Conflict can lead to greater openness and intimacy in relationships if you can push through it. At the end of the play, I wanted to tell Julie how much her life had challenged me in how I relate to the poor. Yet something in me held back; I didn't want to encourage Julie in her good works and in doing so affirm the notion that "good people" are right with God.[10] Julie is not a follower of Jesus – she's "spiritual" yes, but she is not redeemed. She docs not put trust in Jesus to be a mediator between her and God. She is not trusting Jesus for forgiveness of her sin.

Jesus did not come to make bad people good; he came to make dead people alive.

About this same time, I was talking with my teammate Teresa who made a statement that has been rattling around in my head since. She said, *"Jesus did not come to make bad people good; Jesus came to make dead people alive."* It was a simple enough statement, and one I'd probably heard before, but this time it caught my attention. This was exactly what I was feeling with Julie. Julie is doing good things – in many ways

---

10   I never did tell Julie how much her life had challenged me. In hindsight, I wish I HAD told her and used it as a platform to open a Gospel conversation. But I was too fearful – wrongfully fearful - of affirming "the wrong things".

better things than I am. So why would she need Jesus? She's not a bad person who needs be made good. She doesn't have a bad life that needs to be made better. We KNOW that everyone is sinful and everyone needs Jesus, but it's often hard to see it when our friends, co-workers, or family members are such "good" people. Why would "good people" need Jesus?

Of course the "right answer" is that there are no good people. *"There is no one righteous, no not one"* (Romans 3:10). However, depending on how and where you grew up, it's easy to fall into the pattern of believing that Jesus is about making bad people good. I would never have said that is true, and yet that mentality showed up in how I related with Julie. So why do "good people" need Jesus? Even if their actions are good, their souls area "dead in their sin" (Ephesians 2). Jesus did not come to make bad people good; he came to make dead people alive.

You might have heard the parachute analogy. You board a plane, take your seat, and the stewardess comes around offering everyone a parachute. *"Here,"* she says, *"this will make your flight better. It will help you be more comfortable and make your flight more enjoyable."* You take the parachute, put it on, but instead of making you more comfortable just the opposite is true. It pokes and prods in places you'd rather it not. It forces you to sit in an unnatural way, causing you to squirm. The stewardess comes by to offer a beverage service, and because you are squirming she spills coffee on you, burning you and making a mess. Finally, in frustration you throw the parachute to the ground; it's not working. This parachute is not making my life better or helping in any way.

Rewind. You board a plane and the stewardess comes around offering you a parachute. *"Take this,"* she says, *"because at 30,000 feet the plane is going to crash and you will need this parachute to survive."* You gladly take the parachute, put it on, and cling to it as if your life depended on it (because it does). True, the parachute is not very comfortable. It causes you to squirm a little, and it feels unnatural at first. But you know that this parachute is the difference between life and death, so the discomfort doesn't matter. When the stewardess comes by offering a beverage service and spills hot coffee on you because you are squirming, you hardly notice because you are so intent on clinging to the parachute, your hope for life.

The parachute is Jesus – our hope for life. His goal is not to make our life "better" (by worldly standards) or "more comfortable." In fact, Jesus clearly tells us that "*in this life you will have trouble...*" (John 16:32). His goal is not to make bad people good or to make a bad life better. Why did Jesus come? Jesus came that we might have life and have it more abundantly (John 10:10).

✐ ON YOUR OWN

How would you answer the question "Why did Jesus come?" Would you answer it differently to a believer in the U.S. than to a local friend who is not a believer?

Do you know people like Julie? People whose life is so "good" that it's hard to imagine why they need Jesus? How do you relate to them? How do you share Jesus with them? How do you pray for them?

Returning Home

R.A.F.T.ing

Most of us would agree that we want to live with no regrets. Saying goodbye is one of those places in life worth a little forethought to make sure you have no regrets later. R.A.F.T.ing is an acronym I learned while in Kochevnikstan to help me walk through a process of saying goodbye well.

R - RECONCILE

In preparing to say goodbye, the first step is to reconcile any broken relationships. If there is conflict or relational stress "hanging" in the air, take initiative to resolve it. Avoiding the person you have conflict with until you leave may seem easier, but it isn't better. Reconciling a relationship does not mean that you are now best friends but that you are choosing to live by the Scriptural mandate *"as far as it depends on you, live in peace with everyone"* (Rom. 12:18).

A - AFFIRM

It's equally important to intentionally affirm the good relationships you've developed with teammates and local friends. Affirmation is different from appreciation. Appreciation says *"thank you"* or *"I like you,"* but affirmation is specific. Affirmation says, *"I love your laugh because it always makes me smile"* or *"the way you love people challenges me to do the same."* You can give affirmation in a variety of ways: write a note; take someone to lunch or to a place that is special to you both; make a gift for them. Begin affirming people 1-2 months before your departure, starting with your outer circle of friends first and working your way inward to your closest friends.

F - FAREWELL

Most of us think about saying goodbye to people, but it's important to say goodbye to places as well. When I left Kochevnikstan, one the R.A.F.T.ing things I wanted to do was to say farewell to the nearby ski resort. I had many fun staff retreats at this place as well as significant things the Lord taught as I gazed on the beauty of God's creation. Other places you might want to say goodbye to might be your favorite local restaurant, the classroom where you taught, the school where you studied language, or your favorite quiet place in the middle of the city.

T - THINK DESTINATION

Finally, spend time thinking about your destination. This is probably the hardest of the four R.A.F.T.ing things to do since most people tend to "lean" too much and others not enough. "Leaning" is a term that means someone is beginning to withdraw from their current situation and relationships and "leaning" toward their next destination. Leaning too much too soon can be detrimental to finishing well. On the other hand, not "thinking destination" because the future unknowns are too overwhelming can also be detrimental. The goal of "think destination" is to spend enough time thinking and planning for life after you return in a way that frees you up to be all where you are in your final weeks in your country. The goal is both/and: think well for landing in your home culture AND finish well in your host country.

📖 FOR FURTHER STUDY

Read the following verses:

Matthew 5:23-24	Romans 12:14-18
Matthew 18:15	1 Thessalonians 5:11
Colossians 3:13-15	Ephesians 4:29
2 Chronicles 28:2	Nehemiah 2:5-9

What does the Word have to say about each of these R.A.F.T.ing steps? How can you practically apply these verses to your life right now?

Read Paul's farewell to the Ephesian Elders in Acts 20:13-38. What can you learn from Paul about saying goodbye?

REVERSE CULTURE SHOCK

I sat on the floor of my room crying uncontrollably. I was overwhelmed by the excessive wealth I saw in American culture (and I don't even live in a wealthy area). I felt judgmental. I felt frustrated. Most of all I felt disgusted with myself that I belonged to this frivolous system of self-ishness, waste, and shallowness. In a moment of despair, I literally said out loud, "*I wish my house would burn down!*"

Thankfully the Lord does not give into our rashly spoken requests, and while He gently listened to my rants, he was not swayed by my drama queen theatrics. My house did not burn down. That shocking comment from my own mouth snapped me back into reality, and I began to process more clearly exactly what was going on inside of me that led me to such an irrational and extreme thought.

Now I can look back on that time and smile. I am often overly dramatic and find myself thinking of the most extreme circumstances. While my comment was clearly over the top, my emotions at the time were very real. I had spent the summer in Bangkok, Thailand. It was not my first time overseas, but it was my first time on a missions trip and the first time I had been in a place that was awash with poverty. Spectacular skyscrapers of the most modern design stood next to families living in cardboard boxes. I can still picture the sight in my mind: beggars without limbs sitting on the side of the road or children running after you with hands out waiting for something. The worst part about these beggars – I found out later – is that they often have their own version of a "pimp," a person who offers some level of protection and provision for them in exchange for taking all of their earnings from their day of begging. Since that time I've traveled widely and seen much worse poverty, but that was the first time I had been exposed to something so drastically different than the wealthy world I'd grown up in.[1] It was hard to process, hard to know what my response should be to this hopelessness surrounding me. And then I got back to the U.S. to my air conditioned home on acres of green, forested land my family owned, with plenty of food in our pantry and multiple cars in our yard.

1   You may not think you live in a wealthy world, but when you consider that 56% of the world's people live on less that $2 a day it puts things in a different perspective!

I was plagued with guilt (irrational guilt but guilt nonetheless) over the plenty I had in comparison to the little the families living in those cardboard boxes had. So I sat in my room and cried.

This was my very first experience with reverse culture shock. While not everyone experiences reverse culture shock so dramatically, everyone who has lived cross-culturally experiences reverse culture shock at some point and to some degree. An online business dictionary defines reverse culture shock as *"the shock suffered by expatriates returning home after lengthy overseas assignments. It is caused by the fact that the cultural norms of the ex-pat's overseas assignment become natural to them, over their home country's own traditions and customs."*[2]

Reverse culture shock – much like our initial cultural adjustment – can't be avoided. Even if you understand it and understand why you are feeling the way you do, you can't just turn it off.

When going TO a new country we talk about "culture shock." We expect there to be differences and adjustments. We are prepared to change the way that we naturally think about and do things for the sake of advancing the Gospel. But reverse culture shock can be much worse. We often don't expect things to be different, and in fact they probably aren't different. WE are different and experience our home culture differently because of how we have changed. In my example, I had never thought about how wealthy I was compared to the rest of the world. I didn't know anything different. Then I went to Thailand and experienced real poverty first hand. When I came back, I was unprepared for how much I had been changed by that experience, and I saw my old life in a whole new light. Because I'm a person of extremes, I had an extreme response; I became extremely judgmental of American culture. So much so that I wrongly adopted a "I hate America" mentality that spilled over in muttered disapproving comments until someone called me out on it. No culture is perfect, and America is no exception. But when we live cross-culturally we spend a lot of energy

2   http://www.businessdictionary.com/definition/reverse-culture-shock.html

immersing in, learning, and accepting our new culture, and it's easy to become hypercritical of our home culture. We are always hardest on the things we hold most dear.

Reverse culture shock – much like our initial cultural adjustment – can't be avoided. Even if you understand it and understand why you are feeling the way you do, you can't just turn it off. You have to walk through it. It helps to have someone who has been there listen to you rant your frustrations and remind you of truths that you know.

In the two plus decades since that first summer trip, I've been back and forth between my home and host cultures numerous times. Fortunately, I've never experienced reverse culture shock quite like I did that first time, but every time I return to the U.S. there is something new that catches me off guard. On one furlough it was pharmaceutical commercials. It seemed that every other commercial on TV was about how popping some pill could take away any pain, depression, or sadness you possessed. I was appalled by the American health care system promoting what I considered a health, wealth, and prosperity gospel. Another time it was the automated self-service check out stations. Not only was I intimidated by the high tech system, I was also a little disappointed in the move away from real life people interaction. I felt sort of like Sarah Connor from *Terminator*, afraid that computers were eliminating people and taking over the world!

The more you move back and forth between cultures, the more you learn to expect changes, helping you not be so caught off guard by them. You learn coping mechanisms that help you process the new things and adjust your own attitude more quickly. Reverse culture shock is a natural part of the process. Let the Lord use it, like other things, to teach you and refine you and make you more and more like him (God is never caught off guard by reverse culture shock!).

✔ LET'S GET PRACTICAL

The more often you move back and forth between cultures the more you will develop your own coping mechanisms.

Here are a few things that have helped me:

1. Prayer
Weeks (or sometimes months) before I know I'm going to the U.S., I start asking the Lord to prepare me for re-entry. Since I don't know the details of what will catch me off guard, I ask the Lord to prepare me with basic Christ-like attitudes: grace, thankfulness, peace, eternal perspective, others-centeredness, quick to listen, slow to speak, slow to become angry!

2. Thankfulness
Thankfulness is the best tool in my tool belt for combating a negative and judgmental attitude. I focus on being thankful both for the things I love about my home culture as well as the things I love about my host culture.

3. Cast Vision
Often what I see in my home culture is not good. I can become judgmental and criticize, or I can ask the Lord for opportunities to cast vision for another way of thinking. For example, when I came back to the States for the first time after 9/11, Americans were afraid of anything Muslim; here I had been living in a Muslim culture. My experience with my Muslim friends post-9/11 was one of care and concern. My Muslim friends were not terrorists – they hated the terrorism and misrepresentation of Islam as much as I hate the mis-representations of Christianity! When I got back to the U.S. I could have been critical of "Muslim hating" Americans (who didn't know a single Muslim first hand). Instead, God gave me opportunities to share about my own experiences with my Muslim friends and what they thought about the 9/11 attack. It opened doors for great discussions about loving people. I also had opportunities to cast vision and cultivate in others a heart for Muslims to experience the freedom of the true Gospel.

MOVING STREAMS: PERSPECTIVE ON RE-ENTRY

I grew up near the water – ocean, rivers, streams, lakes, and ponds. I love the water and the ways God has written truth into the natural movements of water. Imagine a slow moving stream peacefully flowing along. At some point, there is a fork and the stream splits – not forever but for a time. One part is more narrow, and a collection of some rocks and debris cause the streams to move a little faster, even showing white water at times. This faster, white water stream flows separately from the slower peaceful stream for quite a distance, but eventually they both empty into the same larger river.

Returning to the U.S. after 2 or more years in a cross-cultural situation is like the faster moving stream merging with the slower stream into the same larger river. There are some important lessons we can learn about re-entry from this stream illustration.

BE A LEARNER OF YOUR STREAM

Your life for the last few years has been like the fast moving stream full of obstacles, debris, white water, and the occasional peaceful flow of a quiet stretch. Whether your experience laboring internationally was amazing or challenging (or likely both), there's no doubt it was full of learning new things. Especially the first months, every day felt like a year because of all the new experiences. It's important that you understand this and that you invest time to process and debrief all the experiences, emotions, lessons learned, etc. In the chapter "Communicating Your Experiences" I give some practical suggestions to help you do this. The better you understand your own experiences, the more you will be able to share them with the people you love back home who haven't experienced this same stream.

REALIZE THAT YOURS ISN'T THE ONLY STREAM

Your friends and family back home haven't experienced the same things you have and their interest in hearing about the details or you "divergent" stream will range from wanting every detail to being satisfied with the standard "*it was good*" response. Share as much of your experiences as you can, but the most important thing to remember is that your stream is not the only stream that's been moving. Your friends and family also lived their lives, just as you did, during the years you were away. They have their own experiences and stories that they want to share with you. It's easy for you (and them) to feel like their stories are not as "exciting" as yours are (and that is probably true). But their stories are important to them! One of the biggest mistakes people make in returning home is thinking that they are the only ones who have changed and the only ones who have something new to share. It's natural and understandable, but it's also very self-centered. A big part of re-entry is choosing to be "others-centered" as we talk with people both about our own experiences and ask about theirs.

Let me make a side comment here. I say that it's important to remember that you aren't the only one who has changed, but maybe you are. Maybe the slow moving stream that represents your friend's and family's lives hasn't changed at all. They are the same people they were when you left, just a few years older, but the things the Lord taught you, showed you, and convicted you of make you very different from when you left. In this situation it's easy to become very judgmental of the people you love the most. Either you judge them for not changing or you judge them for not understanding your new perspective. Again, it's natural and understandable, but it's also very self-centered. Be thankful for the changes God has brought about in your life without finding fault with those who haven't changed so much – it is HE who has brought about these changes in you.

Be thankful for the changes God has brought about in your life without finding fault with those who haven't changed so much – it is HE who has brought about these changes in you.

MERGING STREAMS COULD PRODUCE WHITE WATER

Have you ever seen two strong streams come together? At the point of merging, there is white water (i.e. turbulence) until the two merging rivers move forward and become one, finding a mutual rhythm and flow. This is a picture of our merging back into the natural flow of our home culture. It doesn't matter if you do this one time or 100 times.

Every time may be different, some more intense while others calm, but there is always some degree of white water as you re-enter. Accept this. Embrace it. Be a learner of yourself, your family, and your friends as you merge together back into a natural flow of life.

WE ARE ALL PART OF THE SAME RIVER

At the end of the day, we are all part of the same river, whether we are flowing separately along different paths or merged and flowing together along the same path. We are one body (of water). As you return to the U.S. and re-enter the culture – both U.S. culture and your family culture – keep that in mind. It's easy to become judgmental or frustrated, but that's not helpful. It doesn't build bridges or promote understanding. Let the changes in your life because of your experiences merge back into the river and become a force of influence on the whole river to encourage, challenge, and shape.

✎ ON YOUR OWN

As you prepare to return to your home culture, think about your family. What kinds of experiences have they been having that they want to share with you? What are some good questions you can ask them to draw out those experiences? (Think about the kinds of questions you wish people would ask you.)

It's hard to anticipate the "white water" places in our re-entry, but ask the Lord to give you insight into what those things might be. Begin praying now that the Lord would give you wisdom, peace, and graciousness to navigate the white waters you'll encounter.

COMMUNICATING YOUR EXPERIENCES

"How was your trip?" your friend asks you. You think to yourself, *"My trip? I've been gone 2 years and God has completely turned my life upside down and inside out. I wasn't on vacation at the beach!"*

"What did you learn?" a more informed friend asks you about your 1-2 years of service on the field. How do you begin to tell someone with no concept of your experience about all the things God did in your life?

"So, how was it? Did you meet any cool people? (3 second pause) *Oh, let me tell you about what happened to me while you were gone...."* and off goes your friend telling you all about what's been going on with him or her, clearly not very interested in the details of your last few years.

Unfortunately, not everyone is well informed about living and laboring cross-culturally, and even if they are, they often don't know how to ask good questions. Then there are those people who really love you but are only slightly interested in the details of your experiences. They are far more interested in telling you about all that has happened to them while you've been gone. Communicating your experiences can be challenging at best, and at worst, a chore that feels overwhelming. Yet learning to communicate about your life internationally – what you have learned and seen and experienced – is essential not just for the vision it casts for others but for your own emotional health, debriefing, and re-entry.

> *"Not only was the teacher wise, but also he imparted knowledge to the people. He pondered and searched out and set in order many proverbs. The Teacher searched to find just the right words, and what he wrote was upright and true."*
> Ecclesiastes 12:9-10

Solomon was a wise man and imparted that wisdom and knowledge to the people. At the end of Ecclesiastes, we are given the secret of how he passed on his wisdom: *"He pondered and searched out and set in order...[then]...he searched to find just the right words."* Like Solomon, it's important that we think about how to best communicate our experiences to others. Not only does the process help us prepare to share with others, it also forces us to evaluate our experiences for ourselves. It's not experience that is the best teacher but evaluated experience! Here are a few helpful hints on communicating your experiences.

DEBRIEF- GET IT ALL OUT THERE

Before you leave the field spend some time doing a self-evaluation. Like Solomon, take time to "ponder." If you are a journaler, then set aside a day or a few half days to write down everything from how you feel to what you learned to the things that were hard. Or if you journaled throughout your assignment, go back through your journals looking for themes and patterns. If you hate journaling, find another way to unpack your experiences. One of my teammates hated to write so he "journaled" using a tape recorder. If you are artistic, you might want to consider drawing as a way to debrief. Or simply find a quiet place to sit and think – mentally journaling – asking the Lord to guide your thoughts and keep you focused. The key is to spend some extended time reflecting back on your experiences. There's a reason we have the saying that hindsight is 20/20. Looking back at your experiences can give you an understanding of a situation or something the Lord was doing that you didn't have in the midst of it. A few questions that you could ask yourself during this self-debrief:

What have I learned about God and His character?
What have I learned about myself?
What have I learned about relating on a team?
What have I learned about laboring cross-culturally?
What have I learned about loving the lost?

Don't get bogged down at this point in trying to put things in order or saying it just right. Just get it all out there. I encourage you to start setting aside small chunks of time 2-3 weeks before you are scheduled to return home. It may feel like you will have more time once you get back, but chances are that you will be flooded will all kinds of re-entry emotions that will cloud your review of your time in your country.

SUMMARIZE YOUR EXPERIENCE INTO SHORT ANSWERS

Once you've been able to self-debrief, getting all your thoughts and experience "out there," follow the example of Solomon and "set in order" the themes that emerged as you pondered your experiences. The goal here is not to capture everything but to be able to pass on a few of your experiences in a way that will both encourage people as well as honestly share of yourself. I try to summarize my experiences into 4 types of responses:

1. One Word. A one word summary prepares you with an answer to the very bland question: *"How was your trip?"* If you have thought about this one word, then you will not be tempted to default to an equally bland answer like "good" or "great." Let your one word be descriptive and "salty," meaning let it make people curious enough to want more (e.g., life-changing, challenging, upside down, wrecking ball, or a word from the language you've spent time learning). Your one word answer should be honest and reflective of your experiences. Use a Thesaurus, be creative, and ponder what one word the Lord wants to give you. Not only is a one-word summary helpful for communicating, but it also gives you a "hook" for thinking about your own experiences.

2. One minute. For some people a one word answer will be enough, but a creative one-word summary will often open the conversation for a slightly longer answer. I call this the one minute version: a thesis statement about your time cross-culturally that unpacks some of what you learned and experienced. For example, if your one word is "wrecking ball" then your one minute summary might be something like: *"The Lord took a wrecking ball to everything I thought I knew about Him and myself. He tore down a lifetime of wrong thinking and rebuilt a foundation of truth."* (Wrecking ball was my real one word summary after my first 1-year experience cross-culturally).

3. 5-20 minutes. If you are sharing with close friends or family, they probably want to know more than a one minute summary (although not always). A 5-20 minute summary is like a 3 point outline or 5 paragraph essay. It's still short but has a few different points that unpack your "thesis" even further. This is also a good outline to think about if you expect to be sharing at your home fellowship, Sunday school classes, or with donors. In this summary, include a few stories along with the principles of what you've learned (using the previous example, you may share exactly what the wrong views were that you had of God and yourself and what right views he rebuilt). If you want to get really creative, you could even have a 5-20 minute "personal response," focusing on what you learned personally and a 5-20 minute "cultural response" that is more about the country and culture where you lived. Again, the goal is not to have this down to perfection or written word for word on 3x5 cards. The goal is to have a general outline in your mind – one you have thought about (pondered) and summarized (set in order). It's like giving a speech where you have a few key phrases, ones you searched to find just the right wording for, that are anchors for how and what you talk about so that you don't get bogged down in too many details or start rambling and lose your audiences' interest.

4. Longer version. Hopefully, you have a few close friends and family members who really, really want to sit down over coffee or tea and hear everything that you learned and experienced. These will be the people who will ask better questions that draw you out or, if you a verbal processor, who will simply listen to you talk. Many organizations have a debriefing process for people to complete once they return home. If you have the opportunity to debrief either informally or formally, I strongly encourage it!

HAVE 4-5 STORIES IN YOUR REPERTOIRE

In addition to thinking through your one word, one minute, and 5 minute summaries, have a few stories in mind to share. Personally, I get tired of sharing the same stories over and over again. I usually have 5 or more in mind, and I rotate them as I talk to people so that everyone hears one story but they're not all the same. Stories are powerful ways to communicate our experiences, what we've learned, and insights about the country and culture. Stories are what people will remember most.

CULTURAL INSIGHTS

On one trip back to the U.S. after several years of living in Kochevnikstan, I noticed that I was getting really tired of talking to donors, which is unusual because I like visiting donors. I realized that I was tired, because I was talking mostly about the cultural differences, political views, and economic realities of Kochevnikstan rather than talking about God, what He was doing in my life, and in the lives of my friends. The reality is that most people want to know about the cultural things: eating scorpions in China (which I didn't!), political and economic stability in Central Asia, that Holland doesn't take credit cards without chips in them. While those things are fun to talk about and should definitely be part of your story repertoire, it gets old pretty quickly (at least for me). Since these are things that people really want to know, I have learned to think of ways that these discussions can lead me into how God is working (economic instability pushes people to seek security which can only be found in Him) or how the cultural differences challenge me to rethink what is Scriptural versus what is cultural (like the difference between a guilt or shame world view).

Learning to communicate your experiences from laboring cross-culturally is important for two main reasons. First, it's important for us to evaluate our experiences and really learn from them. But it's equally important to use the opportunity to cast vision for our friends, family, donors, and churches for how God is working in the world. We are ambassadors, not only when we are on the field, but also when we are at home sharing with the body how the harvest is plentiful and the laborers are few. Sharing our stories well is a means God uses to stir peoples hearts to pray, to give, to send, to go. Don't underestimate the power of sharing your story and don't short-change people by not being prepared to share it well.

📖 FOR FURTHER STUDY

Read Acts 14:26-28 about Paul's debrief in Antioch.

Read Colossians 4:7-9. What was the purpose for Paul sending Tychicus to Colosse?

Read Proverbs 22:20-22. How can you practically apply this wise counsel?

YOU ARE DIFFERENT

"What is your address?" the receptionist asked. I was sitting in my doctor's office after being back in the U.S. on a Home Assignment for all of 24 hours. The receptionist was not unkind, but it was clear she was ready to move forward quickly from what she considered to be a no-brainer question. The receptionist was right; the address question should be a no-brainer. I mean, everyone knows their address, right? Even little kids can spout off a memorized address that mom and dad have drilled into their heads. But I was temporarily speechless, my mind whirling for the right answer. Which address did she want? My international address (in Kochevnikstan)? My work address (U.S. organization in a different state than my U.S. home)? My U.S. "home" address (from my drivers license, which is my dad's address)? My billing address (which is my brother's address)? My current U.S. address (where I was living while in the U.S. on this home assignment, neither my dad's or brother's address)? Or my local address (where I was staying temporarily in the city where the doctor's office was located)?

I recovered after a few seconds of uncomfortable silence and asked the receptionist which address would be most helpful, briefly explaining my situation (I've learned that people rarely want the long drawn out version of my "dilemma" and that it only serves to make me appear even more schizophrenic than I already feel when I start rattling off a long explanation about the complexities of my life that the average person doesn't understand!). The receptionist was helpful, and we landed on my billing address (which happened to be the same as my insurance address). The interaction only lasted a few minutes, but it felt like longer. I spent the rest of my time in the doctor's waiting room, pondering how such a simple question like *"what's your address?"* could make me feel so out of place and different.

BEING AN ANOMALY
Seven addresses, all of them very real and very legitimate, but to a "normal" person – who is used to having one address at a time – I am an anomaly. It's especially awkward if I call and talk to the credit card company. I've learned to think ahead about my answers, because hesitations about simple questions about your address (or your former

address), don't just make you sound stupid, they make you sound like an identity thief.

Your address may not be the specific question that causes you to be temporarily speechless, but there will be something that makes you feel "out of place" or "crazy" or an "anomaly" (meaning not normal). Be prepared for this – it is normal for people like us!

BEING MISUNDERSTOOD

I am a very organized person. In fact, if you asked anyone I've worked with internationally, they would confirm that I planned ahead to a fault. But my parent's don't me see me that way – especially my mom.[3] She thinks that I am the most loosy-goosey, disorganized, undisciplined, and wait to the last minute decision maker she knows. And in my mom's world, I AM all of those things. My parents have lived in the same city for more than 40 years and in only 2 houses in the last 30 years. On the other hand, I have lived in over 10 places (same city, different apartments) in the last 10 years.

Living overseas – especially in a less structured Asian culture – teaches you to hold plans loosely; even if there is a plan (which there often isn't), it can change in a moment. As cross-cultural workers, not only do we learn out of necessity to adopt some of the cultural norms of our host culture (that are often at odds with our own home culture), but we also learn a whole new "culture" of international travel that affects our ability for things to happen the way we plan.

Kochevnikstan requires ex-pats to have a visa in order to visit and live in the country. While not all countries require American citizens to have a visa in addition to a passport, many countries where we labor DO. This is a whole new world that is "normal" for all our international co-workers but quite unfamiliar to our family and friends in the U.S.

Every time I was in the U.S. on home assignment, part of my prepara-

---

3   Let me just say that my relationship with my mom is very good. She's super supportive of what I do and of me in general. She does not have unrealistic expectations or demands. All in all, our relationship is healthy. THIS issue of being misunderstood is not characteristic of my parents but a reality of the breadth of difference between my very transient "change often" lifestyle and their very stable "one address" lifestyle.

tion to return was getting a visa. I planned for it, allowing time for the visa processing, thinking about where I would be and what address to have my passport and new visa sent. In spite of my planning, there were several times that I was down to the very last day waiting for my visa to arrive so I could actually get on the plane to return. One time I was even delayed in New York City, waiting on my visa for a full week. If you've ever had to get a visa in a less than developed country (and it can be even worse for more developed countries), you know exactly what I'm talking about.

The very worst visa delay was one that affected my parents directly. We were supposed to drive together from my hometown to Atlanta where I would catch my international flight. My visa didn't come, so I couldn't leave (it was being mailed to my parent's address). My parents went on to Atlanta with my stuff, and I was to catch a late afternoon flight and meet them. To make a long story short, nothing worked out as planned, and my mother was so stressed out. She could not understand the "normality" of visa delays. In her world things like this didn't – and shouldn't – happen.

Being different doesn't make you better than other people or worse than them, simply different. And different is often misunderstood.

Whether it's your parent's or friends, visa delays or some other pressure point, there will be times when you and your lifestyle as an international worker will be misunderstood by your mono-cultural friends and family. What we do, the way we live, the uniqueness of our "normal" life (like visa challenges), are not the way mono-cultural Americans live. They aren't wrong anymore than we are wrong, but we are different. In the same way that we make choices to be learners of the differences in our host culture, we must also make choices to be learners of our home culture. With my mom, I learned that my change-often lifestyle was too stressful for her. While I continued to share my life with my parents, I made choices to protect them from some of the "unknowns." I didn't tell them about plans until I was pretty sure they would happen (which contributed to my mom thinking I never planned ahead, but that was better than her being stressed in the middle of my uncertainty). I was cautious to not make promises that might be affected by my transient lifestyle, and I looked for ways to understand their point of view and their world rather than being critical of it.

SOUNDING BOASTFUL WHEN YOU REALLY AREN'T

"We went to the beach in Florida last week and it was so beautiful," my friend shared as she started telling me about her trip. Wanting to contribute to the conversation I chime in, *"I know the white sand beaches in Florida are so much nicer than beaches in Thailand or in Australia. I mean I liked those beaches, but they can't compare to Destin's Emerald Coast."* My friend just looks at me. I know that I've said something wrong, but I'm not quite sure what it is.

One of the perks (in my opinion) of living internationally is that you do more international traveling to exotic places than you would if you lived and worked in the United States. It's likely that you have an annual country and/or regional conference – maybe at a resort in your host country or maybe in some sunny beach paradise (like Thailand or Turkey). Vacation also takes on a whole meaning. In Kochevnikstan even the locals take vacations outside of the country to places like Cyprus, United Arab Emirates, or Singapore. If you live in Europe, a vacation will likely mean a trip to another country rather than a trip to another state. And in Africa, a weekend camping adventure takes on a whole new meaning.

Living in another culture – no matter how developed and comfortable the country – is hard. It wears on you in ways you don't even realize. All the organizations I know strongly recommend and often require workers to "get out" on a regular basis. This is a part of your job and important for the overall health of you and your family or team. But when you start talking to your mono-cultural American friends and family about your "vacation" to exotic places that they probably can't afford to go, it can sound like you are being boastful and bragging about your adventures – even if you are just sharing honestly about your life. Another challenge with sharing about the places you travel is that you can feel like donors will be judgmental of how you are spending money. Why are you going to Thailand for a conference when they could never afford that? It's important to be comfortable in your own skin and come to terms with not only the challenges of your life cross-culturally but also the perks of it!

The key here is not to clam up and never share about your life. But simply be aware of how your friends are responding to the things you share. Be careful about unintentionally "one upping" them as they share about their daily life, work, vacation, etc. The main principle in relating to your home culture is the same as the main principle in going to another culture – be a learner not a judger.

SUMMARY

As part of the re-entry process (whether on a home ministry assignment or permanently returning), it's important to remember that you are different. Your life has not been "normal" in the sense that most people around you experience normal, routine, daily life in America. Your experiences are different than most of your mono-cultural friends, and while some of them will really try to understand and be interested, some of them simply can't relate. Being different doesn't make you better than other people or worse than them, simply different. And different is often misunderstood.

✎ ON YOUR OWN

In what situations might you feel like an anomaly or misunderstood? Think about how you will respond to these situations. How can you use these situations to open doors for deeper conversations with people?

How will you respond when people are indifferent or look at you like you are from another planet? How do you think Jesus felt when people did not understand him? How did he respond?

Practical
Resources

COMMON REACTIONS TO LEARNING NEW THINGS

COMMON WRONG REACTIONS

1. **Condemnation**: *"I should have already known this."*
   Remember, God has you where He wants you; you should not have already known the truth He will reveal.
2. **Blame shifting**: *"Why didn't someone tell me this earlier?"*
   They may have, but you were not ready to hear it. God is sovereign over your past.
3. **Self focus**: *"We need to tell everyone this now!"*
   Everyone has their own needs. It's easy to think others need what you're learning (and they might), but meet people where THEY are.
4. **Judgment**: *"We are 'missing it' in our ministry."*
   Maybe not…the basics are basic, and babies need milk and babies need food. Take time to evaluate where the new truth fits into ministry as a mentor.
5. **Guilt**: *"If I used my time better, I could have already known this."*
   Probably not. God teaches us what we need to know when we need to know it. You must search, but God alone reveals truth. If you were/are in sin about how you spent/spend time, repent and go forward.
6. **Pride**: *"You didn't know that!"*
   Other believers are not less mature because they do not understand this truth you have just learned.

COMMON RIGHT REACTIONS

1. **Thankfulness**: *"Thank you, God, for teaching me something new."*
   Give God the credit for revealing truth to you.
2. **Personal application**: *"How can I apply this to my walk with God?"*
   Great questions! This will move you to understanding and wisdom. How did Jesus do it? Ask God and listen. Write out thoughts as you pray, listen, and get into the Word.
3. **Sharing with others**: *"How can I apply this and pass it along to others in an appropriate way?"*
   We are to *"teach those things I have commanded you."* Be in touch with others' needs and share this new information on their level. Take time to assimilate. Ask mentors for ideas on how to pass it on to others.

ONE ANOTHERING – A 30-DAY EXPERIMENT

For the next 30 days, take a few minutes a day to apply one of the "one another" verses to a teammate, roommate, or friend. Ask the Lord to give you specific opportunities to apply the Scriptural principles in a timely and encouraging way.

1. Matthew 18:15-19 - Restore one another.
2. Mark 9:50 - Be at peace with one another.
3. Acts 2:42-47 - Learn, share, and worship with one another.
4. Romans 12:10 - Honor one another.
5. Romans 12:15 - Rejoice with one another.
6. Romans 12:15 - Weep with one another.
7. Romans 14:13 - Stop passing judgment on one another.
8. Romans 15:2 - Please one another.
9. Romans 15:7 - Accept one another.
10. Romans 15:14 - Instruct one another.
11. 2 Corinthians 2:7-11 - Forgive and reaffirm your love for one another.
12. Galatians 5:13 - Serve one another in love.
13. Ephesians 4:25 - Speak truthfully to one another.
14. Ephesians 4:29 - Speak words that build up one another.
15. Ephesians 4:32 - Be kind and compassionate to one another.
16. Ephesians 5:21 - Submit to one another.
17. Philippians 2:1-5 - Look out for the interests of others.
18. Ephesians 5:19 - Speak to one another in psalms, hymns, & spiritual songs.
19. 1 Thessalonians 5:15 - Be kind to each other.
20. 2 Thessalonians 1:3 - Love one another.
21. 2 Thessalonians 3:15 - Warn one another as brothers.
22. 2 Timothy 2:22-26 - Gently instruct one another in kindness.
23. James 4:11 - Do not slander one another.
24. James 5:9 - Do not grumble against one another.
25. James 5:13-16 - Pray for one another.
26. James 5:16 - Confess your sins to one another
27. 1 Peter 4:9 - Offer hospitality to one another without grumbling.
28. 1 Peter 4:10 - Use all gifts to serve one another faithfully.
29. 1 Peter 5:5 - Clothe yourselves with humility toward one another.
30. 1 John 1:7 - Have fellowship with one another.

GMJGR - A Gospel Dialogue and Diagnosis

Just as a cake has the same essential ingredients regardless of the flavor, the Gospel has the same essential ingredients regardless of time or culture. Below are listed the five key points of the Gospel. Look up the verses in Scripture and look for ones that you could share with people who have questions about each main point of the Gospel. Use the outline to "dialogue" with people and "diagnose" where they are in their understanding (or misunderstanding) of the Gospel.

GOD is holy/perfect
What do you think God is like? Is God perfect? How is God different from man?

Isaiah 55:8-9	Psalms 24:1	Psalms 50:21
Exodus 34:6	John 10:18	Isaiah 40:12-17

MAN is sinful (not holy/perfect)
What is mankind like? Is this true for all men/women everywhere? Why or why not? By your own standard of right and wrong have YOU ever done anything wrong? (Do you think you are perfect?)

Romans 3:10-11	Ephesians 2:1-3	Isaiah 64:6
Romans 6:23	Isaiah 53:6	Psalms 51:5

JESUS is the Mediator between God and Man
Do you believe Jesus was a real, historical person? What is the character and nature of Jesus? Is he different from man? How?

Isaiah 53:5,8	1 Corinthians 15:22	1 Timothy 2:5
Hebrews 1:3	John 14:6	1 Peter 2:22

GRACE, not works, is the means to a relationship with God
What is grace? How does grace affect a relationship with God? How does man receive grace?

Ephesians 2:4-9	Colossians 2:13-15	Romans 9:16-18
John 5:39	2 Timothy 1:9-10	Galatians 2:21

REPENTANCE is our response to the grace of God
What is repentance? What does it mean? Why is it necessary?

Luke 13:3	Romans 2:4	2 Peter 3:9
Romans 10:10, 13	Acts 26:20	Acts 2:38

KINGDOM OF GOD BIBLE STUDY

There are 155 references to Kingdom of God (or heaven) in the New Testament. What is the Kingdom of God and why is it so important and central in Jesus' teaching? The questions below will introduce you to the concept of the Kingdom of God. The verses are not exhaustive but a suggested place to begin.

What is the PURPOSE of the Kingdom of God?

| Proverbs 24:11 | Luke 4:43 | Matthew 9:35 |
| Ephesians 6:10-20 | Mark 1:39 | |

What are the characteristics of the Kingdom of God?

Daniel 2:4, 4:3	Daniel 6:26	Matthew 13:11
Psalms 145:11-13	Matthew 4:23	Matthew 11:11
Psalms 103:9	Matthew 24:13	John 18:36

WHO can be part of the Kingdom?

| Matthew 21:33-46 | Matthew 13:47-50; | Matthew 5:20 |
| Matthew 8:11-12 | 13:24-30 | |

HOW are we to respond to/enter into the Kingdom of God?

Matthew 7:21	Matthew 3:2	Matthew 5:20
Mark 1:14	Matthew 18:1-3	Acts 14:22
Matthew 4:17	Matthew 19:14	

HOW does the Kingdom of God ADVANCE?

| Matthew 4:17, 23 | Ephesians 6:10-18 | Acts 8:1 |
| Matthew 6:10 | Matthew 13:19, 20-33 | |

What are the PROMISES of the Kingdom

| Matthew 6:33 | Matthew 13:43 | Revelation 11:35 |
| Matthew 5:10 | Matthew 24:13 | Daniel 2:44 |

WARNINGS about the Kingdom of God

Matthew 23:13	Matthew 8:12	Matthew 25:30
Matthew 18:5-9	Matthew 13:50	Matthew 21:33-46
Matthew 19:13-14	Matthew 22:13	Mark 1:15

KINGDOM CULTURE VALUES BIBLE STUDY

The way to recognize TRUTH versus LIES is to become an expert on the TRUTH. Matthew 5-7 is called "The Sermon on the Mount". In it Jesus teaches us many principles about Kingdom values and how Kingdom values are different from worldly values.

Read Matthew 5-7.

How many times does "Kingdom" or "Kingdom of Heaven" occur in these 2 chapters?

When Jesus talks about the Kingdom of Heaven in these chapters, what is the specific context?

Make a list of the Kingdom values in these 3 chapters.

List LIES the world (home, host, or other cultures) believes that are opposite of Kingdom values.

Application: Where do you see conflict between Kingdom values and your home and host culture values?

CHOICES I CHOOSE TO MAKE

Have you ever seen the inspiration poster that says, *"Life is 90% what happens to us and 10% how we choose to respond"*? I think it's true. I can choose joy, or I can choose to wallow in my hardships. Choosing the things listed below is NOT about sucking it up and deciding I can do it all on my own. It IS about choosing to believe God's truth – His promises – to call us, make us, humble us, help us to be what He has chosen for us. Yes, I choose, but even that choice I can't make on my own. I need Him to work in me, making me want to choose to obey His will and then helping me do what He wants (Phil. 2:13).

I choose to adapt (Phil. 2:6)
I choose to change my schedule (Mark 6:31-34)
I choose to be uncomfortable in certain settings (John 22:42)
I choose to relate to people different from me (Luke 19:7; John 4:9)
I choose to adjust the way I dress (Phil. 2:7))
I choose to not become defensive (1 Peter 2:23)
I choose to learn and relate to the culture I live in (Luke 2:52)
I choose to speak words that build up and don't tear down (Eph. 4:29)
I choose to stretch my convictions, letting tension exist (Matt. 4:1-11)
I choose to jealously protect my time alone with the Father even when others want to distract me (Mark 1:35-37)
I choose to be joyful (Luke 10:20-21; Heb. 12:2-3)
I choose to live in light of eternity (Phil. 2:9-11)

I would not choose to do these things because of money, or prestige, or power. There is only one reason I choose to radically alter my comfortable lifestyle ---

BECAUSE JESUS DID.

"For Christ's love compels us...[that our] attitude should be the same as that of Jesus..." (2 Corinth. 5:14-15 and Phil. 2:5)

ATTRIBUTES OF GOD

"Thus says the Lord: 'Let not the wise man glory in his wisdom, Let not the mighty man glory in his might, Nor let the rich man glory in his riches; But let him who glories glory in this, That he understands and knows Me, That I am the LORD, exercising loving kindness, judgment, and righteousness in the earth. For in these I delight,' says the Lord."

Jeremiah 9:23-24

WAYS TO USE THIS STUDY

1. Single sitting: I suggest for the first time you do this study that you set aside several hours (perhaps a day of prayer) to "bathe yourself" in the truths of God's character. Looking at all the attributes at one time gives a "helicopter" view of God's character that gets missed as we dive deeper into the individual verses. The first time I did this study was a full day staff training seminar. We literally "ran through" the verses. But at the end of the day, I found that I had insight into the overall nature of God's character and it's application to my life that I would not have noticed if I had worked through the study more slowly.

Look up verses and summarize. Define the attribute and how it affects you. Keep it simple for each individual attribute. At the end of the study write out an overall application – how does the character of God affect your view of God, view of yourself, and view of others.

2. One attribute a day: A second way to use the study would be to take one attribute a day. By keeping a "helicopter" view of the attribute you will see big picture things about this aspect of God's character. This method is especially helpful if you do not have several hours to do the full "run through;" you can do the whole study this way in about 2 weeks.

3. One attribute a week: Finally, you can use the study as a daily verse by verse encouragement of a specific attribute of God's character. This method is especially helpful if you are struggling with a particular problem in which you need to immerse yourself in the truth of a specific aspect of God's character.

Choose 6-7 verses from this attribute to focus on for a week. Each day, look up one verse and write down the truth you discover. Choose a part to meditate on during that day. At the end of the week, summarize the attribute and write down how it affects your view of God, self, and others.

ETERNAL - Limitless; Infinite

FAITHFUL - True; Sure; Safely relied upon; Committed

FORGIVING - To pour out; atonement; To cover over; To pardon

GOOD - His perfection that prompts Him to deal bountifully and kindly with All His creation

GRACIOUS - His unmerited, and unearned love and favor

HOLY - Perfect; Majestic Purity; Separation from Moral Evil

JUST- Fair; Honorable; Righteous; Commitment with Moral Right

KNOWING, ALL - Possessing perfect Knowledge; Never has He learned, been surprised or amazed

LOVING- Steadfast kindness; Eternally committed; Loyalty

MERCIFUL- Tender compassion towards those in misery

OMNIPRESENT- Everywhere at once; "God is Here"

PATIENT - Slow to anger; Longsuffering; Forbearance with the evil

POWERFUL, ALL - Able to bring to pass whatever He pleases; Power belongs to him and him alone

RIGHTEOUS - To be right; He maintains His Holiness in every respect

SOVEREIGN - God's Supremacy exercised in His will and power

TRUTH - Consistent; Reality; Genuine

B.R.I.D.E.

I'm a process-loving, structured, always-want-a-plan kind of person. So during my first year (1991) in Kochevnikstan, when God was teaching me a lot about sin in my heart, I wanted to know: How do I begin to root out this sin? What is the process? What do I need to do?

Romans 12:2 says, *"Do not conform any longer to the pattern of this world, but be transformed by the renewing of your mind. Then you will be able to test and approve what God's will is – his good pleasing and perfect will."*

We can break this down into three parts:
1. **Do not conform** – to the pattern of this world. As with repentance there is a conscious turning away from the habitual patterns. This means I have to first recognize those patterns.
2. **Be transformed** – As I pursue Christ and grow in him, my life is transformed.
3. **Renew your mind** – The battle happens in our minds. Feed my mind truth, believe it, obey it and my actions will follow suit.

As I journeyed through this process of not conforming, being transformed, and renewing my mind I developed this acronym B.R.I.D.E.[1] as a practical reminder of the "steps" I needed to take:

B – Be honest with yourself, God, and others (Ps. 51:6)
R – Recognize the lies; ask God to reveal them (Ps. 134:1, 23-24)
I – Identify the truth; use Scripture (John 17:17)
D – Develop new tastes (Jer. 2:11-13)
E – Engage your heart (Matt. 15:8-9, Ps. 115:3-8)

B – Be honest with yourself, God, and others
As I embarked on this journey of change from the inside out, my commitment was to be honest with myself (Ps. 51:6), with God (Ps. 41:12),

---

1   This is not a "formula" for transformation, nor is it a one time "do this and move on to something else." It's a life-long process based on biblical principles and promises. We never "arrive" until we reach heaven. But applying these principles to your life will form a habit that will eventually become like second nature.

and others (James 5:16). These verses became my prayer and invitation to the Lord to shine light into my "inmost parts." I don't know my "hidden faults" (Ps. 19:12-13), but the One who made me does know them, and He desires to bring them into the light. He desires truth in the deepest parts of my heart. My part is to ask God to reveal the sin in my heart. His part is to do it, and his word promises that he will.

R – Recognize the lies (ask God to reveal them)

Have you ever cut down a tree? Depending on the size of the tree, it's not too difficult to cut off the branches or even to cut down the trunk. But getting rid of the stump – it's an expensive, difficult and time-consuming process. Dealing with lies in our life is like getting rid of a tree stump. Cutting off the branches (trimming the behaviors) is relatively easy. But if you cut off a branch without dealing with the root it will eventually grow back. You have to kill the roots, and killing the roots is a time consuming and difficult process. The older the lie, the longer I've believed and clung to it, the harder it is to kill its roots. We need to learn to recognize the root lies we believe – not just the behaviors but the lies that lead to that behavior.

In Psalms 139:1 God promises that He knows me. He knows the tree, the branches, and the root system. He understands my past and the lies that I believe that I don't even know I believe. He knows what small seed (or lie) was planted, when it was planted, and how it took form. As we journey into the depths of our own hearts to begin to recognize the lies rooted there we need to pray earnestly as the psalmist did, *"Search me, O God and know my heart; test me and know my anxious thoughts. See if there is any offensive way in me and lead me in the way everlasting."*

I – Identify the truth (use Scripture)

Once we've recognized the root lies, we need to combat them with truth from God's word. In John 17, Jesus prays for his disciples and in verse 17 he prays, *"Sanctify them by the truth. Your word is truth."* We are sanctified [transformed] by the truth of God's word taking root in our lives and replacing the "patterns of the world" (Rom. 12:2) that have controlled our behaviors. God desires truth in the inmost parts. Ask Him to show you the lies and replace them with His truth!

Identifying truth and using it to combat the lies we believe is not a once done act, it is a continuous flow of truth that – over time – begins to completely replace the lie(s).

Have you ever cleaned a radiator? It is a 2-part process. First, you have to drain all the water out of the radiator. The water that flows out is usually gross and nasty. Even once the water is drained there is still gunk stuck to the inside walls of the radiator that has built up over time. Step two is to put a hose in the top plug of the radiator and let clean, fresh water flow through it until the water that comes out is nearly as clean as the water that goes in. That is what it's like to "clean" our minds with truth. We have to first "drain" the dirty water that has been sitting stagnant (the lies). But more importantly than that, we have to feed a consistent flow of clean, fresh water (God's Word) through our minds, until the gunk that has built up inside is washed away. Just like cleaning a radiator, this is not something that you can do once and never touch again. It's a process we repeat over and over throughout our lives.

D – Develop life giving tastes
"Taste and see that the Lord is good." Psalm 34:8

In Jeremiah 21:3, Jeremiah accuses the people of committing two sins. Not only have they turned their back on the only one who can truly satisfy all their desires, but they've gone a step farther and are trying to satisfy their desires with "broken cisterns." It would be like drinking sand (believing lies) and not even realizing it when fresh, cool water (truth) is available to us if we only ask. As strange as it might sound, this is exactly what we do. We dig "broken cisterns" in our lives to satisfy our desires. People-pleasing, pornography, productivity, power: we fill our lives with the things we think will satisfy us. Because we put our hope in those things satisfying us, they have a power over us that we can't break free of. To be truly free, we not only have to recognize that we are "drinking sand" and that it doesn't satisfy, but we have to also develop a new taste for fresh spring water. And it's harder than you might think - especially if you've spent your whole life drinking sand.

A friend of mine once told me, *"Say your whole life you have worn your shoes on the wrong feet. You know that it doesn't feel right. But when you put them on the correct feet – that doesn't feel right either."* It takes time, trust and intentionality to develop life-giving tastes.

"It's not that our desires are too strong but too weak. We are like children playing in a mud puddle when a holiday at the beach is available." C.S. Lewis

E – Engage your heart

In Psalms 115:3-8, the psalmist goes through a list of all the ways the *"idols...made by the hands of men"* are not fully alive: *"...mouths that cannot speak, eyes that cannot see..."* etc. In verse 8 he concludes, *"Those who make them will be like them and so will those who trust in them."* In the margin of my Bible I have written: *"Am I actually alive? Do my eyes see? Do my ears hear? Am I passionately embracing life? No passion, no life."*

Jesus also quotes the importance of engaging the heart in Matthew 15:8-9 (from Isaiah 29:13): *"These people honor me with their lips but their hearts are far from me. They worship me in vain; their teachings are but rules taught by men."* Jesus goes on to say, *"Listen and understand. What goes into a man's mouth does not make him 'unclean' but what comes out of his mouth...the things that come out of his mouth come from the heart and these make a man 'unclean'"* (Matt. 15:10-11, 18).

Sin in my heart caused me to spend so much time protecting myself from getting hurt that my heart had become hard, not fully engaged. If you never experience pain (not just physically, but emotionally as well) there's something wrong – you are either dead or diseased.[2]

There is nothing magical about the B.R.I.D.E. process – it's just a tool, a means to end. But it's a tool that has helped me both be aware of the transformation process described in Romans 12:2 and has given me tangible ways to think about intentionally pursuing transformation in my life.

---

2   Dr. Paul Brand is a fore runner in research about leprosy. In his book *The Problem with Pain*, he says that pain is a gift. Lepers lose limbs because they can't feel them. Pain is a God-given safety mechanism that both reminds us we are alive and protects us from destroying ourselves.

H.U.S.B.A.N.D.

Recently I was asked if there was a male version of the female-friend-ly acronym B.R.I.D.E. I'm obviously not a man, and I don't pretend to understand a man's unique struggles with sin. But I do believe that principles are principles for all genders and all generations. My attempt at making a male-friendly acronym for the process of dealing with heart level sin is HUSBAND:[3]

H - Honesty with yourself, God and Others (Ps. 51:6)
U - Uncover the lies (ask God to reveal them) (Ps. 134:23-24)
S - Speak truth to one another
B - Battle for truth in your life (John 17:17; Rom. 12:2)
A - Accountability with other men (1 John 1:5-7)
N - Don't neglect your heart (Matt. 15:8-9, Ps. 115:3-8)
D - Develop life giving tastes (Jer 2:11-13, Ps. 34:8)

See "B.R.I.D.E." for a detailed description of each principle.

---

3   This is not a "formula" for transformation, nor is it a one time "do this and move on to something else." It's a life-long process based on biblical principles and promises. We never "arrive" until we reach heaven. But applying these principles to your life will form a habit that will eventually become like second nature. A few of the principles might seem redundant. Because H.U.S.B.A.N.D. has 7 letters instead of the 5 in B.R.I.D.E. I had to improvise.

UNDERSTANDING BIBLE STUDY

"The fear of the Lord – that is Wisdom; and to shun evil is understanding."

Job 28:28

Look up Understanding in the Strong's Concordance. At least 4 Hebrew words translate as "understanding." What general observations can you make about this word/concept (e.g., times it's used, words it's often combined with, books of the Bible it's most often found in, etc.)? Understanding is NOT about knowing how to fix everything but knowing that I can't and am in desperate need of One who can!

Look at the following verses:

Deuteronomy 32:28   Proverbs 9:6,10   Isaiah 40:14, 28
Proverbs 21:30   Isaiah 43:10

Understanding comes from God and has no limits. We cannot understand on our own. Look at the following verses:

Psalm 147:5   Isaiah 27:11   Deuteronomy 32:28
Proverbs 2:6   Isaiah 1:3   Proverbs 3:5

In the Old Testament God often admonishes his people that they do not understand? Read the following verses. What are the consequences of not understanding?

Isaiah 6:9-10   Isaiah 56:11   Micah 4:12
Isaiah 28:9, 19   Jeremiah 4:22   Ezra 28:4
Isaiah 44:18-19   Jeremiah 9:12   Hosea 4:14

God gives men understanding/discernment to accomplish the specific purposes He has for them. What understanding (or abilities) did God give to each of these people?

Deuteronomy 1:13   1 Kings 7:14   2 Chronicles 26:5
Deuteronomy 36:1   1 Chronicles 12:32   Ezra 8:16,18

How do you get wisdom/understanding? Why is it important?

Proverbs 3:13, 19   Proverbs 8:1-14   Proverbs 23:23
Proverbs 4:1-7   Proverbs 16:16

Proverbs 23:23 implies that it costs something to get understanding. What will it cost YOU to get understanding?

Walk through Proverbs 2:1-9. What are the conditions for acquiring understanding?

Read through Psalm 139. How does the Lord know and understand YOU (make a list)? How does this make you feel loved? What does this practically mean in your life – that the Lord KNOWS you? Spend time giving thanks to the Lord for His love and understanding.

JOB'S JOURNEY TOWARD UNDERSTANDING

Understanding is more than head knowledge. It is a deeper discernment that can only come though practical experience. Understanding does NOT mean getting all the answers we want. It does NOT mean that we understand why something has or has not happened. Understanding is knowing that God is God, and He can do whatever He wants. Understanding begins with a reverence of the Lord that causes us to shun evil (Job 28:28).

Consider Job's story:
Job wants to understand what is happening to him and why (Job 6:24). He begins to think that if God would only listen, he could argue with God so that God would see things Job's way (13:1-2). The longer the pain plagues him the bolder he gets to the point of subtly demanding (23:5) and accusing God of not wanting to listen (23:11-13). But God intervenes and begins to question Job (Job 38:3). God does not give Job answers to his questions or complaints (Job 38:4, 36). He does not explain His behavior so that Job understands why God has been doing what He's been doing. But Job begins to understand who God is - that God is God and Job is not. This is true understanding – not seeing the detailed explanation but simply knowing that God is in charge (Job 42:1-6)

Read through Job 28. What does Job's meditation teach us about understanding?